The Executive Function Playbook in Action

The Executive Function Playbook in Action

ACTIVITIES AND EXERCISES TO SUPPORT KIDS WITH ADHD

MICHAEL McLEOD

JB JOSSEY-BASS™

A Wiley Brand

Contents

Welcome to the Playbook in Action

If you're reading this, chances are you're raising or supporting a child who struggles with focus, follow-through, emotional regulation, frustration tolerance, or independence. You may be feeling overwhelmed, unsure of what works, or tired of trying strategies that seem to miss the mark. You're not alone—and you're in the right place.

The Executive Function Playbook in Action was created to do more than explain executive functioning—it was designed to put it into motion. This workbook is a hands-on, real-world companion to my book *The Executive Function Playbook* and brings to life the core executive function skills that help children move from reactive to reflective, disorganized to purposeful, and dependent to independent.

This workbook is based on the same principles I use every day at GrowNOW:

- Kids don't grow from lectures.
- They don't grow from behavior charts.
- And they don't grow by being reminded over and over.

They grow through internal skill-building, consistent boundaries, and relationship-driven experiences that challenge them to think, reflect, adapt, and regulate—on their own.

This is not just a workbook for kids. It's a tool for parents and adults to use with children. Each page is designed to spark insight, dialogue, accountability, and growth. Every activity is rooted in real-world parenting challenges and based on what truly works for kids with ADHD and executive function challenges.

How This Workbook Is Structured

This workbook is divided into individual activity pages with each one targeting a specific executive function skill, such as:

Self-regulation: The ability to manage impulses, emotions, and behavior

Self-motivation: The ability to initiate and follow through on tasks, especially when they're boring or hard

Self-evaluation: The ability to reflect, assess progress, and learn from mistakes

Self-awareness: The ability to recognize personal strengths, challenges, and impact on others

Social executive functioning: The ability to navigate relationships, consider others' perspectives, and manage conflict

Verbal and nonverbal working memory: The ability to hold and use past experiences and internal language to guide behavior

Each page is built with intention. Here's what you'll find:

- A clear title that names the strategy or topic
- The executive function skill being strengthened
- A thorough explanation (for the adult) of why this page matters
- Step-by-step instructions for implementation
- Built-in reflection questions, prompts, or drawing spaces for children
- A key message, closing thought, and a research reference on every page

Some pages are designed to be filled out by the child with your help. Others are just for you—the parent, teacher, or clinician—to reflect, realign, and step confidently back into your leadership role.

What to Expect, and What Not to

This workbook does not promise quick fixes. It doesn't rely on sticker charts, rewards, or external motivators that fall apart the moment a child isn't being watched. It offers something more meaningful: a way to build the internal foundation your child needs to thrive—not just at home or in school but for life.

As you go through these pages, you may start to see patterns. You'll see how often emotional outbursts are really about a lagging skill. You'll recognize that "bad behavior" often stems from underdeveloped internal language or delayed self-regulation. And you'll begin to shift from constantly reminding and reacting to instead coaching, modeling, and empowering.

You may also feel uncomfortable at times—and that's okay. Some pages ask hard questions about screen time, parenting roles, or how consistent your boundaries really are. This workbook isn't just about helping your child—it's also about strengthening your leadership as a parent. Because when the adult becomes more regulated and intentional, the child almost always follows.

You can complete the pages in any order. Some families work on one page per week. Others revisit the same page multiple times as new challenges arise. Use this book as a living tool—a place for honest reflection, calm direction, and steady progress.

And the most important note: The number-one rule of ADHD parent coaching is to "use less language." This is the trap so many parents unintentionally fall into: talking too much and giving too many lectures. When you do this, it opens the door for more arguing and negotiating, and as we know, the ADHD brain is conflict seeking. So, once you start talking, you are giving your child the stage, the microphone, and the spotlight to start running the entire house with their emotions and behaviors, which then leads to full-on parenting burnout. Many of the worksheets within this workbook are about creating that structure that ADHD kids thrive under. This is exactly why so many kids with ADHD do better at school than they do at home—school is structured, home is unstructured. How do we make home more structured? Specific boundaries that are written down and final; they're non-negotiable. This is exactly what many of these worksheets do—they help the parent to write down expectations, family rules, house rules, and accountability. The worksheet ends all discussions, all negotiations, all arguing—it is written down, and it is final. These worksheets help you reclaim your parental authority by ending all negotiations and arguing and by writing down your parental guidelines and finalizing them as permanent written scripture.

ADHD Hope

Your child doesn't need perfection. They need clarity, connection, and consistency.

You are not failing. You are learning—and so is your child.

Thank you for showing up, leaning in, and doing the hard but transformational work of parenting a child with ADHD and executive function challenges. You are your child's most important teacher. This workbook is here to support you every step of the way.

Let's begin.

Mike

CHAPTER 1

The Foundational Skills

Understanding and Strengthening Nonverbal and Verbal Working Memory

Welcome to the first chapter of *The Executive Function Playbook in Action*. This chapter is devoted to the two most essential—but often invisible—building blocks of executive functioning: nonverbal working memory and verbal working memory. These are the internal skills that form the foundation for every other executive function your child will need to succeed academically, socially, and emotionally.

Many of the challenging behaviors we see in children with ADHD—impulsivity, forgetfulness, reactivity, difficulty following multistep directions—are not signs of defiance or laziness. They are signs that these internal systems are underdeveloped. Simply put, the child is missing the tools that allow them to stop, think, and reflect before they act.

In this chapter, we focus on giving those tools back.

Nonverbal working memory is the ability to visualize and mentally "replay" past experiences. It allows a child to picture what happened yesterday, imagine how someone felt, or anticipate what might happen next. When this skill is weak, the child struggles to learn from experience, repeats the same mistakes, and often seems stuck in the moment without the ability to pause or adjust.

Verbal working memory is the ability to use internal language to guide behavior. This is the inner voice that helps a child talk themselves through a task, remember the steps to a routine, or calm themselves during a moment of frustration. Without it, children often rely entirely on external prompts and reminders—and struggle to function independently.

The pages ahead are designed to strengthen these two foundational skills through structured reflection, visualization, and language-building exercises. They include prompts like:

- "What did I do yesterday, and how did it turn out?"
- "What will future me need from me right now?"
- "What can I say to myself when I'm starting to feel upset?"

These aren't just worksheets—they're tools to build internal systems.

You'll also find pages that encourage the use of imagery, drawing, and storytelling to help children hold onto key emotional experiences, recall them when needed, and apply them in new situations. Over time, as these skills strengthen, you'll see a child who is better able to pause, reflect, regulate, and self-direct.

Before children can manage time, plan assignments, or handle social challenges, they must be able to remember and talk themselves through what has already happened—and what needs to happen next. This chapter is where that journey begins.

Take your time with these pages. Revisit them as needed. And most importantly, complete them alongside your child. Your presence, modeling, and emotional regulation are just as foundational as the skills we're building here.

Let's begin laying the groundwork—one internal skill at a time.

Activity 1.1: Practicing the GrowNOW Predictions Review Model

Executive function skills strengthened: Nonverbal working memory, verbal working memory

OVERVIEW

One of the most significant cognitive challenges faced by children with ADHD is difficulty holding onto mental representations of time, outcomes, and internal experiences. This difficulty—known as *working memory impairment*—is a hallmark executive function deficit. In *The Executive Function Playbook*, we emphasize that without strong nonverbal working memory (mental imagery) and verbal working memory (self-talk), students struggle to plan ahead, regulate their emotions in the moment, and learn from experience.

The **GrowNOW Predictions Review Model** was developed to directly strengthen these internal cognitive systems through an evidence-based process. It is rooted in neurodevelopmental research showing that individuals with ADHD benefit most from *guided mental rehearsal, explicit language strategies,* and *structured reflection* before and after tasks. In short, they learn best through experience—but only when that experience is processed, previewed, and reviewed with support.

This page walks families through a step-by-step approach to improving future thinking (visualizing and talking to themselves through what's ahead) and hindsight reflection (learning from what just happened). These are the very skills needed to break cycles of impulsivity, task avoidance, and time blindness—and to move toward independent goal-directed behavior.

INSTRUCTIONS FOR PARENT, TEACHER, CLINICIAN, AND CHILD (COMPLETE TOGETHER)

Use this worksheet before and after a task, activity, or part of the day (such as going to school, starting homework, playing a sport, or going to a new place). This can be done daily or used situationally to build a habit over time.

Step 1: Predictive Visualization (Mental Movie)

Before beginning the task, guide your child to close their eyes, put their head down, and make a mental movie of what the task or day ahead will look like.

Coach them to visualize:

◆ Where they'll be
◆ What they'll be doing
◆ How they think they will feel
◆ What challenges might come up
◆ What success will look like

This strengthens nonverbal working memory—the brain's internal "camera" that helps children picture themselves in the future. It's the same skill used by successful athletes, public speakers, and leaders who mentally rehearse before performance.

Step 2: Record the Predictions

Now have your child write (or dictate) the specific predictions they made during their visualization. These should be short, clear, and tied to internal experience, not just external outcomes.

Examples:
◆ "I'll feel tired at the beginning but get more focused after 10 minutes."
◆ "I'll probably want to quit when it gets boring, but I'll keep going."
◆ "I think it will take 20 minutes to finish."
◆ "I'll feel proud when I turn it in."

Step 3: Create a Self-Talk Script

Help your child create a verbal self-coaching statement—a short script they can say in their head during the task to stay focused and regulated. This builds verbal working memory, the internal voice used for planning, problem-solving, and motivation.

Examples:
- "Stay calm. You know how to do this. Just take it one step at a time."
- "If I get distracted, I'll just come back to the goal."
- "I've done this before—I can do it again."
- "Keep going until it's done. Then I can relax."

Encourage repetition of the same script in future tasks to build familiarity and internalization.

Step 4: Do the Task or Activity

Now your child does the task. You don't need to guide them through this step—just allow them to apply what they've visualized and rehearsed. If they become dysregulated or frustrated, gently prompt them to return to their mental movie or self-talk script.

Step 5: Predictions vs. Reality—Review and Reflect

After completing the task, come back together and compare what was predicted vs. what actually happened. This builds insight, self-monitoring, and adaptive learning. Help your child identify:

- Where their predictions were accurate
- Where things went differently
- How they felt about the outcome
- What they'd do the same or differently next time

This final step strengthens *hindsight*—a crucial executive function skill that allows individuals to build adaptive strategies over time, rather than repeat the same mistakes or emotional reactions.

KEY MESSAGE

Working memory is not just about remembering facts—it's about holding onto internal experiences long enough to plan, act, and reflect. The Predictions—Review Model gives children a structure to visualize the future, talk themselves through the moment, and learn from the past. Over time, this builds the internal architecture for independence, regulation, and resilience.

CLOSING THOUGHT

Kids with ADHD often live in the "now." They act without thinking, and they forget what they've learned. This isn't due to laziness or defiance—it's neurological. But the brain can grow. With repetition and coaching, your child can develop the internal skills to become their own guide. This worksheet is not just a strategy—it's a mirror that helps them see who they can become.

RESEARCH REFERENCE

Klingberg, T. (2010). Training and plasticity of working memory. *Trends in Cognitive Sciences*, 14(7), 317–324. https://doi.org/10.1016/j.tics.2010.05.002

Activity 1.2: The Brain Coach, Part 1

Executive function skills strengthened: Verbal working memory

OVERVIEW

One of the most powerful tools a child can develop for executive function growth is the ability to talk to themselves—*on purpose*. In the Barkley-Vygotskian model of ADHD, as discussed by Dr. Russell Barkley, verbal working memory is the internal voice we use to guide ourselves, regulate behavior, and stay on task. This inner voice is often underdeveloped in children with ADHD, which can lead to difficulties with impulse control, self-direction, and task completion—especially for tasks that feel boring or offer no immediate reward.

In *The Executive Function Playbook*, I emphasize that the development of self-talk is a teachable skill, not a fixed trait. Children need consistent modeling and opportunities to practice talking themselves *through* challenges, rather than reacting emotionally *to* them.

This worksheet introduces the concept of the "Brain Coach"—a friendly, internal guide that children can access anytime, anywhere. Originally introduced by Ryan Wexelblatt (known as the ADHD Dude and co-host of the *ADHD Parenting Podcast*), this concept provides kids with a concrete, empowering way to begin building an internal support system.

By externalizing the idea of a brain coach—something "real" they can rely on—adults can help students begin to develop the skill of self-directed speech, which is crucial for emotional regulation, motivation, problem-solving, and time management.

INSTRUCTIONS FOR THE ADULT (PARENT, TEACHER, OR CLINICIAN)

This section is designed to be a *conversation and practice tool*. Begin by explaining the concept and then work through the worksheet prompts together.

Step 1: Introduce the Brain Coach Concept

Explain that inside everyone's brain is a quiet, helpful voice that can remind them of what matters, guide them through challenges, and keep them focused on the future.

Say something like:

> "Everyone has a Brain Coach inside their head. This coach helps us stay on track, even when things feel boring, frustrating, or hard. Your Brain Coach is your best helper—it never yells, and it always wants you to succeed. We're going to learn how to hear it and use it."

Make it playful, concrete, and positive. Younger kids may enjoy drawing their brain coach. Older kids may want to choose a name or personality for theirs.

Step 2: Identify Situations Where the Brain Coach Is Needed

Guide your child to name some common situations where their Brain Coach could be helpful:

- Starting a nonpreferred task
- Getting distracted in class
- Feeling frustrated during homework
- Wanting to give up quickly
- Facing something new or uncertain
- Trying to stay calm during an argument

Step 3: Practice Sample Brain Coach Scripts

Now, together they come up with three to five phrases their Brain Coach could say in those situations. These are simple, actionable self-talk lines that can be mentally repeated during moments of challenge.

Examples:
- "You've done hard things before. Just get started."
- "Keep going—don't stop now."
- "You can do this for five more minutes."
- "Stay calm, take a breath, think it through."
- "One step at a time."

Encourage consistency. These same phrases can be used across situations to help the child internalize them as default scripts.

Step 4: Reinforce Brain Coach Awareness During the Day

Encourage the child to check in with their Brain Coach throughout the day—especially during transitions or moments of stress. Adults can prompt with questions like:

- "What would your Brain Coach say right now?"
- "Did your Brain Coach help you during math today?"
- "Next time you feel stuck, try asking your Brain Coach for help."

Over time, this builds the habit of **intentional self-talk**, a foundational skill of verbal working memory and long-term executive function growth.

Why This Matters

Children with ADHD often lack a strong "mental narrator" to help guide behavior. Instead, they react quickly and emotionally in the moment. Teaching them to access and strengthen their inner Brain Coach helps build the essential pause between thought and action.

Verbal working memory enables:

- Future thinking
- Goal persistence
- Emotional self-regulation
- Planning and follow-through

This page gives kids a starting point for that lifelong skill—and gives adults a structured way to coach it consistently.

KEY MESSAGE

Self-talk isn't just helpful—it's essential. Children with ADHD must be explicitly taught to develop their inner voice so they can guide themselves through discomfort, distraction, and challenge. The Brain Coach gives them a tool they can access anytime—and the words to use when they do.

CLOSING THOUGHT

No child is born with a fully developed inner voice—but every child can build one. With practice and support, your student can learn to become their own guide, their own motivator, and their own calming presence. The Brain Coach isn't imaginary—it's the first step toward independence.

RESEARCH REFERENCE

Barkley, R. A. (2012). *Executive Functions: What They Are, How They Work, and Why They Evolved.* Guilford Press.

Activity 1.3: The Brain Coach, Part 2
Executive function skills strengthened: Verbal working memory

OVERVIEW

Building on the previous activity, this page deepens a child's understanding of their internal voice—specifically when they are under stress, dysregulated, or not acting like their "best self." Children with ADHD often default to negative or rigid internal scripts in moments of failure, boredom, or frustration. These internal reactions may sound like: "I can't do this," "This is stupid," "I'm bad at this," or "Nothing ever goes right." Left unaddressed, these thought patterns reinforce low motivation, poor emotional regulation, and learned helplessness.

Verbal working memory—the ability to guide oneself with internal speech—is one of the most crucial executive function skills for maintaining goal-directed behavior under pressure. In *The Executive Function Playbook*, we emphasize the critical role of intentional self-talk in breaking impulsive cycles, managing emotions, and maintaining momentum.

This page helps the adult guide the child to intentionally create the voice they want to hear when they're at their lowest. It's a shift from reactive, unconscious thinking to deliberate, positive internal guidance. In effect, the child is not just imagining a brain coach—they are building the *blueprint for their own self-regulation system.*

INSTRUCTIONS FOR THE ADULT (PARENT, TEACHER, OR CLINICIAN)

Begin by reviewing what the Brain Coach is: an internal guide who always supports the child's success. Then explain that this page is about preparing for moments when things go wrong—when the child is feeling upset, impulsive, ashamed, angry, or off-track.

Emphasize that the Brain Coach is:

◆ Positive, even when things feel hard
◆ Kind, never mean or judgmental
◆ Flexible, reminding them there's always another way
◆ Regulating, helping them calm down
◆ Motivating, helping them take the next step forward

You can say:

"Everyone has moments when they're not at their best. What matters is what we do next—and what we say to ourselves in that moment. Today we're going to decide what we want our Brain Coach to tell us when we feel that way."

STEP-BY-STEP GUIDANCE

1. **Set the context.**

    Ask your child:
    - "What does it mean to *not* be your best self?"
    - "What are some times you feel really frustrated, angry, or like you're about to give up?"

        Use real examples from home or school to ground the discussion.

2. **Brainstorm responses from the brain coach.**

    Work with your child to come up with three phrases or short scripts they want their Brain Coach to say in those moments. Keep them:
    - Short and easy to remember
    - Encouraging and noncritical
    - Flexible and realistic

3. **Review some examples.**
    - "It's okay to mess up. You can try again."
    - "You're not stuck. Take a breath, and then figure out what's next."
    - "This is hard, but you've done hard things before."
    - "Even if today wasn't great, you still get to try again tomorrow."

4. **Practice tone and voice.**

    Once the child chooses their three Brain Coach lines, have them say each one out loud using a calm, kind, and encouraging tone. This helps them hear the difference between helpful and unhelpful self-talk.

5. **Make it routine.**

    Adults can reinforce this by asking:
    - "What did your Brain Coach say when you felt upset today?"
    - "Which Brain Coach line helped you the most today?"
    - "Do we need to change or add a new Brain Coach phrase for tomorrow?"

Why This Matters

Kids with ADHD often internalize the message that something is "wrong" with them—especially when they struggle to control their behavior or emotions. Giving them a compassionate, empowering internal voice interrupts this cycle and replaces shame with growth.

Verbal working memory isn't just for planning or remembering—it's the tool children use to *talk themselves through* discomfort, distraction, and disappointment. This activity helps that tool become stronger, more available, and more effective—especially during the hardest moments of the day.

KEY MESSAGE

In moments of dysregulation or difficulty, children need a voice that keeps them grounded and focused—not one that adds pressure or shame. When they choose what their Brain Coach says ahead of time, they build the inner tools to navigate emotional challenges with greater control and confidence.

CLOSING THOUGHT

What we say to ourselves when no one else is watching shapes who we become. Helping a child script that voice with kindness, flexibility, and motivation is one of the most powerful interventions we can offer.

RESEARCH REFERENCE

Vygotsky, L. S. (1962). *Thought and Language* (E. Hanfmann & G. Vakar, Trans.). MIT Press.

Activity 1.4: Nonverbal Working Memory
Executive function skills strengthened: Nonverbal working memory

OVERVIEW

Nonverbal working memory is the ability to mentally visualize experiences—past, present, and future—without relying on language. In *The Executive Function Playbook*, this skill is described as the "mental movie screen" that allows children to reflect on the past, anticipate consequences, and picture themselves moving through time and tasks. Dr. Russell Barkley refers to nonverbal working memory as a foundational executive function because it allows individuals to pause, reflect, and apply lessons from previous experiences—what we commonly refer to as hindsight.

For children with ADHD, this internal movie screen is often underdeveloped or underutilized. They may struggle to hold on to recent memories, reflect on yesterday's choices, or mentally rehearse the steps needed for a task. Instead, they operate in the present moment, heavily influenced by impulse and emotion. Without consistent access to hindsight, it becomes nearly impossible to learn from past experiences or make thoughtful decisions.

This page guides adults in helping children activate and strengthen their nonverbal working memory through a daily reflection routine. The goal is to slow down the mind, develop awareness of patterns, and give the brain space to simulate and reflect—skills that are often undermined by excessive screen time and overstimulation.

INSTRUCTIONS FOR THE ADULT (PARENT, TEACHER, OR CLINICIAN)

This page is intended to be used at the beginning of the day or before a meaningful task (e.g., school, homework, practice). You will guide the child in a quiet mental rehearsal exercise to strengthen their ability to recall, reflect, and imagine.

This daily mental rehearsal—just two minutes a day—can become a powerful anchor in the development of executive functioning skills such as goal-setting, emotional regulation, time awareness, and future planning.

STEP-BY-STEP GUIDANCE

1. **Set the scene.**

   Have the child sit comfortably, close their eyes, and put their head down if that helps them focus. Explain that they are going to create a mental movie of yesterday. No talking, no moving—just imagining.

   Say:

   "I want you to watch a movie in your mind of what happened yesterday. Just sit quietly and let the day play out in your imagination. You can start from the morning and go all the way to bedtime."

2. **Wait silently for two minutes.**

   Use a timer if needed. No prompts during this period—let the child sit in silence and work their mental movie screen.

3. **Ask guided reflection questions.**

   After the two minutes, use the following questions to facilitate thoughtful discussion and help the child connect visual memory with insight:
   - "Can you walk me through what happened yesterday—from start to finish?"
   - "What went well?"
   - "What didn't go so well?"
   - "How did you feel during different parts of the day?"
   - "Did anything or anyone help you stay on track?"
   - "Where did things start to go off course?"
   - "What could you have done differently?"
   - "What did you do well that you're proud of?"
   - "What are your goals or plans for today, based on what you remember?"

4. Connect past to present.

Help the child use what they remembered and reflected on to set intentions for the current day. This builds a sense of cause and effect and helps children apply learning from their past to shape future behavior.

Why This Matters

Nonverbal working memory is not just a memory skill—it is the internal mechanism that gives children access to *hindsight*. Without it, patterns are not recognized, lessons are not internalized, and behavior remains reactive.

In today's fast-paced, screen-saturated world, children are rarely bored. But boredom plays a crucial developmental role: it creates the mental space for imagination, memory, and reflection to flourish. Screens, on the other hand, hijack attention and offer endless stimulation, preventing the brain from developing the cognitive patience and imagery needed for deep reflection.

This activity helps re-establish that space. It gives children the mental stillness they need to "see" their life with clarity and to use the past as a compass for growth.

KEY MESSAGE

True executive functioning begins with memory—not just of facts, but of experience. When children can mentally replay the past and visualize themselves in it, they gain insight, foresight, and control. This is the heart of self-regulation and personal growth.

CLOSING THOUGHT

Children don't grow from chaos. They grow from reflection. Every quiet moment spent imagining yesterday is a step toward building a better tomorrow. This daily practice is a simple, powerful way to help them pause, process, and plan—one mental movie at a time.

RESEARCH REFERENCE

Alloway, T. P., & Alloway, R. G. (2010). Investigating the predictive roles of working memory and IQ in academic attainment. *Journal of Experimental Child Psychology, 106*(1), 20–29. https://doi.org/10.1016/j.jecp.2009.11.003

Activity 1.5: GrowNOW Video Journals

Executive function skills strengthened: Self-evaluation

OVERVIEW

Students with ADHD often struggle with *self-monitoring*—the ability to track their own performance, reflect on their behavior, and make adjustments without being told.

In *The Executive Function Playbook*, we explore how this challenge is closely tied to deficits in working memory, emotional regulation, and delayed internal development of self-talk and self-reflection.

Traditionally, journaling has been used as a powerful tool to support emotional insight, identity formation, and goal-setting in youth. However, students with ADHD frequently find written journaling to be tedious, slow, and frustrating. Writing requires sustained attention, emotional regulation, task initiation, memory retrieval, and motor output—skills already underdeveloped in this population.

Instead of forcing a model that doesn't fit, this page introduces an innovative adaptation: video journals. By using the child's natural comfort with screens and their interest in seeing themselves on camera, we can preserve the *benefits* of journaling while removing the *barriers*. Video journals allow students to speak freely, reflect in real time, and access a record of their own words, thoughts, and goals—without relying on writing.

This practice supports the development of self-evaluation, the executive function skill that allows individuals to step outside of themselves, observe their own behavior, and make deliberate changes. Over time, regular use of video journals can increase independence, strengthen internal motivation, and reduce overreliance on adult prompting.

INSTRUCTIONS FOR THE ADULT (PARENT, TEACHER, OR CLINICIAN)

Set this up as a regular, low-pressure habit—daily or a few times per week. Use a phone, tablet, or laptop camera. The video doesn't need to be long (two to five minutes is enough), and it does not need to be watched by anyone else unless the child wants to share it.

What matters most is that the child is practicing thinking about their day, setting intentions, and evaluating outcomes.

Make it part of the routine: morning video + evening video.

STEP-BY-STEP GUIDANCE

Morning Video Journal (Before the Day or Task Begins):

Record a short video with your child answering the following four prompts. Adults can ask the questions off-camera or let the child speak freely in sequence.

1. **What are my goals for today?**
   Encourage one to three short goals. These can be behavioral, emotional, academic, or social.

2. **What does my perfect day look like?**
   This prompt builds future thinking and intentionality. It invites the child to visualize their own ideal and align their behavior with it.

3. **What do I want to avoid today?**

   Help them build awareness of common distractions, pitfalls, or emotional triggers. This develops internal monitoring and anticipation.

4. **How do I want to feel at the end of the day?**

   This connects the day's goals to an internal emotional outcome (pride, relief, confidence, calm), strengthening emotional regulation and forward planning.

Evening Video Journal (After the Day or Task Ends):

At the end of the day, record a second video to reflect on how things went. Guide the child through the following three prompts:

5. **What went well today?**

   Help the child celebrate small wins. This builds confidence and reinforces progress.

6. **What didn't go well?**

   Encourage honesty without shame. The goal is to normalize setbacks as learning opportunities.

7. **What are my goals for tomorrow?**

   Support the child in carrying forward momentum or addressing what needs improvement. This reflection-to-action loop builds long-term self-reliance.

Why This Matters

Self-evaluation is a critical component of executive function growth—and one of the most overlooked in ADHD treatment. Children who don't regularly reflect on their choices and outcomes tend to repeat mistakes, misread their own progress, and remain dependent on adult prompts for change.

By using technology *as a tool* instead of a distraction, this activity makes self-reflection accessible and engaging. Children begin to build a digital library of their own insights, thoughts, and growth over time. This process nurtures internal motivation, metacognition, and a stronger sense of ownership over their decisions and behavior.

KEY MESSAGE

Video journals are a developmentally appropriate and ADHD-friendly alternative to written reflection. When students consistently set goals, reflect on outcomes, and visualize their success using their own voice and face, they grow in self-awareness, emotional control, and independence.

CLOSING THOUGHT

When children see themselves, they begin to know themselves. Video journaling turns passive experience into active reflection. It transforms everyday moments into lessons—and turns students into the authors of their own growth story.

RESEARCH REFERENCE

Pennebaker, J. W., & Smyth, J. M. (2016). *Opening up by writing it down*. Guilford Press.

Activity 1.6: My Core Memory

Executive function skills strengthened: Nonverbal working memory, verbal working memory

OVERVIEW

Children with ADHD often struggle to access their past experiences in a way that guides their present behavior. When they become emotionally dysregulated, they may act impulsively or feel overwhelmed, as if the moment will never end. This is because both nonverbal working memory (the ability to mentally visualize a past experience) and verbal working memory (the ability to use internal self-talk) are often underdeveloped. As a result, they lack the internal tools to recall positive emotional states or use calming language with themselves during distress.

This page guides the child to intentionally retrieve a meaningful, positive "core memory"—one filled with joy, calm, love, or fun—and teaches them how to store that memory as a tool they can revisit when their emotions spiral. By building this skill, the child learns to tap into positive self-regulation strategies from within, rather than relying solely on external reminders or interventions.

This memory becomes a mental anchor—a personal moment of joy they can return to again and again.

INSTRUCTIONS FOR THE ADULT

Begin this activity during a calm, quiet moment. Ask the child to close their eyes (if comfortable) and reflect on one of their happiest, most peaceful memories. Reassure them that it doesn't need to be big or dramatic—sometimes the smallest memories hold the most emotional power.

Use gentle prompting to help them recall the details:

◆ Where were you?
◆ What were you doing?
◆ Who was with you?
◆ What made you feel so good?
◆ What were the sounds, smells, or colors?

Then encourage the child to draw any part of the memory—it can be literal or abstract. The image doesn't need to be perfect; what matters is that it represents a feeling they want to hold onto.

STEP-BY-STEP GUIDANCE

1. **Create a safe reflective space.**

   Say: "Let's think back to one of the best memories you've ever had. A time you felt calm, happy, loved, or excited. Let's see if we can bring it back into our minds."

2. **Complete the reflection prompts.**

   Help the child write or dictate responses to:
   - "Where were you?"
   - "What were you doing?"
   - "Who were you with?"
   - "How did you feel?"

3. Reinforce emotional vocabulary and sensory detail.

4. **Draw the memory.**

   Invite the child to sketch something from that moment. It might be a beach, a dog, a favorite meal, or just colors and shapes that represent how they felt.

5. **Build the connection to regulation.**

   Guide the child through this key idea:

   "You felt that way before. That calm, happy feeling is *still inside you*. You can bring it back anytime—even when things feel hard."

6. **Practice visualization as a regulation strategy.**

   Teach the child how to pause and silently picture this memory during moments of stress or overwhelm. Reinforce:

   "Your memory is a superpower. Use it to remind your body that you've felt peace before—and you can feel it again."

KEY MESSAGE

You've already felt joy, calm, and safety before—and that memory is always with you. It's yours to carry and yours to return to when life gets hard.

CLOSING THOUGHT

Self-regulation begins with internal access to peace. When children learn to visualize a calm, joyful memory and connect it to their emotional state, they build the inner tools of resilience, reflection, and hope. Memory is not just a record—it's a resource.

RESEARCH REFERENCE

Siegel, D. J. (2012). *The Whole-Brain Child: 12 Revolutionary Strategies to Nurture Your Child's Developing Mind.* New York: Random House.

Activity 1.1: Practicing the GrowNOW Predictions Review Model

1. Stop, close your eyes, put your head down, and make a mental movie of what the day, task, or activity will look and feel like.
2. Record your predictions here.

_____

_____

3. Create a self-talk script to coach yourself through to the end goal.

_____

_____

_____

4. Complete the plan, task, or activity.
5. Once completed, record the event below. How does it compare to the prediction?

_____

_____

_____

Activity 1.2: Brain Coach, Part 1

1. Name of your Brain Coach:

2. Draw a picture of your Brain Coach in the space provided:

Activity 1.3: Brain Coach, Part 2

The Brain Coach is always:

- ◆ Positive
- ◆ Kind
- ◆ Flexible
- ◆ Regulating
- ◆ Motivating

What are three things you want your Brain Coach to tell you when you are *not* your best self?

1. _____

2. _____

3. _____

Activity 1.4: Nonverbal Working Memory

At the beginning of the day, follow these steps:

1. Take one to two minutes to visualize what happened yesterday.
2. Describe what happened.

_____

_____

3. What went well? What didn't go well? How did you feel about it?

_____

_____

_____

4. Based on what happened yesterday, what are your goals or plans moving forward?

_____

_____

5. What did you do well yesterday?

_____

_____

6. What could you do differently today?

_____

_____

Activity 1.5: GrowNOW Video Journals

Morning Video Journal: Record a short video with your child at the start of the day and have them answer the following four prompts.

1. What are my goals for today?

    i. _____

    ii. _____

    iii. _____

2. What does my perfect day look like?

_____

_____

_____

3. What do I want to avoid today?

_____

_____

_____

4. How do I want to feel at the end of the day?

_____

_____

_____

Evening Video Journal: At the end of the day, record a second video to reflect on how things went. Guide the child through the following three prompts:

1. What went well today?

_____

_____

_____

2. What didn't go well?

_____

_____

_____

3. What are my goals for tomorrow?

_____

_____

_____

Activity 1.6: My Core Memory

Think of one of your most favorite memories you have ever had in your entire life.

Where were you?

_____

What were you doing?

_____

_____

Who were you with?

_____

How did you feel?

_____

_____

Draw that feeling here.

```



```

How do we make ourselves feel this way?

_____

_____

_____

CHAPTER 2

Self-Awareness

Helping Children Recognize Themselves, Their Choices, and Their Impact

Self-awareness is the gateway skill to meaningful change.

In this chapter, we turn our attention to one of the most critical executive function skills—the ability to observe and understand oneself. Self-awareness allows a child to reflect on their behavior, recognize how their actions affect others, and begin to take responsibility for how they show up in different environments: at home, at school, and in social situations.

For many children with ADHD and executive function challenges, self-awareness is underdeveloped or inconsistent. These children often react quickly, move impulsively, or say things without realizing the emotional weight of their actions. They may struggle to connect cause and effect or to understand why they were disciplined, redirected, or misunderstood. Without this internal understanding, behavior becomes cyclical and progress stalls.

The worksheets in this chapter are designed to slow things down. They help children look inward with support, identify their patterns, and begin building a stronger internal lens through which they can view themselves.

Here, you'll find exercises that guide your child to reflect on:

- ◆ Who they are in different settings (home, school, social)
- ◆ How their actions make others feel
- ◆ What their core strengths and challenges are
- ◆ How they want to be seen—and what might get in the way

These pages don't ask the child to be perfect. They invite the child to be honest.

When a child becomes more aware of how they operate in the world, they are better positioned to grow. They begin to realize, "I actually do act differently with certain people. I can change how I show up. I'm capable of doing better when I understand myself."

The development of self-awareness doesn't happen through lectures or consequences. It happens through guided reflection, thoughtful dialogue, and meaningful adult presence. That's why these pages are meant to be completed with you—so that you can help connect the dots, provide nonjudgmental insight, and reinforce what your child may not yet see in themselves.

As you work through this chapter, remember: self-awareness is not a switch—it's a muscle. It's built gradually, through calm conversations and consistent feedback, until the child begins to carry that lens on their own.

Let's help your child become the kind of person who not only notices their actions—but chooses better ones.

Activity 2.1: The Comfort Zone, Part 1
Executive function skills strengthened: Self-awareness

OVERVIEW
Many students with ADHD and executive function challenges develop a rigid comfort zone early in life. This is often due to repeated negative experiences with effort, failure, or unfamiliar tasks. Over time, they begin to internalize the belief that only certain activities are "safe" or "worth doing"—while everything else feels threatening, boring, or overwhelming.

From a brain development perspective, this makes sense: students with executive function struggles experience heightened sensitivity to emotional discomfort and difficulty initiating tasks that don't offer immediate reward. As a result, avoidance becomes their default coping strategy. This can lead to stalled growth, underdeveloped coping skills, and a fear-based approach to learning and life.

This exercise helps children (and their caregivers) *visualize the path* from safety to struggle to success—and recognize that growth only happens when we step beyond what's familiar.

INSTRUCTIONS FOR PARENTS AND CHILDREN (COMPLETE TOGETHER)
On the diagram provided, you'll see four nested zones: Comfort Zone, Fear Zone, Learning Zone, and Growth Zone. Together, take time to reflect on and *label each zone* with real-life examples from your child's experience.

Use these guiding questions:

Comfort Zone
"Where do I feel safest?"

- ◆ What are the activities or routines your child prefers and repeats daily?
- ◆ Are there specific environments or people they gravitate toward because they feel in control?

Examples:
- ◆ Watching YouTube or gaming instead of doing homework
- ◆ Repeating the same drawings or topics over and over again
- ◆ Talking only to one or two "safe" friends at school
- ◆ Refusing to try new foods or go to new places

Fear Zone
"What makes me want to quit or run away?"

- ◆ What tasks, settings, or situations lead to avoidance, frustration, or shutdowns?
- ◆ What thoughts hold them back (e.g., "I'll mess up," "People will judge me," "This is too hard")?

Examples:
- ◆ Reading aloud in class
- ◆ Joining a group activity where rules are unclear
- ◆ Trying a subject they think they're "bad at"
- ◆ Writing without being told exactly what to say

Learning Zone
"What can I learn by trying—even if it's hard?"

- ◆ What's one thing they might gain by sticking with a challenging task just a bit longer?
- ◆ What life skills are being built through effort, even if the outcome isn't perfect?

Examples:
- ◆ Learning to manage frustration during a board game
- ◆ Asking a new peer to join in a game
- ◆ Practicing a math problem until it starts to make sense
- ◆ Learning to deal with "boring" tasks with focus and patience

Growth Zone
"What kind of person could I become if I keep going?"

- What amazing long-term strengths, goals, or dreams are possible if they push through?
- What do they admire in others that they could one day build in themselves?

Examples:
- Becoming a confident speaker
- Making a new friend or teammate
- Discovering a hidden talent
- Becoming more independent with schoolwork, chores, or social skills

KEY MESSAGE

Executive function grows when discomfort is managed, not avoided. When children with ADHD push just slightly beyond what's comfortable—and feel supported doing it—they begin to trust themselves, manage frustration, and build internal motivation. Growth doesn't mean leaping into the deep end. It means taking one small step outside the bubble, then another.

This worksheet is a visual way to show your child that what feels scary now can lead to pride, purpose, and independence in the future. Complete it together. Talk about your own comfort zones too. Make it real, shared, and empowering.

CLOSING THOUGHT

There are many executive function skills that are worked on when describing the Comfort Zone. First, we are developing self-awareness and helping the student become more self-aware of their likes and dislikes, and strengths and needs. Next, we are focusing on self-regulation and self-motivation toward nonpreferred tasks, outside of their small and narrow comfort zone. Finally, we develop self-evaluation, and their ability to look back on their day and ask themselves: "Did I leave my comfort zone today? If I didn't then I did not learn or grow."

RESEARCH REFERENCES

Carver, C. S., & Scheier, M. F. (1998). *On the Self-regulation of Behavior*. Cambridge University Press.

Dweck, C. S. (2006). *Mindset: The New Psychology of Success*. Random House.

Activity 2.2: The Comfort Zone, Part 2

A Personal Reflection on Avoidance, Goals, and Growth

Executive function skills strengthened: Self-awareness, self-evaluation

OVERVIEW

Students with ADHD and executive function challenges often struggle to bridge the gap between where they are and where they *want* to be. This exercise builds on Activity 2.1 by helping children name their habits, hopes, and hesitations—all in one place. It offers a clear, structured way for families to explore the internal barriers that stand between comfort and growth.

Many children live in cycles of avoidance: they stick to what's easy, dream big about what they *could* achieve, but get stuck in fear, frustration, or self-doubt. This page is a way to break that cycle—by putting language to what's really going on inside and bringing parents into the conversation with empathy and strategy.

INSTRUCTIONS FOR ADULT AND CHILD (COMPLETE TOGETHER)

Take your time working through each of the three sections below. Use your own examples and lived experiences—there are no wrong answers. The goal is to bring clarity, not perfection.

1. Comfort Zone

Prompt: *"What are three tasks or activities I do often because they feel safe or easy?"*

These are routines, hobbies, or behaviors your child gravitates toward. They're not necessarily bad—but they may offer comfort without challenge. Identify what your child repeats often without much effort.

Examples:
- Rewatching favorite shows or YouTube videos
- Playing the same video game daily
- Sitting out during group discussions or new activities
- Only doing homework when told exactly what to do

2. Growth Zone

Prompt: *"What are three meaningful goals I would like to accomplish?"*

This is where your child can dream. What are the things they *wish* they could do, achieve, or feel proud of—even if they feel far away right now?

Examples:

◆ Making more friends or joining a group
◆ Getting better at math or writing
◆ Becoming more organized and independent
◆ Being able to talk to the teacher when confused

Encourage bold but realistic goals. Use this section to get hopeful and forward-focused.

3. Fear Zone

Prompt: *"What are three fears, thoughts, or doubts that are holding me back from reaching my goals?"*

This is often the most powerful and important section. Be gentle and curious. Fear often shows up as avoidance, perfectionism, or negativity.

Examples:

◆ "What if I mess up and people laugh?"
◆ "I don't know how to start."
◆ "It's too hard—I'll never be good at it."
◆ "People will think I'm weird."

KEY MESSAGE

Parents: Listen closely to these answers. This section gives you insight into the internal struggles that executive function coaching and supportive parenting can begin to shift.

CLOSING THOUGHT

When kids begin to see their comfort zone not as a permanent home, but as a resting place between challenges, they develop resilience. This page offers them the self-awareness and vocabulary to name where they are—and where they want to go. And with your support, they can start moving.

RESEARCH REFERENCES

Locke, E. A., & Latham, G. P. (2002). Building a practically useful theory of goal setting and task motivation. *American Psychologist, 57*(9), 705–717. https://doi.org/10.1037/0003-066X.57.9.705

Dweck, C. S. (2006). *Mindset: The New Psychology of Success*. Random House.

Activity 2.3: *The Comfort Zone, Part 3*

Executive function skills strengthened: Self-awareness, self-evaluation

OVERVIEW

One of the foundational themes explored in *The Executive Function Playbook* is the idea that executive function growth does not occur in a vacuum—it must be built through guided experience, emotional safety, and self-reflection. This workbook page is designed to help students begin that process of internal reflection by thinking deeply about the habits and patterns that define their behavior in both the Comfort Zone and the Growth Zone.

For children with ADHD and executive function challenges, there is often a sharp contrast between the desire to achieve and the instinct to avoid. These opposing forces create what we refer to here as "the space between fear and growth." Without structured reflection and adult co-regulation, students often remain unaware of this internal push-pull dynamic. That's where this page becomes essential: it helps children put language to their emotional and cognitive patterns, which is a core skill in developing self-awareness, metacognition, and long-term executive function strength.

By guiding students to reflect on the *why* behind their behavior—not just the *what*—we help them begin to see that thoughts, habits, and feelings can be examined, challenged, and reshaped. This is also a meaningful opportunity for parents to gain insight into how their child's brain interprets challenge, risk, and change.

INSTRUCTIONS FOR ADULT AND CHILD (COMPLETE TOGETHER)

On this page, you'll find five reflective questions. These are not rapid-fire prompts. Take time with each one. Parents, ask follow-up questions. Be curious. Stay engaged. The goal is to help your child build the *internal language* and emotional vocabulary that forms the bedrock of long-term growth.

You can use writing, drawings, or spoken answers. There are no wrong responses—just patterns to uncover.

1. What Did I Learn About Myself?

After working through the earlier Comfort Zone activities, what realizations did your child have about how they respond to challenges? Did they recognize habits of avoidance, surprising strengths, or patterns of fear?

Tip: Parents, share what *you* observed in your child during the earlier exercises. Use supportive language. ("I noticed that you had some really honest answers when we talked about fears.")

2. What Do Comfort Zone Habits Do for Me?

Here, your child should identify the short-term benefits of staying in the comfort zone. These habits serve a purpose—even if they're limiting long-term.

Examples:

◆ "They make me feel calm or safe."

◆ "I know I can be successful when I do these things."

◆ "I don't get in trouble when I stay quiet or don't try."

This helps children understand *why* they rely on these patterns and reduces shame around avoidance.

3. What Do Growth Zone Habits Do for Me?

Now shift to the long-term benefits of stepping outside the comfort zone—even if they feel difficult at first. Growth Zone behaviors are uncomfortable but rewarding.

Examples:

◆ "I feel proud after I try something new."

◆ "I learn what I'm good at."

◆ "I get better at handling frustration."

◆ "I surprise myself and other people."

Parents can help here by reminding the child of specific times when they took a risk and succeeded—or when they learned something important by trying.

4. What Is My Brain Telling Me That Holds Me Back?

This is a powerful prompt to uncover *automatic thoughts* that may be unspoken but deeply influential. Children with ADHD often develop cognitive distortions or internal narratives such as:

◆ "I'm not good at this."

◆ "If I mess up, people will laugh."

◆ "It's too hard, so why try?"

◆ "I always forget stuff. I'm just not smart."

Identifying these thoughts is the first step in building cognitive flexibility—a key executive function skill—and replacing unhelpful beliefs with empowering ones.

5. How Do I Feel in Each Zone, and Who Does It Make Me?

This is a reflective and emotional check-in. Help your child think about how they feel *emotionally* in the Comfort Zone vs. the Growth Zone—and what identity those feelings start to shape.

Examples:

- ◆ "In the comfort zone, I feel relaxed but bored. It makes me feel like I'm stuck."
- ◆ "In the growth zone, I feel nervous but proud. It makes me feel stronger."
- ◆ "In the fear zone, I feel embarrassed. It makes me want to hide."

Understanding these emotional patterns helps your child reframe discomfort not as failure—but as *the starting point of growth*.

KEY MESSAGE

Self-awareness is not something children are born with—it is taught, modeled, and practiced over time. When children with ADHD begin to name their thoughts, explore their fears, and reflect on their emotions, they develop the foundational skills of meta-cognition, cognitive flexibility, and emotional regulation—all of which are essential executive functions.

CLOSING THOUGHT

The space between fear and growth is often where the most meaningful transformation happens. It's where your child learns who they are, what they're capable of, and how to persevere. By doing this reflection with them—not for them—you're building a life-long tool they can return to again and again. Growth starts with language, and language starts with reflection.

RESEARCH REFERENCE

Zimmerman, B. J. (2002). Becoming a self-regulated learner: An overview. *Theory Into Practice, 41*(2), 64–70. https://doi.org/10.1207/s15430421tip4102_2

Activity 2.4: Best Self–Words, Part 1
Executive function skills strengthened: Self-awareness

OVERVIEW

In *The Executive Function Playbook*, we emphasize that executive function development is not just about skills—it's about identity. A child's self-concept, or the way they see themselves in relation to the world, directly impacts how they behave, regulate emotions, set goals, and respond to feedback. For students with ADHD and executive function challenges, their self-perception is often shaped more by what they're *told* about themselves ("disruptive," "lazy," "not working to potential") than by who they *actually are* or strive to be.

This activity helps children build an intentional, positive internal identity—one that they can use to guide their behavior and decision-making. This worksheet is grounded in both cognitive-behavioral and social-emotional learning frameworks. It is designed to cultivate self-awareness, one of the most foundational executive function skills.

By identifying their "best self-words," children are empowered to think not just about what they *do*, but who they are becoming. These words serve as internal anchors—reminders of the traits they value and the version of themselves they want to bring forward, even during moments of stress, distraction, or peer pressure.

INSTRUCTIONS FOR PARENT AND CHILD (COMPLETE TOGETHER)

Use the question prompt on this worksheet to spark meaningful conversation:

"If someone were to say: 'Describe [your name] in three words,' what three words would you want them to use?"

These are the child's best self-words—positive traits they hope to embody, express, and grow into over time. The goal is not perfection but intention. Once chosen, these words become reference points for future behavior.

STEP-BY-STEP GUIDANCE

1. **Brainstorm freely.**
   Begin by listing as many positive traits as possible—kind, honest, curious, hard-working, helpful, brave, patient, etc. You can use examples from books, admired adults, teachers, athletes, or role models they know.

2. **Narrow it down.**
   Choose the three that resonate most with how your child wants to be seen—not just by others, but by themselves. These are aspirational, yet attainable.

3. **Watch for surface-level or dopamine-driven words.**
   Some children (especially those with ADHD) may default to words like:
   - "Funny" (often linked to impulsive behaviors for quick social feedback)
   - "Cool" or "popular" (driven by external validation or appearance)

4. These aren't inherently bad, but help your child explore *why* they chose them. If they're tied to attention-seeking or image over character, guide them gently toward deeper self-concept traits.

5. **Look at some example guidance:**
   "It's great that you like being funny. That's part of your personality! But let's think about other qualities too—like being brave, thoughtful, or determined. These are the kinds of traits that stick with you, even when things get hard."

6. Write the final three words.

Have your child write their three best self-words in the space provided on the worksheet. They can decorate or illustrate the words as well.

7. Discuss what they mean in action.

For each word, ask:

- "What does this word look like at school? At home?"
- "How do people act when they show this trait?"
- "What would it look like to live like this word tomorrow?"

WHY THIS MATTERS

Children with ADHD often struggle to pause, reflect, and consciously choose behavior. By choosing words to define their ideal self, we give them a powerful framework for internal motivation and intentional behavior.

This activity strengthens self-awareness, emotional vocabulary, and goal-directed behavior—all core components of executive functioning. It also serves as a gentle way to introduce self-regulation without using punishment or external rewards.

KEY MESSAGE

When children have a positive internal identity—and can name the kind of person they want to be—they are far more likely to make behavior choices that align with that identity. Best Self-Words become a quiet compass, helping them return to their core values even when emotions or distractions pull them off track.

CLOSING THOUGHT

Kids become what they practice. And what they practice starts with how they see themselves. These three words aren't just labels—they're seeds. With reflection, guidance, and repetition, they grow into habits, and habits shape lives.

RESEARCH REFERENCE

Oyserman, D., Elmore, K., & Smith, G. (2012). Self, self-concept, and identity. *Handbook of Self and Identity* (2nd ed., pp. 69–104). The Guilford Press.

Activity 2.5: Best Self-Words, Part 2
Executive function skills strengthened: Self-awareness

OVERVIEW

This follow-up activity builds directly on the previous "Best Self-Words" worksheet, transitioning from identity formation to *daily behavior alignment*. In *The Executive*

Function Playbook, one of the core principles emphasized is the importance of helping children with ADHD externalize internal goals—putting language and structure around the kind of person they want to be, and then consistently tracking whether their behaviors are supporting that vision.

Children with executive function challenges often struggle with self-monitoring and consistency. They may understand a concept in theory (e.g., "I want to be kind") but have difficulty noticing their actions in real time or reflecting back on their day to determine whether they lived up to those values. This page serves as a bridge between *self-image* and *action*—a tool to help students begin living out their best self-words in practical, observable ways.

This worksheet is meant to be completed daily or weekly as part of a short check-in. It is designed to build a regular habit of accountability, reflection, and self-directed growth—all of which are central to long-term executive function development.

INSTRUCTIONS FOR THE ADULT (PARENT, TEACHER, OR CLINICIAN)

Guide the child or student through this reflection by referring to the three best self-words they identified in Activity 2.4. If needed, revisit those words together to reinforce their meaning and significance.

Then, using the template provided, help the child provide one concrete example for each word that shows how they *embodied that trait* during the day.

This process builds the critical skill of self-awareness—the ability to recognize and evaluate one's own behavior, especially in alignment with internal values.

STEP-BY-STEP GUIDANCE

1. **Start with a brief review.**
   Say: "Let's remember your three best self-words. Today we're going to check in and see if you did anything that showed those words in action."

2. **Support retrieval with gentle prompts.**
   Many children with ADHD may struggle to remember what they did earlier in the day, or may say "I don't know." Help by offering time anchors and behavioral cues:
   • "Let's think back to this morning. Did anything happen at breakfast, during school, or during your game that showed you being [word]?"
   • "Did you help anyone? Did you stay calm even when something was frustrating?"
   • "When did you feel proud of yourself today?"

3. **Document specific actions.**
   For each word, write down one example of behavior that reflects that trait. If the child can't think of one, ask what they *could do tomorrow* to embody that word more clearly.

Example output:

- *Best Self-Word: Brave* → "I raised my hand in class even though I was nervous."
- *Best Self-Word: Kind* → "I let someone else use the swing before me at recess."
- *Best Self-Word: Focused* → "I finished my homework without being reminded."

4. **Emphasize consistency over perfection.**

   This is not about always getting it right. It's about building awareness and intention over time. Even small actions count.

WHY THIS MATTERS

Many children with ADHD operate in a reactive mode. They move from one task to another without much reflection or sense of continuity. This activity helps slow down their thinking, connect behavior to identity, and build a daily rhythm of reflection and growth.

When repeated regularly, this habit builds the foundation for:

- Greater internal motivation
- Improved behavior regulation
- A stronger, values-based self-concept
- Long-term executive function resilience

KEY MESSAGE

Executive function is not just about finishing tasks—it's about aligning actions with values. When children practice noticing and naming the moments when they live out their best traits, they grow in self-awareness, confidence, and intentionality.

CLOSING THOUGHT

Kids don't become their best selves by accident. They become their best selves by noticing what matters, trying again tomorrow, and learning to measure success in more than just grades or gold stars. This page teaches them how to do that—one word, one action, one day at a time.

RESEARCH REFERENCE

Dweck, C. S. (2006). *Mindset: The New Psychology of Success.* Random House.

Activity 2.6: Impact on Others
Executive function skills strengthened: Self-awareness, perspective-taking

OVERVIEW
A core theme in *The Executive Function Playbook* is the importance of teaching children with ADHD to recognize how their behavior affects the people around them. While most students can intuitively understand social cause and effect, children with executive function challenges often struggle with this process. They may act impulsively, speak without thinking, or disregard social cues—not because they lack empathy, but because they lack real-time awareness and reflection.

This page supports the development of self-awareness by building the skill of perspective-taking—the ability to step outside oneself and consider how one's words and actions shape the emotional experiences of others. Many students with ADHD live in the "now," highly focused on their own needs and emotions in the moment. This page helps expand their awareness beyond the self, offering a simple but powerful structure for understanding social impact.

By consistently linking behavior to consequences—not in the form of punishment, but in terms of how others feel and react—children can begin to internalize social norms and develop a more adaptive, respectful, and emotionally intelligent behavioral style.

INSTRUCTIONS FOR THE ADULT (PARENT, TEACHER, OR CLINICIAN)
This is a collaborative worksheet to be completed alongside the child or student. Begin with a neutral, supportive tone. This is not a disciplinary exercise—it is a learning experience designed to increase social insight and emotional intelligence.

Use the two-column format:

- **Left column:** "When I do/say. . ."
  Here the child names a specific behavior or verbal action they commonly exhibit.
- **Right column:** "Effect on others"
  Here, the child identifies the emotional or behavioral response their action may cause in peers, adults, or family members.

Draw the arrow between each column to emphasize the *connection* between the child's behavior and its social consequences.

STEP-BY-STEP GUIDANCE

1. Introduce the concept.

Say:

"Everything we do or say creates a ripple. It doesn't just affect us—it affects the people around us. Today we're going to think about how certain actions make other people feel or react. This helps us understand the power of our behavior."

2. Brainstorm real-life examples.

Help the child identify specific actions they've done at home, in school, or with peers.

Examples of "When I do/say. . .":

- "Interrupt my teacher."
- "Call out in class."
- "Roll my eyes at my parent."
- "Refuse to clean up."
- "Say thank you."
- "Help someone with a tough problem."

3. Explore the impact in the right column.

For each action, help the child reflect on how it makes others feel or what it causes them to do.

Examples of "effect on others":

- "The teacher gets frustrated and skips my turn."
- "My classmates stop listening to me."
- "My parent feels disrespected."
- "My friend feels appreciated."
- "My teacher feels proud of me."
- "My brother gets upset and leaves the room."

4. Encourage nuanced thinking.

Discuss how the same action can have different effects depending on tone, timing, or setting. Build flexibility and insight into social context.

5. Reflect and discuss patterns.

After several rows are complete, ask:

- "Which of these actions makes you feel proud?"
- "Which ones cause problems for you?"
- "What's something you could do differently tomorrow?"

WHY THIS MATTERS

For many students with ADHD, the gap between intention and impact is wide—and often invisible. They may not realize that their behaviors are causing breakdowns in relationships, classroom conflicts, or emotional distance at home. Conversely, they may not notice the positive impact of helpful or respectful behaviors.

This activity develops empathy, accountability, and emotional insight by making those connections visible. Over time, children who regularly reflect on the effects of their actions are better able to pause, consider outcomes, and make more prosocial choices.

KEY MESSAGE

Self-awareness includes understanding that our behavior doesn't happen in a vacuum. Every action has a ripple effect. Teaching children to link their words and actions to how others feel helps them develop empathy, emotional intelligence, and social maturity.

CLOSING THOUGHT

The most powerful lessons in life aren't taught through lectures—they're learned through reflection. When a child begins to understand their impact on others, they gain a sense of agency, responsibility, and connection. These moments of insight are the building blocks of true character.

RESEARCH REFERENCE

Barkley, R. A. (2012). *Executive Functions: What They Are, How They Work, and Why They Evolved.* New York: Guilford Press.

Activity 2.7: How Am I Different?
Executive function skills strengthened: Self-evaluation, self-awareness

OVERVIEW

Children and teens with ADHD often behave very differently depending on the environment they're in. While some may appear quiet and compliant at school, they may be emotional, impulsive, or resistant at home. Others may struggle more in structured environments and appear more regulated in familiar, comfortable spaces. These shifts are often misunderstood by adults and can lead to confusion, blame, or frustration—especially for parents.

In *The Executive Function Playbook*, we discuss how behavior is always a reflection of the *interaction between the brain and the environment*. Children with ADHD are highly responsive to the demands, expectations, and relationship dynamics around them. This workbook page is designed to help adults and children examine those environmental influences and reflect on how context shapes behavior.

This activity uses a Venn diagram to help students compare and contrast how they act, feel, and perform in two key settings: home and school. By analyzing the differences and similarities, children can build greater self-awareness and begin to understand *why* they may act one way in school and another at home—not because they're being manipulative or "masking," but because their brain responds differently based on the structure, expectations, and emotional safety of the environment.

This distinction is crucial for building empathy, insight, and consistency across settings.

INSTRUCTIONS FOR THE ADULT (PARENT, TEACHER, OR CLINICIAN)

Use the two overlapping circles on the worksheet to facilitate an open-ended discussion with the child. Label one circle "School" and the other "Home." The shared space in the middle represents behaviors, feelings, or traits that remain consistent across both environments.

Guide the child through each part of the diagram with patience and curiosity. This is not about judgment—it's about understanding how the brain functions across different settings.

STEP-BY-STEP GUIDANCE

1. **Start with the school circle.**

   Ask questions to explore how the child typically acts, feels, and performs at school:
   - "How do you feel most days at school?"
   - "Do you raise your hand or stay quiet?"
   - "Do you follow rules easily or feel frustrated?"
   - "What's hard for you in the school environment?"
   - "What helps you stay calm or focused at school?"

2. Encourage the child to think about the structure of school, classroom rules, teacher expectations, and peer dynamics.

3. **Move to the home circle.**

   Now shift to the home setting:
   - "How do you act differently at home?"
   - "Are there things you say or do at home that you wouldn't at school?"
   - "Do you feel more free or more frustrated at home?"
   - "What do you like most about being home?"
   - "What's harder for you at home than at school?"

4. Help the child reflect on the looser rules, unconditional relationships, and emotional triggers that are more likely to surface in a home environment.

5. **Fill in the middle overlap.**

   Ask:
   - "What stays the same no matter where you are?"
   - "What strengths or challenges follow you in both places?"
   - "Are there behaviors or feelings that are just part of who you are?"

6. This helps children build a stable sense of identity while recognizing the role of context.

ADDRESSING THE "MASKING" NARRATIVE

Social media has popularized the idea that children with ADHD "mask" their symptoms at school and then collapse at home from exhaustion. While this narrative may feel validating to some, research does not support masking as a widespread phenomenon in ADHD.

Instead, what's often happening is environmental reactivity. School environments are:

◆ Highly structured
◆ Conditional (rewards/consequences based)
◆ Rule-driven and externally regulated

Home environments tend to be:

◆ Loosely structured
◆ Unconditional (family bonds, safe attachments)
◆ Emotionally loaded with fewer formal boundaries

Children aren't faking or hiding symptoms—they are responding to different external stimuli, levels of accountability, and emotional safety. This page helps make those dynamics visible and discussable, without blame or oversimplified labels.

WHY THIS MATTERS

Students with ADHD benefit enormously from reflection that connects *how* they behave to *where* they are and *what's expected of them*. When they begin to understand the role of environment in their own self-regulation, they become more empowered to generalize skills across settings—and more compassionate toward themselves when things feel harder at home or school.

This also opens the door for parents and educators to create more consistent structures and expectations across environments to support executive functioning.

KEY MESSAGE

Children with ADHD don't behave randomly—they behave *situationally*. Recognizing how their actions change across home and school helps them develop the self-awareness to carry their strengths across environments and adapt more flexibly.

CLOSING THOUGHT

When children understand that who they are is shaped by where they are, they begin to see behavior as something they can influence—not just something that "happens" to them. This awareness is the first step toward consistent, empowered self-regulation.

RESEARCH REFERENCE

Dawson, P., & Guare, R. (2018). *Smart But Scattered: The Revolutionary "Executive Skills" Approach to Helping Kids Reach Their Potential.* New York: Guilford Press.

Activity 2.8: Impact on SELF
Executive function skills strengthened: Self-awareness

OVERVIEW

In *The Executive Function Playbook*, we stress that one of the most critical—and most delayed—skills in children with ADHD is the ability to connect present behavior to future consequences. These students often live in the "now," responding impulsively to their current thoughts and emotions, with limited access to hindsight or forethought. Without structured opportunities to reflect on their own choices and patterns, they remain unaware of how their behavior affects their own outcomes—academically, socially, emotionally, and personally.

This worksheet builds on the concept of external cause and effect (previously explored in the "Impact on Others" page) and turns the lens inward. The goal is to help students recognize that their actions don't just affect others—they shape their own experience. This reflection is the foundation of self-directed learning, self-regulation, and long-term independence.

By visually mapping specific behaviors to internal outcomes, students can begin to take greater ownership of their decisions—not because they're being told to but because they're beginning to see and *feel* the patterns for themselves.

INSTRUCTIONS FOR THE ADULT (PARENT, TEACHER, OR CLINICIAN)

Guide the student through a calm, thoughtful reflection using the two-column structure:

- ◆ **Left column:** "When I choose. . . / When I do. . ."
  The student selects specific, real behaviors or actions they engage in regularly—both helpful and unhelpful.
- ◆ **Right column:** "Impact on SELF"
  The student identifies the emotional, social, or functional outcome of that behavior. This includes how they feel, what happens to their motivation or confidence, or how it affects their progress.

The goal is not to label behaviors as "good" or "bad," but to make visible how actions lead to consequences that either support or interfere with their own goals and well-being.

STEP-BY-STEP GUIDANCE

1. **Start with real examples.**

   Begin by prompting the child to think about actions or choices they make in their daily life. These can include:
   - Procrastination
   - Staying up late
   - Completing a task early
   - Asking for help
   - Losing their temper
   - Ignoring instructions
   - Taking deep breaths before reacting

2. **Record the behaviors.**

   Write each one in the left column under "When I choose... / When I do. . ."

3. **Explore internal impact.**

   For each behavior, guide the child to reflect on how it affects *them*—their energy, mood, mindset, goals, or relationships. Use prompts such as:
   - "How do you feel afterward?"
   - "What happens to your day when you do that?"
   - "Does it help you feel more or less confident?"
   - "Does this move you closer to or further from your goals?"

4. **Examples might include:**
   - "I stay up late → I'm tired and cranky the next day."
   - "I take my time on my work → I feel proud and get good feedback."
   - "I yell when I'm frustrated → I feel bad later and people avoid me."
   - "I ask for help when I'm stuck → I feel calmer and get back on track."

5. **Encourage honesty without shame.**

   Create a space for honest reflection without making the child feel criticized. Focus on growth and learning. If they struggle to articulate impact, share your own observations gently.

WHY THIS MATTERS

Many students with ADHD are caught in behavior loops—they repeat the same choices without understanding why they're stuck. This activity gives them the chance to pause and examine the connection between their *own actions* and their *own experience.*

By externalizing this process through a visual chart, children begin to develop the metacognitive muscles needed to reflect, adapt, and improve over time. Over weeks and months, these exercises help replace blame and reactivity with insight and intentionality.

KEY MESSAGE

Self-awareness means noticing not just what we do, but how what we do shapes our own life. Helping children see the link between their choices and their experience gives them the power to self-correct, self-advocate, and self-direct.

CLOSING THOUGHT

True independence doesn't come from constant adult reminders—it comes from a child knowing how their own actions move them forward or hold them back. This page helps plant that seed of self-discovery and strengthens their ability to own their journey.

RESEARCH REFERENCE

Best, J. R., Miller, P. H., & Naglieri, J. A. (2011). Relations between executive function and academic achievement from ages 5 to 17 in a large, representative national sample. *Learning and Individual Differences, 21*(4), 327–336.

Activity 2.9: My Goals → My Actions
Executive function skills strengthened: Self-awareness

OVERVIEW

Executive function development relies heavily on the ability to connect intentions with behavior—a skill that many students with ADHD find especially challenging. While they may be able to identify what they *want* (e.g., better grades, improved friendships, more independence), they often struggle to translate those goals into actionable steps. This disconnect stems from underdeveloped self-awareness, weak planning skills, and difficulty linking long-term outcomes with daily choices.

In *The Executive Function Playbook*, we stress the importance of explicitly teaching students to recognize that goals are not abstract wishes—they are built through actions. This page offers a simple structure to help students make that connection visible. It encourages them to reflect on their aspirations and then immediately tie those goals to *something specific they've done*—even if it's small—that moved them closer.

This practice nurtures personal responsibility, agency, and growth mindset. Over time, students who engage in this kind of reflection begin to see that their daily decisions are not random—they are either aligned with their goals or pulling them off track. That shift in perspective is central to building internal motivation and long-term success.

INSTRUCTIONS FOR THE ADULT (PARENT, TEACHER, OR CLINICIAN)

Use this page as a daily or weekly reflection activity. The goal is not to fill the page quickly, but to help the child think deeply and deliberately about their goals and how their actions align—or don't.

Guide them to identify three meaningful, realistic goals in the left column, and then link each goal to one specific step or behavior they've recently taken in the right column.

STEP-BY-STEP GUIDANCE

1. **Identify three personal goals.**

   In the left-hand column titled "My Goals," support the child in choosing three goals that are personally meaningful and developmentally appropriate.

   Encourage variety across academic, behavioral, emotional, or social domains. These can include:
   - "Get better at reading out loud."
   - "Stay calm when things don't go my way."
   - "Make a new friend."
   - "Be more organized with my homework."
   - "Try to be more respectful at home."

2. Avoid vague goals like "be better" or "be good." Make them observable, relatable, and motivating.

3. **Draw the connection to action.**

   For each goal, help the child reflect on a specific action they took that moved them closer to achieving it. Write this in the right-hand column under "Steps I Take to Reach Goal."

   Examples:
   - *Goal: Be more organized* → "I packed my backpack the night before school."
   - *Goal: Be calmer at home* → "I took deep breaths instead of yelling when I was frustrated."
   - *Goal: Improve in math* → "I stayed in for help during recess and asked the teacher questions."

4. **Celebrate small wins.**

   Emphasize that even small actions count. The point of this activity is not perfection but progress awareness. Every choice that aligns with a goal builds the child's sense of competence and agency.

5. **Use prompts to guide thinking.**

   If the child struggles to identify actions, use guiding questions:
   - "What's something you did today that you feel proud of?"
   - "Did you do anything that helped you feel closer to this goal?"
   - "If not yet—what could be a good next step?"

WHY THIS MATTERS

Children with ADHD often struggle with follow-through not because they lack ambition, but because they lack a cognitive bridge between their desires and their behaviors. This page helps build that bridge. It trains the brain to scan for alignment between what the child *wants* and what the child *does*—and that's a skill that fuels lifelong independence.

This simple habit also helps reduce prompt dependence. When children regularly reflect on their own choices and connect them to outcomes, they become more internally motivated and less reliant on adult feedback or correction.

KEY MESSAGE

Executive function is not about doing everything right—it's about noticing what matters, making a plan, and taking steps that move you forward. When students begin linking goals with specific behaviors, they take ownership of their growth.

CLOSING THOUGHT

Children don't reach their goals all at once—they get there one decision, one moment, one action at a time. This page helps them see that every small step matters, and every choice counts toward building the future they want.

RESEARCH REFERENCE

Zelazo, P. D., & Carlson, S. M. (2012). Hot and cool executive function in childhood and adolescence: Development and plasticity. *Child Development Perspectives, 6*(4), 354–360.

Activity 2.10: My Goals → My Steps Backward, Sometimes
Executive function skills strengthened: Self-awareness

OVERVIEW

A vital component of executive functioning—and a key principle throughout *The Executive Function Playbook*—is learning how to reflect on *not just what helps us grow, but what holds us back*. Many children and teens with ADHD exhibit patterns of behavior that are unintentionally self-sabotaging. These behaviors aren't rooted in laziness or defiance, but rather in impulsivity, emotional dysregulation, and a lack of awareness around how their actions interfere with their own success.

This page is designed to help students pause and notice the disconnect between what they want and what they sometimes do. By comparing their goals to the behaviors that pull them off course, they begin to develop true self-awareness—the ability to identify internal obstacles, take ownership of patterns, and begin choosing differently.

This exercise is not about shame, guilt, or highlighting failure. It's about building insight in a safe, constructive way so that students can begin to name their own barriers and learn to interrupt them with support.

INSTRUCTIONS FOR THE ADULT (PARENT, TEACHER, OR CLINICIAN)

Work alongside the child or student using the two-column format. Emphasize that this page is about learning from the past, not judging it. Use a calm, supportive tone to reinforce the idea that everyone takes steps backward sometimes—what matters is noticing the pattern and learning from it.

The structure:

- **Left column:** "My Goals"—three personal goals identified by the student
- **Right column:** "Things I do that keep me from achieving my goal (my steps backward)"—one self-sabotaging behavior linked to each goal

STEP-BY-STEP GUIDANCE

1. **Identify three meaningful goals.**

   Ask the child to name three goals they care about. These can be academic, emotional, behavioral, or social. Help them be specific and realistic.
   Examples:
   - "Stay out of trouble in class."
   - "Make more friends."
   - "Finish homework on time."
   - "Get better at managing my emotions."
   - "Earn more screen time by completing chores."

2. **Explore behaviors that get in the way.**

   For each goal, guide the child to reflect on one thing they do—a habit, action, or choice—that makes it harder to reach that goal. Normalize the idea that *everyone* has habits that make things harder.
   Examples:
   - *Goal: Stay out of trouble in class* → "I call out to make people laugh."
   - *Goal: Make more friends* → "I tease people when I don't know what to say."
   - *Goal: Finish homework on time* → "I pretend I don't have any homework."
   - *Goal: Manage my emotions* → "I yell before I stop to think."
   - *Goal: Earn more screen time* → "I argue with my parents when they ask me to do chores."

3. **Encourage reflection, not excuses.**

   Once each step backward is named, ask reflective follow-ups:
   - "Why do you think you do that?"

- "What are you feeling right before it happens?"
- "What could help you catch yourself next time?"

4. This helps deepen metacognition and emotional insight.
5. **Keep the focus on progress.**
   Emphasize that awareness is a huge step forward. Once a behavior is named, it can be addressed. Let the child know that everyone takes steps backward sometimes—and part of growing up is learning how to notice and reset.

WHY THIS MATTERS

Children with ADHD often repeat the same behaviors without realizing they're undermining their own goals. This activity interrupts that loop. It helps students begin to see that their actions carry consequences not only for others, but for themselves. Over time, this strengthens internal accountability and self-directed learning—key components of mature executive functioning.

When children become aware of their own roadblocks, they also become more open to strategies that can help them change. They begin to feel more in control—not just of their behavior but of their outcomes.

KEY MESSAGE

Self-sabotage isn't a character flaw—it's often a habit rooted in avoidance, emotion, or fear. By helping children notice how they step away from their goals, we empower them to step back in with clarity and intention.

CLOSING THOUGHT

Progress isn't a straight line. It's a winding path filled with learning moments. This page helps children discover that even their missteps are part of their growth story—and that each time they reflect, they move one step closer to becoming who they're meant to be.

RESEARCH REFERENCE

Seligman, M. E. P., & Csikszentmihalyi, M. (2000). Positive psychology: An introduction. *American Psychologist, 55*(1), 5–14.

Activity 2.11: My Brain: What Stimulates It?
Executive function skills strengthened: Self-awareness

OVERVIEW

Understanding how the ADHD brain seeks stimulation is one of the most important foundations of executive function development. As explained in *The Executive Function*

Playbook, children and teens with ADHD are not lacking intelligence or ability—they are dealing with a brain that craves stimulation and novelty to feel engaged, alert, and motivated. This neurological reality is rooted in dopamine dysregulation, a key component of ADHD.

This page is built around a core metaphor: the brain is like a phone battery that needs charging. But instead of a power outlet, the ADHD brain seeks dopamine—and it learns very early in life how to get it. Some sources of stimulation are healthy and productive (e.g., exercise, music, social play, creative expression). Others, while effective in the short term, are harmful in the long run (e.g., video games, arguing, risk-taking, defiance).

This worksheet guides children, with the support of a parent or clinician, to explore *what charges their brain*, and to evaluate whether that stimulation is helpful or harmful. It lays the groundwork for self-awareness, impulse control, and long-term behavioral change by teaching kids to recognize their brain's patterns.

INSTRUCTIONS FOR THE ADULT (PARENT, TEACHER, OR CLINICIAN)

Use this page to open up a curious, nonjudgmental discussion with the child or teen. Say something like:

> "All brains like to feel energized, just like a phone needs to be charged. But for people with ADHD, their brains are constantly looking for ways to feel more alive, alert, and stimulated. Let's figure out what your brain uses to 'charge up'—and then let's think through whether those things are helping you or getting in your way."

You'll work together to identify three specific activities or behaviors that tend to give the child a sense of energy, excitement, or alertness. These are not always "good" or "bad"—the goal is not shame or praise but insight. Once listed, each one is followed by an arrow pointing to the right, leading to the questions:

> "Is this helpful?"

> "Why or why not?"

This leads to deeper conversations about managing stimulation in healthy, sustainable ways—rather than falling into harmful cycles of overstimulation and burnout.

WORKSHEET STRUCTURE

Visual Prompt:

Illustration of a human brain plugged into a wall via a phone charger, symbolizing how the brain recharges through stimulation.

What Stimulates My Brain?	→	Is This Helpful? (Yes or No)	Why or Why Not?
Example: Watching YouTube	→	No	Too hard to stop; makes homework harder
Example: Listening to music	→	Yes	Helps me focus while working
Example: Arguing with parents	→	No	Feels powerful in the moment, but makes everyone upset

Three blank rows are included for the adult and child to complete together in the Activity 2.11.

WHY THIS MATTERS

This activity gives children the language and insight to describe what their brain craves—and to evaluate those cravings from a functional standpoint. Many students with ADHD don't realize that their choices are driven by a neurological need for stimulation. Helping them develop this awareness can transform how they understand their behavior—and how they begin to make healthier decisions.

It also gives parents a framework to address problematic behaviors without shame, shifting the conversation from "Why are you doing this?" to "What is your brain getting out of this?"

This reframing allows adults to become coaches instead of critics—and allows children to develop self-control from a place of empowerment, not punishment.

KEY MESSAGE

The ADHD brain is constantly seeking stimulation. Learning what charges your brain—and whether it's helping or hurting—is one of the most powerful self-awareness tools you can develop.

CLOSING THOUGHT

You can't change what you don't understand. But once you understand your brain's habits, you can begin to shape your life in ways that are healthier, calmer, and more in your control.

Activity 2.1: The Comfort Zone, Part 1

Fill in each zone of the diagram using real-life examples.

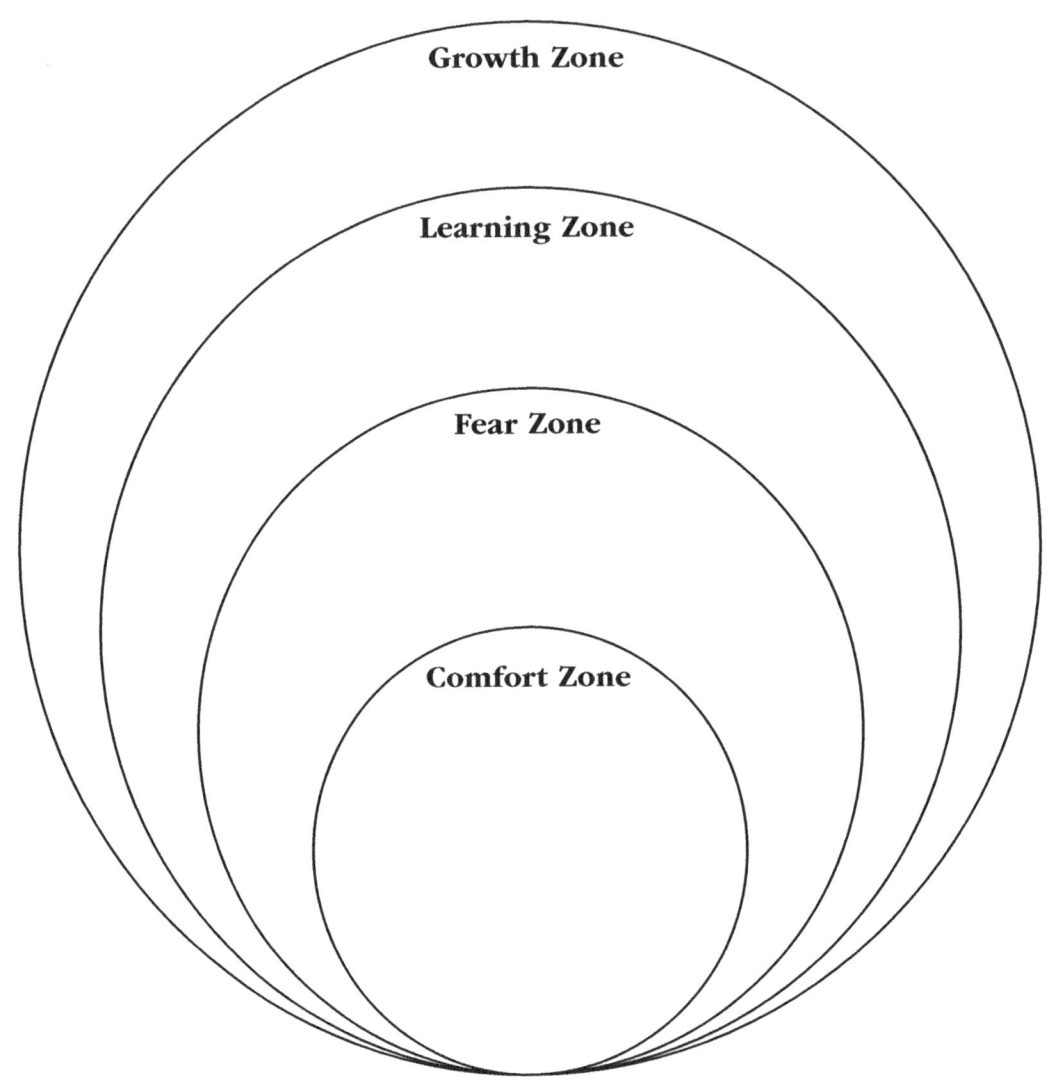

Activity 2.2: The Comfort Zone, Part 2

COMFORT	GROWTH ZONE	FEAR ZONE
What are three tasks/ activities I do in the comfort zone? Examples: (1) iPhone, (2) Video games, (3) YouTube	What are three goals I would like to accomplish? Examples: (1) More friends, (2) Improved grades, (3) Join a club/sport	What are three fears stopping me from getting to the growth zone? Examples: (1) People won't like me, (2) I can't resist my phone, (3) I won't be good
_____ _____ _____	_____ _____ _____	_____ _____ _____

Activity 2.3: The Comfort Zone, Part 3

The learning zone is the space between fear and growth.
   Developing Self-Awareness

1. What did I learn about myself?

_____

_____

2. Comfort zone habits: What do they do for me?

_____

_____

3. Growth zone habits: What do they do for me?

_____

_____

4. What is my brain telling me to hold me back?

_____

_____

5. How do I feel in each zone, and who does it make me?

_____

_____

_____

_____

Activity 2.4: Best Self-Words, Part 1

Create a list of three best self-words: words you would want someone to describe you as.

If someone were to say, "Describe (your name) in three words," what three words do you hope they would say?

1. _____

2. _____

3. _____

Activity 2.5: Best Self-Words, Part 2

Give one example of how you embodied each word today:

1. _____

2. _____

3. _____

Activity 2.6: Impact on Others

When I do/say. . .   The effect on others is. . .

1. _____ → _____

2. _____ → _____

3. _____ → _____

Activity 2.7: How Am I Different?

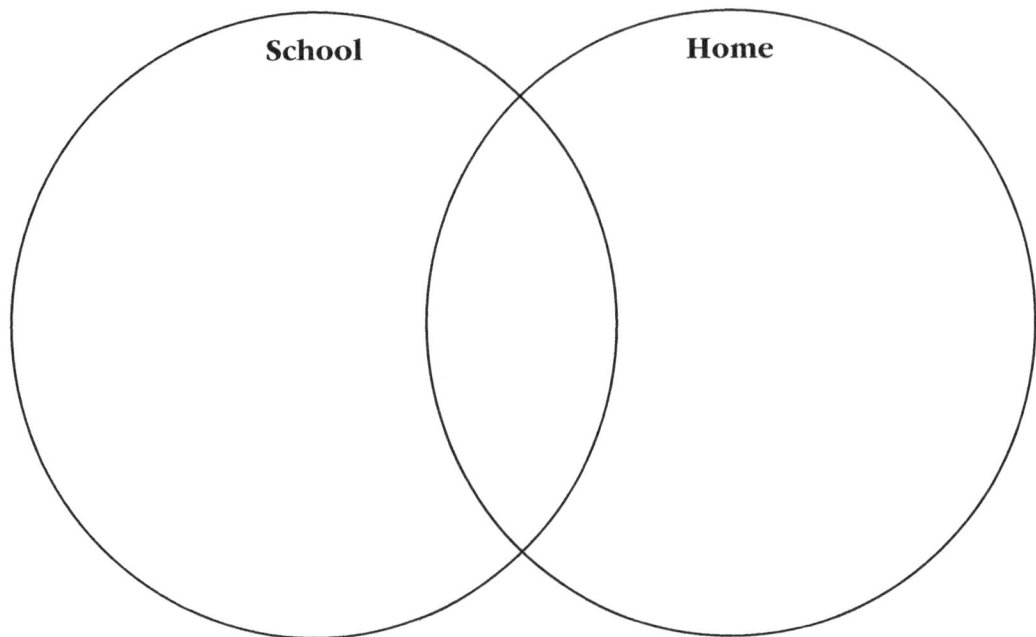

Activity 2.8: Impact on SELF

When I choose/do. . .   The effect on myself is. . .

1. _____ → _____

2. _____ → _____

3. _____ → _____

Activity 2.9: My Goals → My Actions

Goal: Steps I take to reach goal:

1. _____ → _____

2. _____ → _____

3. _____ → _____

Activity 2.10: My Goals → My Steps Backward, Sometimes

Goal: Things I do that keep me from
                                          achieving this:

1. _____ → _____

2. _____ → _____

3. _____ → _____

Activity 2.11: My Brain: What Stimulates It?

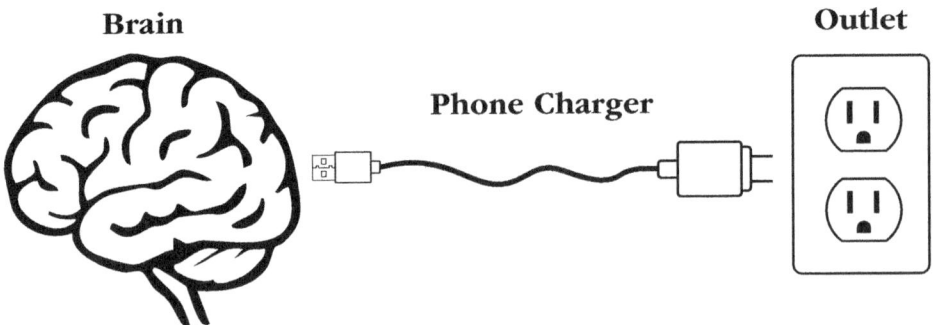

Brain   **Outlet**

Phone Charger

What are the things that stimulate *my* unique brain?

                                                    Yes   No

1. _____ → Is it helpful?   ☐   ☐

Why?

_____

                                                    Yes   No

2. _____ → Is it helpful?   ☐   ☐

Why?

_____

                                                    Yes   No

3. _____ → Is it helpful?   ☐   ☐

Why?

_____

CHAPTER 3

Self-Regulation

Helping Children Manage Their Emotions, Language, Body, and Behavior

If there's one chapter that captures the heart of what executive function challenges look like in daily life, it's this one.

This chapter focuses on self-regulation—the ability to pause, process, and respond intentionally rather than react impulsively. It is the core executive function skill that governs how children manage their emotions, words, movements, tone, energy, and behaviors. And for kids with ADHD, this skill is not just delayed—it's often missing entirely.

In *The Executive Function Playbook*, we reframe ADHD not as an attention problem but as a self-regulation disorder. This distinction matters. Children with ADHD can focus just fine—on video games, favorite activities, or high-stimulation environments. The real challenge is their ability to regulate that attention, shift it as needed, and manage their internal state when faced with frustration, boredom, disappointment, or unpredictability.

Self-regulation is what allows a child to:

- ◆ Calm themselves before lashing out
- ◆ Think before they speak
- ◆ Handle disappointment without a meltdown
- ◆ Recognize that an emotion is temporary
- ◆ Shift from "I can't" to "I can figure this out"

These are the very skills that determine how a child functions in the real world. Without self-regulation, a child may have potential—but lack the tools to access it. And while rewards, consequences, and behavior charts might help in the short term, they don't build internal control. That's what this chapter is here to do.

The worksheets in this chapter are carefully designed to help children:

◆ Identify their triggers and warning signs
◆ Strengthen the internal scripts they can use in difficult moments
◆ Practice healthy strategies for calming their body and brain
◆ Reflect on past outbursts without shame—and learn from them
◆ Create predictable routines and responses to dysregulation

These are not surface-level strategies. They are rooted in what we know about the developing brain—and the executive system that supports emotional regulation, impulse control, and delayed gratification.

Each page in this section is built to slow down the moment, increase reflection, and provide real tools your child can begin to internalize. You'll also notice that many pages ask you, the adult, to reflect as well—because your own emotional regulation plays a critical role in shaping your child's.

In *The Executive Function Playbook*, we talk about the importance of building "future thinking," "pause power," and "self-directed internal language." This chapter puts those ideas into practice. You'll help your child pause long enough to notice what's happening, think about their choices, and build the muscle memory to make better decisions the next time around.

Remember, your child is not choosing to overreact or explode. They are doing the best they can with the tools they have. This chapter is about giving them better tools—and using them together, one moment at a time.

Let's help your child go from reactive to reflective—and learn how to regulate from the inside out.

Activity 3.1: Ready vs. Not Ready, Part 1
Executive function skills strengthened: Self-awareness, self-regulation

OVERVIEW
Emotional self-regulation is one of the most foundational and most challenging executive function skills for children and teens with ADHD. One of the core messages emphasized in *The Executive Function Playbook* is that dysregulation is not the time for instruction, correction, or coaching—it's the time for space and safety. This page is a

powerful tool to help students build the essential awareness of their own emotional state: am I "ready" or "not ready"?

"Ready" does not mean perfection or compliance—it means the child is regulated, available for help, and functioning at a baseline level where they can listen, think, respond appropriately, and engage socially. "Not ready" means the opposite: the child is dysregulated, emotionally flooded, and unable to process language or interact productively with others.

INSTRUCTIONS FOR THE ADULT (PARENT, TEACHER, OR CLINICIAN)

This page is *not* meant to be filled out by the child. Instead, the adult models what it looks like to *observe* and *understand* regulation in real time. This is done by identifying and writing down the clear signs of when the child is "ready" vs. when they are "not ready." The adult writes; the child watches and learns.

1. **Label observable signs of regulation and dysregulation.**

   In the "Ready" column, list what the child looks, sounds, and acts like when regulated:
   - "You make eye contact."
   - "You can answer questions calmly."
   - "You stay in your space and don't yell."
   - "You listen and respond to feedback."
   - "You can work with others."

2. **In the "Not Ready" column, list dysregulation indicators:**
   - "You raise your voice or yell."
   - "You walk away or slam a door."
   - "You interrupt or talk over others."
   - "You shut down, won't speak, or lash out."
   - "You cannot be reasoned with or soothed with words."

3. **Make the differences clear and compassionate.**

   Explain that *everyone* has moments of being "not ready." This is not a bad thing—it's just part of being human. But in these moments, we all need the same thing: *space and time to return to baseline.* Kids must learn that help, coaching, and connection are only possible when they are *ready.*

4. **Explain the role of adults during dysregulation.**

   Remind the child of a key principle from *The Executive Function Playbook*:

   "Language makes dysregulation worse."

When a child is dysregulated, they cannot process words, logic, or problem-solving. It is the adult's job to step away, stay calm, and allow the child space to self-regulate. Repeating directions, arguing, or talking only escalates the moment.

Why This Skill Matters

Children with ADHD often have difficulty identifying their internal states. They may go from 0 to 100 without realizing they were even dysregulated in the first place. This page helps make those patterns visible and explicit.

It also strengthens the child's ability to eventually *self-identify* when they are approaching dysregulation—and to choose to follow their safety plan or take space on their own. The more familiar they become with what "ready" feels like and looks like, the more likely they are to seek regulation before behavior escalates.

This is also an essential page for parents, teachers, and clinicians who may feel powerless or reactive in the face of a dysregulated child. It gives adults permission to stop talking and to remove themselves from the interaction when "helping" is no longer possible.

Tips for Adults Using This Page

Review before you need it: This page should be reviewed when the child is *already* calm—not during a moment of dysregulation.

Display it visibly: Keep this page visible in the home or classroom as a visual reminder.

Use visuals or icons: Some students may benefit from cartoon faces or traffic lights (green = ready, red = not ready) as visual cues.

Narrate transitions: Model aloud: "I can see you're not ready right now, and that's okay. I'm going to step away so you can have space."

KEY MESSAGE

Regulation is the foundation of all executive functions. If a child is not regulated, no learning, helping, or parenting can happen effectively.

CLOSING THOUGHT

The most powerful growth moments don't happen during dysregulation—they happen *after*. When a child learns to recognize their "not ready" state and use space to return to calm, they are building the lifelong muscles of emotional independence and resilience.

Activity 3.2: Ready vs. Not Ready, Part 2

Executive function skills strengthened: Self-awareness, self-regulation

OVERVIEW

Building on the foundational insights from the previous page, this exercise expands a child's understanding of their own internal state by helping them explicitly connect their behavior to how *others* will respond. In *The Executive Function Playbook*, we emphasize that children with ADHD often struggle with perspective-taking—not only how they feel in a moment but how their behavior shapes the reactions of others around them.

This page bridges that gap. It helps children and teens understand:

◆ *"When I am regulated, I invite support."*

◆ *"When I am dysregulated, I push others away—because they cannot help me at that time."*

For students with ADHD who crave connection but often sabotage it during dysregulated moments, this can be a profound shift in awareness.

INSTRUCTIONS FOR THE ADULT

This worksheet is designed to be collaborative. Adults—whether parents, teachers, or clinicians—work directly with the child to fill in the blanks. Use real-life language and examples specific to the child's behavior patterns and support needs.

The two prompts to complete are:

1. **When [child's name] is READY, parents and teachers can:**
    → This is where you help the child identify how others can step in and be helpful when they are calm and available for support.
    Examples:
    • "Give reminders."
    • "Talk about next steps."
    • "Ask questions or give encouragement."
    • "Help problem-solve a situation."
    • "Work as a team."
2. **When [child's name] is NOT READY, parents and teachers can:**
    → This is where you help the child understand what adults will do when they are dysregulated.
    Examples:
    • "Give space."
    • "Step away quietly."

- "Stop talking."
- "Let you follow your safety plan."
- "Wait until you're calm before helping."

Make sure the child understands that these responses are not punishments—they are logical, respectful, and protective actions meant to preserve emotional safety for *everyone*.

Why This Skill Matters

Children with ADHD often don't realize how much power they have in shaping how others respond to them. They may view adult behavior as unpredictable, unfair, or overly strict. In reality, most adult responses are a direct reaction to the child's internal regulation. This page helps children internalize this sequence:

My regulation → invites support. My dysregulation → requires space.

This creates a new pathway to motivation: if I want others to help me, I need to work on becoming ready first. That's self-regulation.

The Deeper Message for Parents and Teachers

As *The Executive Function Playbook* discusses, ADHD is not a behavior problem—it is a regulation and skill development challenge. When we teach kids what it *looks like* to be in a "ready" state and how their internal state determines how others interact with them, we build both their *emotional intelligence* and *relational awareness*.

This is not just helpful for school success—it is essential for life success.

Suggestions for Use

- **Review it together:** Revisit this page after moments of dysregulation to reflect and reinforce awareness.
- **Use visuals or icons:** Create a chart or traffic light visual using these statements as cues.
- **Model your own states:** Adults can narrate their own regulation ("I'm feeling dysregulated, so I'm going to take a breath before I speak").

KEY MESSAGE

How others treat us is often a reflection of our current emotional state. When we are calm and regulated, we invite collaboration and support. When we are dysregulated, we must first focus on returning to calm before connection is possible.

CLOSING THOUGHT

When children realize they have the power to influence how adults respond to them—simply by managing their own emotional state—they begin to take true ownership of their behavior. That is the essence of growing up with executive function skills.

Activity 3.3: Ready vs. Not Ready, Part 4

Executive function skills strengthened: Self-awareness, self-regulation, social perspective-taking

This page builds on the previous exercises by helping children and teens take a more proactive and reflective approach to managing their dysregulation. The primary goal is to help them identify personal triggers that lead to dysregulation ("Not Ready"), determine specific strategies to help themselves return to regulation ("Ready"), and deepen their understanding of how their behavior impacts others around them.

Students with ADHD and executive function challenges often lack awareness of the sequence of events that leads to an outburst or dysregulated episode. They tend to experience intense emotions without understanding the antecedents, and they struggle to recognize how their actions affect others in the moment. This lack of insight makes it incredibly difficult for them to break the cycle of dysregulation.

In this activity, adults are encouraged to sit down with the child to explore three crucial components:

1. **Triggers:** "These are the things that make me Not Ready."
   This helps the student identify patterns in their day—specific situations, tasks, or interactions that are most likely to push them out of regulation. Examples may include: "Being rushed in the morning," "Getting corrected in front of classmates," or "Having to stop a preferred activity."

2. **Regulation strategies:** "To become READY again, I can do these three things. . .."
   This builds self-regulation by encouraging the student to generate and agree on personal calming strategies or self-soothing activities. These must be practical and realistic for the environment (e.g., taking a break, deep breathing, stepping outside, going to a quiet corner). These skills align with research on cognitive-behavioral interventions and mindfulness-based regulation strategies that have been shown to improve emotional and behavioral control in children with ADHD.

3. **Perspective-taking:** "When I am READY, I make others feel _____."
   This section helps develop empathy and perspective-taking. It encourages the child to think about the emotional impact they have on the people around them when they are regulated and functioning at their best. This promotes a sense of social responsibility and emotional intelligence, key areas that are often delayed in neurodiverse youth.

Adults may need to scaffold this conversation, offering real-life examples and gentle reminders of past scenarios. This is not about punishment or shame—it's about developing insight and building metacognitive awareness, which Dr. Russell Barkley and other EF experts cite as core executive function skills that support long-term success.

KEY MESSAGE

Helping children identify their triggers, regulation strategies, and impact on others deepens their self-awareness and equips them with practical tools for emotional control and social success.

CLOSING THOUGHT

Emotional regulation isn't just about calming down—it's about understanding what sets you off, having a plan to recover, and recognizing how your behavior shapes the way others experience you. These are the building blocks of emotional maturity and resilient relationships.

Activity 3.4: Emotion → Action

Executive function skills strengthened: Self-regulation

This worksheet is designed to help students slow down and recognize the link between their emotions and their actions—something that is often impaired in children and teens with ADHD and executive functioning challenges. At the core of this activity is the concept of response inhibition—the ability to pause before acting, which is a foundational executive function that allows for emotional control, planning, and socially appropriate behavior.

ADHD brains are wired for immediacy. When emotions arise, especially frustration, embarrassment, or boredom, children may act impulsively without thinking through the consequences. Emotional responses like yelling, storming off, or refusing to comply can happen before their rational brain has a chance to intervene. That's why this activity introduces a stepwise structure for helping students recognize emotional cues in their body and re-route their responses through self-regulation strategies.

This worksheet follows a three-part sequence:

1. **Emotion to impulse mapping:**
   "When I feel _____, my body tells me to _____."

   This helps the student identify a core emotion and the immediate, often automatic behavioral response that follows. For example:

   "When I feel overwhelmed, my body tells me to shut down and avoid everything."

This reflection helps increase interoceptive awareness—recognizing internal bodily cues that signal emotional states, which is a crucial but underdeveloped skill in many neurodiverse learners.

2. **Introducing the pause:**
   "But when I Stop, Breathe, and talk to my Brain Coach. . ."
   Here, we activate the "pause button." This is the moment of interruption that helps transition from a reactive to a reflective state. It incorporates the GrowNOW internal skills model, specifically the use of verbal working memory (internal self-talk) via the Brain Coach concept to engage the rational, goal-directed parts of the brain. This moment of pause is often missing in ADHD behavior but is essential for emotional growth.

3. **Intentional action:**
   ". . .I am able to _____ instead."
   Now, the child identifies a better action—one that aligns with their goals and values rather than with the emotional impulse. This final reflection helps reinforce healthier behavioral patterns and creates a mental script the student can return to in future situations.

This kind of cognitive restructuring exercise draws from the principles of cognitive-behavioral therapy (CBT) but simplifies it into a visual and language-supported scaffold that is developmentally appropriate for children. It helps them learn that emotions are not the enemy—they're data. But without regulation, emotions can take the steering wheel.

KEY MESSAGE
You don't have to act on every feeling you have. With practice, you can pause, listen to your brain coach, and choose a better path forward.

CLOSING THOUGHT
Self-regulation begins with awareness. By learning to recognize the space between emotion and action, children develop the power to choose how they respond—not just react. That's where true growth begins.

Activity 3.5: Safety Plan
Executive function skills strengthened: Self-regulation

This workbook page is designed specifically for students who experience moments of significant emotional dysregulation during the school day—episodes that may lead to disruptive, aggressive, or unsafe behaviors. These moments are not signs of a "bad child" but rather indicators that the student lacks access to the self-regulation tools and structure needed in that moment.

The goal of this page is to proactively build a predictable plan—so when a student begins to feel dysregulated, they know exactly what to do, and the adults around them know how to respond consistently.

This page is completed with the student and school staff. It includes four clearly labeled sections:

1. **When I feel dysregulated at school, I know that I can...**

   (These are healthy, safe actions the student is allowed to take when emotions rise.)

   Examples:
   - Ask for a break using a predetermined signal or card.
   - Take three deep breaths and count backward.
   - Get a drink of water.
   - Use a fidget or sensory tool at my desk.

2. **I can go to these safe places in the school to calm down...**

   (Designated spaces where the student can regulate safely without causing disruption.)

   Examples:
   - The guidance counselor's office
   - The regulation or sensory room
   - A quiet desk in the hallway
   - The main office (if monitored and appropriate)

3. **I will use these calming strategies when I arrive...**

   (Specific strategies tailored to the student that will help bring them back to baseline.)

   Examples:
   - Listen to music with headphones.
   - Stretch or do wall push-ups.
   - Journal or draw in a notebook.
   - Use a weighted lap pad and rest quietly for five minutes.

4. **When I am ready again, I will...**

   (Clear steps for reintegrating into class or returning to routine.)

   Examples:
   - Return to class and tell the teacher "I'm ready now."
   - Write a short reflection about what happened.
   - Review expectations with a staff member before rejoining.
   - Pick up where I left off with my schoolwork.

This worksheet helps all staff members support the student in the same, consistent way. It also helps the student internalize the message that dysregulation is not shameful—it's manageable when we have a plan and the right tools in place.

KEY MESSAGE

A self-regulation safety plan gives students structure, predictability, and tools to manage big emotions before they escalate.

CLOSING THOUGHT

We don't wait for storms to arrive to build shelter. This safety plan is the student's shelter—a place they know they can go, and what they can do, when emotions become too much.

Activity 3.1: Ready vs. Not Ready: Part 1

(1) Ready _____ (child's name) _____

Characteristics:

_____

_____

_____

(2) Not Ready _____ (child's name) _____

Characteristics:

_____

_____

_____

Activity 3.2: Ready vs. Not Ready: Part 2

(1) When _____ (child's name) is <u>ready</u>, parents and teachers can:

_____

_____

_____

(2) When _____ (child's name) is <u>NOT ready</u>, parents and teachers can:

_____

_____

_____

Activity 3.3: Ready vs. Not Ready: Part 4

These things make me <u>NOT Ready</u> (child's name). _____

_____

_____

_____

To become <u>Ready</u> _____ (child's name), I can:

_____

_____

_____

When I am <u>Ready</u> _____ (child's name), I make others feel:

_____

_____

_____

Activity 3.4: Emotion → Action

When I feel _____, my body tells me to _____.

But when I stop, breathe, and talk to my Brain Coach, I am able to
_____ instead.

Activity 3.5: Safety Plan

When I feel dysregulated at school, I know that I can. . .	I can go to these safe places in the school to calm down. . .
I will use these calming strategies when I arrive. . .	When I am ready again, I will. . .

CHAPTER 4

Self-Motivation

Helping Kids and Teens Take Initiative, Persist Through Challenges, and Follow Through

Self-motivation is the ability to start something hard, stick with it when it gets uncomfortable, and finish it even when it's no longer exciting. For children and teens with ADHD, this skill is often one of the most misunderstood—and most underdeveloped.

In *The Executive Function Playbook*, we explore the uncomfortable truth that many kids with ADHD are not struggling with attention—they are struggling with activation. They know what needs to be done. They may even want to do it. But the internal engine that drives most people to start, persist, and complete tasks is often quiet or missing entirely. That's not laziness—it's a lagging executive function skill.

Self-motivation is what allows a child to:

- ◆ Start a nonpreferred task without being reminded
- ◆ Stay with it through boredom or frustration
- ◆ Complete it without giving up or melting down
- ◆ Take ownership over their responsibilities
- ◆ Work toward a goal without needing a reward every time

This chapter includes a collection of worksheets that bring those motivational systems to life. These pages are not designed to push your child harder—they're designed to build the internal scaffolding they need in order to push themselves.

The activities in this chapter help your child:

◆ Visualize their future self and connect actions to long-term goals
◆ Break down overwhelming tasks into smaller, manageable steps
◆ Reflect on the benefits of persistence—even when no one is watching
◆ Replace helpless statements like "I can't" with action-based thinking
◆ Learn how to self-start instead of waiting to be told what to do

In *The Executive Function Playbook*, we talk about the importance of future thinking, internal language, and task initiation—and how these skills must be explicitly taught to children with ADHD. This chapter is where that teaching happens in practice.

Each page is a step toward helping your child move from external motivation ("Will I get a reward?") to internal motivation ("This is hard, but I can do it—and it's worth doing"). You'll begin to see your child build what we refer to in the playbook as "future-you thinking"—the ability to take action now in service of a better outcome later.

As always, these worksheets are meant to be completed together. Your role as the adult is not to provide the motivation, but to coach, guide, and model what it looks like to work through discomfort. Many of these activities will also highlight the importance of consistency, structure, and connection—because children build self-motivation when they know what's expected and believe someone is walking alongside them.

Initiation. Persistence. Completion. These aren't character traits—they are teachable skills. And this chapter is where the work begins.

Let's help your child learn to take the first step—even when it's hard—and keep going until they're proud of what they've done.

Activity 4.1: Getting That Feeling

Executive function skills strengthened: Self-motivation, self-awareness

Motivation doesn't always come before action—sometimes, it comes *from* the action. One of the greatest challenges for students with ADHD is initiating tasks that seem boring, difficult, or unimportant in the moment. Their executive function delays—especially with delayed gratification and working memory—make it hard to *remember* how good something feels *after* it's done. This worksheet helps build that internal connection between effort and reward by making the emotional payoff *visible and memorable*.

INSTRUCTIONS FOR STUDENT AND ADULT TO COMPLETE TOGETHER

List three things you've done recently that were hard to start or not that exciting at first—but once you did them, you felt really good about it afterward.

What I Did	How I Felt Before I Started	How I Felt After I Finished
Example: Cleaned my room	Overwhelmed and annoyed	Proud and calm—it looked great afterward
Example: Studied for my math test	Bored and frustrated	Accomplished and surprised I remembered stuff
Example: Helped my sister with homework	Didn't want to do it at all	Happy I helped and that she said thank you

Why This Matters

Children with ADHD often say "I don't want to!" when asked to do something hard—but what they *mean* is, "I'm afraid I won't feel good while doing it." This worksheet gives them real, concrete proof that the *outcome* is often worth the effort. It builds a feedback loop between action and positive emotion. That's self-motivation in action.

When a student can recall and internalize the positive feeling they get *after* completing a challenging or nonpreferred task, they build the cognitive muscle to push through the initial discomfort the next time that task comes around.

KEY MESSAGE

The feeling of success doesn't come before the hard work—it comes *because of it.*

CLOSING THOUGHT

When you take action—even on something small—you prove to yourself that you can do hard things. That feeling of pride, relief, and strength? That's what makes you want to keep going. Keep chasing *that* feeling.

Activity 4.2: Wants and Needs

Executive function skills strengthened: Self-motivation, self-awareness

A key developmental milestone for children and teens with ADHD is learning to distinguish between *wants* and *needs*—especially when it comes to functioning independently in school, at home, and in social relationships. This worksheet is designed to build that internal awareness and develop the executive function skill of delayed gratification. Students often operate from a "now brain," focused only on immediate comfort or stimulation. This worksheet helps bridge the gap between short-term wants and long-term goals by creating a visual representation of the important (but less preferred) tasks that need to get done.

INSTRUCTIONS

With an adult (parent, teacher, or clinician), the child will complete the following chart by first listing what they *want* to do in each setting, followed by what they actually *need* to do to be successful, respected, and well-liked.

Setting	What I Want to Do	⮕ What I Need to Do
At School	Play on my Chromebook, make my friends laugh	⮕ Pay attention to the teacher, stay on task, and ask for help when needed
At Home	Watch YouTube, play video games, avoid chores	⮕ Help clean up, do my homework, follow the evening routine
With Friends	Talk only about my interests, be the leader all the time	⮕ Listen to others, take turns, do what *they* want to do sometimes too

Why This Matters

Students with ADHD often struggle to understand that while their wants are real and valid, they don't always align with what's necessary to succeed in structured environments or relationships. This worksheet gives them an intentional moment of reflection and planning—clarifying that "doing what I need to do" leads to longer-lasting rewards like trust, respect, and independence.

By connecting wants and needs side by side, the student begins to internalize the concept that effort leads to growth, and growth opens more opportunities for choice and freedom in the future.

KEY MESSAGE

Wants give us comfort—but meeting our needs gives us success.

CLOSING THOUGHT

Life won't always give you what you *want* in the moment—but when you consistently do what you *need* to do, you'll build the life you *want* over time.

Activity 4.3: Who Am I?

Executive function skills strengthened: Self-motivation, self-evaluation, self-awareness

Children and teens with ADHD often struggle with self-concept, particularly when their days are filled with redirection, correction, and comparison. Over time, this can wear down their motivation and inner drive, creating a false internal narrative: "I'm not good at anything" or "I can't do this." That's why this page is designed as a grounding daily activity—to re-anchor their sense of identity, personal strengths, and purpose.

This worksheet can be completed each morning as a simple yet powerful exercise in self-affirmation and intention-setting. It helps the student reflect on who they are *today*, what they bring to the world, and how they can continue to grow.

INSTRUCTIONS

With an adult, the child or teen fills out the prompts. These answers can change and evolve over time, and that's the point—growth is a process.

This last statement ("Every day I have to. . .") is especially important. It's meant to clarify that there are non-negotiable expectations in life—routines, responsibilities, and values that, when practiced consistently, make life easier and more rewarding.

Why This Matters

This worksheet helps students internalize the idea that while ADHD may impact their day-to-day functioning, it does not define their identity. They are whole, valuable individuals who have strengths, areas for growth, and personal responsibilities. It also reinforces that effort, not perfection, is what drives success over time.

When done daily or weekly, this page becomes an executive function ritual—one that sets a tone of resilience, ownership, and personal empowerment.

KEY MESSAGE

You are a work in progress—and that's exactly how growth happens.

CLOSING THOUGHT

Knowing who you are, where you shine, and where you're still growing is the foundation of lasting self-motivation. You're not behind—you're becoming.

Activity 4.4: Letter to My Friday Future Self

Executive function skills strengthened: Nonverbal working memory, verbal working memory, self-awareness, self-motivation

This exercise helps students develop the essential executive function of *future thinking*—the ability to visualize their future self and use that vision to guide present-day decisions. Many students with ADHD struggle with time blindness. They live in the now, acting impulsively and emotionally without realizing that their current behaviors ripple into their future experiences.

This worksheet gives students a powerful tool to build motivation and clarity for the week ahead by imagining the version of themselves they *want* to become by Friday.

INSTRUCTIONS

On Monday, sit with the student and complete the following reflection or letter. If they are a younger student, this can be a discussion with you writing down their ideas. Older students may write their own letter.

Prompt

"On Monday, I will talk about or write about who I want my Friday Future Self to be and how I want him/her to feel."

Students will then reflect on and complete the prompts.

Weekly Follow-Up (Friday Reflection)

At the end of the week, revisit the letter and reflect:

◆ Did I become the version of myself I wanted to be?
◆ What helped me get there?
◆ What got in the way, and how can I do better next week?

Why This Matters

Students with ADHD often respond better to *concrete visualizations* than vague instructions. This page helps them *see* who they're becoming and gives them ownership over their personal development. When they begin a week with the end in mind, they can make better in-the-moment choices—even when tempted by distraction or frustration.

It's also a gentle reminder that their time and their effort *matter*. The adult's role here is to guide the student in using internal language to coach themselves toward success—one week at a time.

KEY MESSAGE

Every decision you make today builds the story your Friday self will tell. Make it a story you're proud of.

CLOSING THOUGHT

Your future self is always watching. Be the kind of person you'd want to become.

Activity 4.5: An Emotion of the Future

Executive function skills strengthened: Self-motivation

This workbook page focuses on helping students understand one of the most powerful concepts behind lasting motivation: *future-driven emotion*. When students with ADHD learn to delay gratification and visualize a positive emotional outcome, they are more likely to make healthy, productive choices in the present.

Many impulsive behaviors stem from the belief that "now is all there is." This page helps counter that mindset by teaching the student that what they do *now* has a direct impact on how they feel *later*. It gives them the language to connect actions to outcomes—an essential internal skill for executive function growth.

INSTRUCTIONS

With the help of an adult, the child or teen completes the following sentence frames:

- In the future, I want to feel:
- To feel that way, I need to do this *now*:

For example:

- *In the future, I want to feel proud and strong.*
- *In order to feel proud and strong, I need to do this now: finish my homework and go for a walk.*

The adult may prompt the child to think of specific settings:

- How do you want to feel this weekend?
- How do you want to feel after the school day?
- How do you want to feel next summer?

Help them understand that real, lasting happiness and pride often come after effort—not avoidance.

Discussion Prompts for Deeper Reflection
- What things make you feel great afterward—even if they're hard at first?
- What are some things that feel good in the moment but don't help you feel better later?
- What would your "best self" choose to do right now?

Why This Matters
Emotion is the most powerful driver of action for all humans. For kids with ADHD, tapping into *positive emotional forecasting* is one of the most effective ways to move them away from screen-based, short-term dopamine rewards and toward meaningful, lasting experiences.

We are not forcing kids to *do* something—they are choosing to move toward how they *want to feel*. That's internal motivation.

KEY MESSAGE

If you want to feel proud, calm, happy, and strong *later*—make choices now that move you closer to that feeling.

CLOSING THOUGHT

Every action you take is a vote for the kind of person—and the kind of emotions—you want to feel in your future.

Activity 4.6: I'm Bored!

Executive function skills strengthened: Self-regulation, self-motivation, verbal working memory

This workbook page addresses one of the most common and frustrating phrases heard by parents of kids with ADHD: "I'm bored!" For these children, boredom is more than discomfort—it's often intolerable. Because their brains are wired to seek stimulation and instant gratification, boredom can feel like a crisis. And for parents, this constant plea for stimulation often results in frustration and fatigue.

But here's the truth: boredom is not the enemy. In fact, learning to sit with boredom, to tolerate it, and to move through it constructively is an essential life skill—and one that helps build the foundation of executive functioning.

INSTRUCTIONS FOR PARENTS AND CAREGIVERS

On this page, list a set of **parent-approved** and **screen-free** boredom options that the child can turn to independently. These should be reasonable, safe, and realistic activities the child can do without needing you to be their constant entertainment system.

Use sentence stems like:

◆ When I say "I'm bored," I can choose to:

These might include activities like:

◆ Build something with Legos
◆ Draw or color
◆ Do a puzzle
◆ Read a graphic novel
◆ Write in your journal
◆ Go outside and ride your bike
◆ Create your own comic strip
◆ Listen to calming music

◆ Organize your room or desk
◆ Make up a new game with a sibling or pet

Be sure to review and update this list regularly with the child, so they feel involved in choosing meaningful options.

Guidance for Adults

◆ Avoid the temptation to swoop in and solve boredom. That only deepens the dependency.
◆ Instead, when your child says, "I'm bored," gently redirect them to this worksheet.
◆ Reinforce the idea that boredom is a starting point, not a problem to be fixed by someone else.

Boredom tolerance is like a muscle—it must be stretched and strengthened. ADHD kids need opportunities to build this tolerance so they can persevere in real-life settings that won't always be stimulating or immediately rewarding.

KEY MESSAGE
Boredom isn't a bad thing—it's a chance to get creative, take initiative, and grow.

CLOSING THOUGHT
The more you practice managing boredom, the stronger and more independent your brain becomes. Every time you choose a new activity instead of complaining, you are training your brain to be more focused, flexible, and self-motivated.

Activity 4.7: Now and Later
Executive function skills strengthened: Self-motivation

OVERVIEW
Self-motivation is not about doing something simply because an adult told you to. It is the internal spark that drives individuals—especially children—to engage in purposeful, goal-directed behavior. For children with ADHD and executive function challenges, this spark often needs to be intentionally developed through structured reflection and guided language. Many of these children struggle with future thinking—the ability to connect their present actions with long-term goals and consequences. Instead, they live reactively in the present moment, often opting for short-term gratification over long-term benefit.

This workbook page helps children begin to internalize the idea that their present behavior builds their future. By creating a visual and verbal link between their dreams ("I want my future to look like. . .") and their daily responsibilities ("So right now I have to. . ."), this page teaches basic cause-and-effect reasoning, builds internal language for future planning, and fosters a sense of ownership over their goals.

INSTRUCTIONS FOR THE ADULT

Sit down with the child in a quiet, distraction-free environment. Begin by discussing the concept of the future self—an idea that can often feel abstract or irrelevant to children with ADHD. Use this page to help them start building a bridge between now and later by identifying what they want their life to look like down the road and then brainstorming steps they can take today to move toward that future.

Be patient. Some children may struggle to articulate long-term goals. Provide examples, offer encouragement, and celebrate any effort to think ahead—even if the ideas seem unrealistic or immature. What matters is the process of connecting actions to outcomes.

STEP-BY-STEP GUIDANCE

1. **Introduce future thinking.**
   Explain: "Everyone has a 'future self'—a version of us that exists a few months or years from now. That future is shaped by what we do today."
2. **Complete the first prompt together.**
   Read the statement: *"I want my future to look like. . ."*
   Encourage the child to think out loud. You can prompt them with questions such as:
   • What kind of job do you want?
   • Where do you want to live?
   • What kind of friends or family do you want around you?
   • Do you want money, travel, free time, fun?
3. Let the child draw or write in the space provided.
4. **Shift to the present.**
   Read the next statement: *"So, right now I have to. . ."*
   Help the child identify at least one or two concrete actions they can take today to begin working toward that future.
   Examples:
   • If they want to be a video game designer → "So right now I have to practice coding or drawing."
   • If they want to have lots of friends → "So right now I have to practice being kind and flexible."

5. Use positive framing.

Avoid framing this as a punishment or demand. Instead, highlight how empowering it is to take action now that can lead to something exciting later.

6. Review and reflect.

Ask the child how it feels to have a goal and a plan. Praise their ability to connect the dots between today and tomorrow.

KEY MESSAGE

Self-motivation grows when children see that their present actions matter. By teaching them to visualize the future they want—and linking it to actionable steps they can take now—we shift motivation from external reminders to internal purpose.

CLOSING THOUGHT

Many children with ADHD live in the "now" and rarely consider the "later." But when we help them build the language and structure to think ahead, we empower them to take charge of their lives. Motivation is not just about willpower—it's about making the future feel real today.

RESEARCH REFERENCE

Barkley, R. A. (2012). *Executive Functions: What They Are, How They Work, and Why They Evolved*. New York, NY: Guilford Press.

Activity 4.1: Getting That Feeling

When I: It makes me feel:

1. _____ → _____

2. _____ → _____

3. _____ → _____

Activity 4.2: Wants and Needs

School

What I want to do: What I need to do:

_____ → _____

_____ → _____

_____ → _____

Home

What I want to do: What I need to do:

_____ → _____

_____ → _____

_____ → _____

Social

What I want to do: What I need to do:

_____ → _____

_____ → _____

_____ → _____

Activity 4.3: Who Am I?

My name is _____

My strengths are

_____

_____

_____

I can grow at

_____

_____

_____

Every day I have to

_____

_____

_____

Activity 4.4: Letter to My Future Self (Monday → Friday)

On *Monday*, I will talk about or write about who I want my *Friday Future Self* to be and how I want them to feel.

Dear Friday Future Self,

Activity 4.5: An Emotion of the Future

In the future, I want to feel _____.

To feel that way, I need to do this *now:*

_____

_____

_____

Activity 4.6: I'm Bored!

When I say "I'm bored," I can choose to:

Activity 4.7: Now and Later

I want my future to look like:

So right now, I have to:

_____

_____

_____

CHAPTER 5

Self-Evaluation

Helping Kids Learn from the Past, Reflect in the Present, and Build a Better Future

One of the most frustrating patterns parents report—and one of the most painful to witness—is this: a child or teen with ADHD continues to make the same mistakes over and over again, even after consequences, reminders, conversations, and tears. Nothing seems to stick. Nothing seems to change.

This is not laziness. This is not defiance. This is a lack of self-evaluation—a crucial executive function skill that allows us to reflect on our actions, process the outcomes, and adjust our behavior going forward.

This chapter is all about building that skill, from the inside out.

In *The Executive Function Playbook*, we explore how many children and teens with ADHD have trouble forming an internal "pause and reflect" system. They often live in the moment, reacting based on impulse and emotion rather than reason or reflection. As a result, they may not notice how their behavior impacts others. They may not connect yesterday's actions to today's consequences. They may not even remember how they got into trouble in the first place.

Without self-evaluation, there can be no real growth. Mistakes are repeated. Apologies are hollow. And the child begins to believe they are "bad" or "broken," when in reality, they are simply underdeveloped in this one foundational skill.

The good news? Self-evaluation can be taught. It just needs to be broken down, modeled, practiced, and—most importantly—made safe.

This chapter helps children begin to ask:

- What did I do yesterday?
- How did it affect others—and myself?
- What can I do differently today?
- Who do I want to become, and what's holding me back?
- How do my actions shape my identity and future?

These aren't easy questions. But they are life-changing.

Each worksheet in this chapter is designed to gently guide your child through moments of reflection—without shame, lectures, or fear. These pages create space for honest conversation, pattern recognition, and future-focused goal setting. They help your child begin to see themselves as a learner, not a failure—and to understand that reflection is not about guilt, but about growth.

In *The Executive Function Playbook*, we explain that self-evaluation is the link between working memory and self-regulation. Kids must be able to pull past experiences into their present thinking in order to behave differently. These worksheets help them make that link. They move your child from, "I don't know why I did that," to, "Next time, I'm going to try this instead."

You'll find pages that:

- Explore past behaviors and their emotional consequences
- Identify "steps forward" and "steps backward" in achieving goals
- Reflect on patterns, routines, and reactions that need to change
- Reinforce accountability in a calm, structured way
- Celebrate growth—even when it's small or slow

The goal here is not to make your child feel bad. The goal is to help them think better—to become the kind of person who learns from mistakes, self-corrects, and takes pride in progress.

With enough modeling, safety, and repetition, these reflection tools will begin to strengthen your child's nonverbal working memory, helping them carry yesterday's experiences into today's decisions.

This is the key to long-term growth.

When your child learns how to reflect—really reflect—they stop needing to be told the same thing over and over again. They stop blaming others. They stop hiding. And they start owning their actions, their growth, and their future.

Let's begin the journey of helping your child see themselves clearly—not with judgment but with hope. Once they believe they can grow, they will.

Activity 5.1: GrowNOW Video Journals

Executive function skills strengthened: Self-evaluation

OVERVIEW

Students with ADHD often struggle with *self-monitoring*—the ability to track their own performance, reflect on their behavior, and make adjustments without being told. In *The Executive Function Playbook*, we explore how this challenge is closely tied to deficits in working memory, emotional regulation, and delayed internal development of self-talk and self-reflection.

Traditionally, journaling has been used as a powerful tool to support emotional insight, identity formation, and goal-setting in youth. However, students with ADHD frequently find written journaling to be tedious, slow, and frustrating. Writing requires sustained attention, emotional regulation, task initiation, memory retrieval, and motor output—skills already underdeveloped in this population.

Instead of forcing a model that doesn't fit, this page introduces an innovative adaptation: video journals. By using the child's natural comfort with screens and their interest in seeing themselves on camera, we can preserve the *benefits* of journaling while removing the *barriers*. Video journals allow students to speak freely, reflect in real time, and access a record of their own words, thoughts, and goals—without relying on writing.

This practice supports the development of self-evaluation, the executive function skill that allows individuals to step outside of themselves, observe their own behavior, and make deliberate changes. Over time, regular use of video journals can increase independence, strengthen internal motivation, and reduce overreliance on adult prompting.

INSTRUCTIONS FOR THE ADULT (PARENT, TEACHER, OR CLINICIAN)

Set this up as a regular, low-pressure habit—daily or a few times per week. Use a phone, tablet, or laptop camera. The video doesn't need to be long (two to five minutes is enough), and it does not need to be watched by anyone else unless the child wants to share it.

What matters most is that the child is practicing thinking about their day, setting intentions, and evaluating outcomes.

Make it part of the routine: morning video + evening video.

STEP-BY-STEP GUIDANCE

Morning Video Journal (Before the Day or Task Begins):

Record a short video with your child answering the following four prompts. Adults can ask the questions off-camera or let the child speak freely in sequence.

1. **What are my goals for today?**

   Encourage one to three short goals. These can be behavioral, emotional, academic, or social.

2. **What does my perfect day look like?**

   This prompt builds future thinking and intentionality. It invites the child to visualize their own ideal and align their behavior with it.

3. **What do I want to avoid today?**

   Help them build awareness of common distractions, pitfalls, or emotional triggers. This develops internal monitoring and anticipation.

4. **How do I want to feel at the end of the day?**

   This connects the day's goals to an internal emotional outcome (pride, relief, confidence, calm), strengthening emotional regulation and forward planning.

Evening Video Journal (After the Day or Task Ends):

At the end of the day, record a second video to reflect on how things went. Guide the child through the following three prompts:

5. **What went well today?**

   Help the child celebrate small wins. This builds confidence and reinforces progress.

6. **What didn't go well?**

   Encourage honesty without shame. The goal is to normalize setbacks as learning opportunities.

7. **What are my goals for tomorrow?**

   Support the child in carrying forward momentum or addressing what needs improvement. This reflection-to-action loop builds long-term self-reliance.

WHY THIS MATTERS

Self-evaluation is a critical component of executive function growth—and one of the most overlooked in ADHD treatment. Children who don't regularly reflect on their choices and outcomes tend to repeat mistakes, misread their own progress, and remain dependent on adult prompts for change.

By using technology *as a tool* instead of a distraction, this activity makes self-reflection accessible and engaging. Children begin to build a digital library of their own insights, thoughts, and growth over time. This process nurtures internal motivation, metacognition, and a stronger sense of ownership over their decisions and behavior.

KEY MESSAGE

Video journals are a developmentally appropriate and ADHD-friendly alternative to written reflection. When students consistently set goals, reflect on outcomes, and visualize their success using their own voice and face, they grow in self-awareness, emotional control, and independence.

CLOSING THOUGHT

When children see themselves, they begin to know themselves. Video journaling turns passive experience into active reflection. It transforms everyday moments into lessons—and turns students into the authors of their own growth story.

RESEARCH REFERENCE

Pennebaker, J. W., & Smyth, J. M. (2016). *Opening Up by Writing It Down*. Guilford Press.

Activity 5.2: Who Gets Which Version of Me?

Executive function skills strengthened: Self-awareness, self-evaluation

OVERVIEW

A key theme in *The Executive Function Playbook* is helping students recognize that executive function development is not just about skills—it's about *relationships*. Children and teens with ADHD often struggle to understand the social and emotional dynamics of how they "show up" in different settings and with different people. They may not realize that they present very differently depending on who they're with—and that these differences are often shaped by comfort level, emotional safety, triggers, and internal regulation.

This worksheet guides students through a powerful and challenging self-reflection: exploring the version of themselves that different people in their life typically *get* vs. the version that those people *need* from them. It helps students begin to recognize the relational impact of their behavior and the opportunity they have to take greater ownership of how they interact with others.

This exercise strengthens self-awareness by helping students name emotional patterns and relationship dynamics, while also developing self-evaluation by imagining how their behavior could shift to meet relational needs more effectively.

INSTRUCTIONS FOR THE ADULT (PARENT, TEACHER, OR CLINICIAN)

This activity is emotionally complex and may require significant scaffolding and support. Approach it with empathy, curiosity, and care. Let the student know that this is not about being "wrong" or "bad" but about growing in understanding how their behavior affects others—and how they can become more intentional in relationships that matter.

Each relationship has two lines:

◆ **Gets**—What version of you does this person usually see (e.g., silly, serious, avoidant, angry, helpful, distracted)?

◆ **Needs**—What version of you would best support this relationship (e.g., calm, focused, respectful, honest, engaged)?

Relationships listed:

◆ Mom
◆ Dad
◆ Siblings
◆ Teachers
◆ Friends
◆ Classmates

STEP-BY-STEP GUIDANCE

1. **Normalize the concept.**

   Start by explaining that everyone shows up a little differently depending on who they're with—and that's normal. But sometimes the version we give isn't the version the other person *needs*. And sometimes, we're not even aware of the difference.

   You might say:

   "The way we act with Mom might be different than how we act with our friends or teachers. This activity helps us notice those patterns, so we can figure out where we might want to grow."

2. **Begin with easy relationships.**

   Start with one relationship that feels safe or less emotionally charged—like a friend or a teacher. Ask:
   • "What kind of version of you does this person usually see?"
   • "Are you funny with them? Quiet? Helpful? Easily frustrated?"
   • "What do you think they really *need* from you to make the relationship better or stronger?"

3. **Offer concrete examples to help guide the child.**

   Example:
   • *Teacher gets*: The distracted version of me.
   • *Teacher needs*: The listening and focused version of me.

4. Move through the list one by one.

Be patient and encourage honesty. Help the student recognize that they are not "bad" for how they show up—it's about awareness and growth.

Continue through each person:

- *Mom gets*: The angry and yelling version of me.
- *Mom needs*: The calm and talking version of me.
- *Friends get*: The funny and silly version of me.
- *Friends need*: The respectful and kind version of me.

5. Affirm strengths, not just deficits.

Some "gets" may already align well with "needs." Celebrate those. This builds confidence and shows that the student already has relational strengths they can carry into other areas.

6. Use as a bridge to behavior change.

Once the chart is complete, ask:

- "Which relationship do you most want to work on?"
- "What's one small way to bring more of the 'needed' version of you to that person tomorrow?"
- "How can I help you remember that version when things get tough?"

WHY THIS MATTERS

Children with ADHD are often unaware of the ripple effect their behavior has on others—not because they lack empathy but because they struggle to pause and reflect. This page helps externalize those relational patterns in a way that feels safe, structured, and full of opportunity.

Over time, this type of self-reflection helps students strengthen:

- ◆ Emotional intelligence
- ◆ Social insight
- ◆ Relationship repair skills
- ◆ Personal accountability

And perhaps most importantly—it helps students realize they have the power to show up differently, starting now.

KEY MESSAGE

Who we are with others is something we can shape. When we become aware of the version of ourselves we're showing—and the version others need—we build stronger relationships and a stronger sense of self.

CLOSING THOUGHT

You are not just one version of yourself. You are many—and you get to choose which one shows up. This page is your mirror and your map: it shows you where you've been in your relationships and how to become who you want to be in them.

Activity 5.3: Cause and Effect

Executive function skills strengthened: Nonverbal working memory, verbal working memory, self-evaluation, self-awareness, self-regulation

This workbook page helps students with ADHD develop future thinking by reinforcing a simple but critical executive function principle: *what I do now affects what I can do later.*

Because the ADHD brain struggles to visualize future outcomes and track time, students often act in the moment—choosing immediate comfort or distraction over long-term benefit. This worksheet helps them connect *present effort* with *future reward* through the structure of cause and effect.

Students are asked to fill in two parallel columns:

♦ **Column 1: "If I get this done now. . ."**
  (Examples: "Finish my math homework," "Clean out my backpack," "Study for tomorrow's quiz," "Complete my reading log")
♦ **Column 2: ". . .then I'll be able to do this later:"**
  (Examples: "Play outside," "Watch a show," "Relax without being stressed," "Get praised by my teacher," "Feel proud of myself")

This visual mapping activates *nonverbal working memory* by encouraging students to mentally simulate their day, and *verbal working memory* by naming both the effort and the outcome. It also teaches *emotional regulation* and *delayed gratification*, as students come to understand that discomfort is temporary—and relief, joy, and reward are on the other side of follow-through.

This exercise also provides a clear, practical way for parents, teachers, and therapists to coach the student in using planning language and internal motivation to complete tasks they might otherwise avoid.

KEY MESSAGE

You don't have to love the task—just remember why it matters. When you finish what's hard now, you unlock what feels good later.

CLOSING THOUGHT

Doing what's boring or difficult in the moment is a superpower. It gives you more control over your day and leads you to the fun, relaxed version of yourself you're working toward.

Activity 5.4: What Do the Distractions Do for Me?

Executive function skills strengthened: Self-regulation, self-awareness, verbal working memory

This worksheet guides students to take a deeper look at their most common distractions and understand the emotional payoff those distractions offer in the moment—vs. the longer-term consequences they often create. The ADHD brain thrives on novelty, stimulation, and instant gratification, which makes it incredibly hard to resist distractions in school settings. But resisting distraction is not just about willpower—it's about *understanding what the distraction does for you* and whether it's truly helpful or harmful.

The worksheet provides a list of common distractions (e.g., school laptop games, talking in class, making others laugh, scrolling on a phone, daydreaming, passing notes, wandering the classroom) and then guides the student to answer two key reflection prompts for each:

- "What do I like about this distraction?"
- "What happens after I do it?"

For example:

- **Distraction:** Playing games on school laptop
  - *What do I like about it?* "It's fun and takes my mind off the work."
  - *What happens after I do it?* "I fall behind and have more homework later."
- **Distraction:** Making others laugh during class
  - *What do I like about it?* "It makes me feel important and liked."
  - *What happens after I do it?* "People laugh but don't take me seriously. I miss out on learning and get in trouble."

Through this process, the student uses *verbal working memory* to reflect on the purpose of their impulsive behavior and *self-awareness* to track the emotional and academic consequences. This begins to rewire the internal narrative from "I always mess up" to "I'm learning what works for me and what doesn't." It helps the student create space between impulse and action, and develop self-talk scripts that lead to better outcomes.

KEY MESSAGE

Distractions feel good for a second—but they often make things harder later. When you understand what they really do for you, you can choose something better.

CLOSING THOUGHT

Every distraction is a chance to practice self-control. You can't always avoid temptation, but you can always choose to think twice. That's how you take back control of your day.

Activity 5.5: Yesterday Was a Learning Experience

Executive function skills strengthened: Self-evaluation, nonverbal working memory

OVERVIEW

Executive function growth requires more than just planning for the future—it requires the ability to look back, reflect, and learn from past experiences. Children with ADHD and executive function challenges often struggle to internalize past outcomes. They may repeat the same impulsive behaviors, social missteps, or task-avoidant patterns, not because they don't care but because their nonverbal working memory—the ability to hold and replay mental "videos" of past experiences—is underdeveloped.

This page helps strengthen both self-evaluation and nonverbal working memory by guiding children through a structured process of reflecting on a recent moment, identifying what it gave them (a consequence, a feeling, a result), and deciding what they will do differently today. It transforms a reactive child into a reflective one—someone who begins to notice patterns, learn from them, and take ownership of personal growth.

INSTRUCTIONS FOR THE ADULT

This page should be used in a calm, safe space—either at the start of the day, as part of a morning routine, or after a moment of challenge. Invite the child to revisit something that happened *yesterday* or recently—not to dwell on it or assign blame but to mine it for insight.

Use a neutral tone. Avoid lecturing, punishing, or bringing up shame. The focus here is not on what went wrong but on what can be learned and improved. Support the child as they fill in each blank with their own words, and help them dig deeper by prompting with open-ended questions.

STEP-BY-STEP GUIDANCE

1. **Begin with gentle curiosity.**

   Ask: "Let's think about something from yesterday. What's something you did that you're still thinking about today?"

Avoid labeling the moment as a mistake—treat it as an experience worth reflecting on.

2. **Fill in the first statement.**

   "Yesterday I _____"

   Let the child describe the action or choice in their own words. Prompt with:
   - "What did you do?"
   - "What part of the day stands out to you?"
   - "What decision did you make yesterday that matters today?"

3. **Explore the outcome.**

   "It gave me _____"

   This is where the child reflects on the result—what happened because of that action? It may be emotional ("I felt embarrassed"), social ("I lost a friend's trust"), academic ("I had to redo my work"), or neutral. Help the child think critically without judgment.

4. **Plan for change.**

   "Today I will _____"

   Support the child in identifying one small, concrete change they can make today. Tie it back to their personal growth:
   - "So today, I'll slow down before speaking."
   - "Today, I'll write things down so I remember."
   - "Today, I'll ask for help before I get frustrated."

5. **Reinforce with encouragement.**

   Praise the effort to reflect and change, even if the child struggles to express themselves clearly. This process builds the mental replay system needed for growth.

KEY MESSAGE

Every experience is an opportunity to grow. By learning from yesterday, we can make smarter, kinder, more thoughtful choices today.

CLOSING THOUGHT

Children grow when they are taught how to reflect, not just told what to do. This page fosters the kind of internal processing—looking back, analyzing outcomes, and adapting—that is essential to real-world independence and long-term executive function success.

RESEARCH REFERENCE

McCloskey, G., Perkins, L. A., & Van Divner, B. (2009). *Assessment and Intervention for Executive Function Difficulties*. Routledge.

Activity 5.6: Who Am I Becoming?

Executive function skills strengthened: Self-evaluation, nonverbal working memory

OVERVIEW

A critical component of executive function development is the ability to evaluate one's own behavior over time and recognize how choices influence the trajectory of one's life. Many children with ADHD and executive function delays struggle with self-monitoring and future-minded thinking. Their brains often operate in the "now," making it difficult for them to reflect on whether they're moving toward or away from their goals.

This workbook page guides the child to explore the concept of identity—not just who they are right now but who they are becoming through their daily decisions. It helps children connect to their nonverbal working memory by recalling meaningful past actions and strengthens self-evaluation by identifying which actions are consistent with their goals and which are not. The simple "steps forward" and "steps backward" framework makes abstract identity development accessible and practical.

INSTRUCTIONS FOR THE ADULT

Use this page during a reflective moment—at the end of a week, after a meaningful conversation, or following a challenging behavioral pattern. Begin by anchoring the child in their ideal self: who they hope to be in the future. Let this be authentically theirs, even if their goals are unconventional or still forming.

Then work together to identify specific actions the child has taken recently. Categorize them into two types:

- ◆ "**Steps Backward**": Moments or choices that created distance from their ideal self
- ◆ "**Steps Forward**": Moments or choices that moved them closer to that ideal

Help the child recognize that identity is shaped by choices—not all at once, but bit by bit, day by day.

STEP-BY-STEP GUIDANCE

1. **Start with the big picture.**

   Read and complete: *"Who I want to be _____."*

   Encourage the child to imagine the kind of person they want to become. Prompt with questions like:
   - "What do you want to be known for?"
   - "What kind of friend, student, or teammate do you want to be?"
   - "What kind of adult do you want to grow into?"

2. **Identify steps backward.**

In the first set of boxes, write or discuss three specific actions or choices that pulled the child further away from their goal. These could be impulsive behaviors, avoidance, dishonesty, negative self-talk, or quitting too soon.

Emphasize: "This isn't about blaming—this is about noticing patterns so we can grow."

3. **Identify steps forward.**

In the second set of boxes, identify three specific actions or choices that brought them closer to the person they want to become. These may be small: staying calm during a disagreement, finishing homework without reminders, or apologizing to a friend.

4. **Compare and reflect.**

Help the child notice what made the "forward" steps possible. Were they more focused? Did someone support them? What was different in those moments?

5. **Affirm the process.**

Reinforce that both kinds of steps are part of the learning journey. Every day offers the chance to choose again.

KEY MESSAGE

Who you are becoming is shaped by the small choices you make every day. By recognizing which choices move you forward—and which ones hold you back—you can take control of your growth.

CLOSING THOUGHT

Identity is not fixed—it's something we build with our actions. When children are taught to reflect with intention, they begin to step into their future with purpose. They don't just *wish* to become someone—they begin to *act* like it.

RESEARCH REFERENCE

Zelazo, P. D., & Carlson, S. M. (2012). Hot and cool executive function in childhood and adolescence: Development and plasticity. *Child Development Perspectives*, 6(4), 354–360.

Activity 5.7: People Need Me

Executive function skills strengthened: Self-evaluation

OVERVIEW

One of the most meaningful ways to cultivate self-evaluation is by helping children recognize that their actions impact others. Children with ADHD and executive function delays often become hyper-focused on their own internal experiences—how overwhelmed, frustrated, or distracted they feel in the moment. This self-absorption is not selfishness; it's a result of underdeveloped metacognition and perspective-taking skills.

This page helps children step outside of themselves and see that they are part of a larger system—their classroom, their family, their community—and that others depend on them. By identifying specific responsibilities and reflecting on the outcomes of follow-through vs. forgetfulness, this activity strengthens the child's ability to self-monitor, self-evaluate, and take greater ownership of their role in the lives of others. It also begins to develop prosocial motivation—a powerful tool for internalizing responsibility.

INSTRUCTIONS FOR THE ADULT

Use this page during a calm and reflective moment. Begin by discussing the concept of responsibility—not just as a list of chores or tasks but as a way to show care, maturity, and dependability. Guide the child to identify specific, real-world responsibilities they currently have toward others (not just themselves). These might include:

- Helping a sibling
- Bringing something to school
- Feeding a pet
- Remembering to say thank you
- Being ready for carpool on time

Help the child explore both sides of the equation: what happens when they follow through and what happens when they don't. Focus on real consequences and emotional impact, not shame or blame.

STEP-BY-STEP GUIDANCE

1. **Define responsibility together.**
   Ask: "What does it mean to be responsible for someone else?" Discuss how small actions help others feel cared for, respected, or safe.
2. **Complete the first prompt.**
   "My responsibilities toward others are:"

   Encourage the child to list two to three tasks or actions where others are counting on them. These can be home-based, school-related, or social.

3. **Explore positive outcomes.**
   "When I get it done:"

   In this section, discuss and write down what happens when the child success-
   fully completes their responsibilities. Prompt with:
   • "How does it help others?"
   • "How do you feel when it's done?"
   • "What's the result or reward—even if it's not a prize?"
4. **Explore missed opportunities.**
   "When I do not get it done:"

   Without judgment, talk about what typically happens when responsibilities are
   missed. This could include someone feeling disappointed, plans getting delayed,
   or the child feeling guilty or frustrated. Focus on natural consequences.
5. **Draw the contrast.**
   Guide the child to compare both columns and reflect on how their choices
   influence others' emotions, routines, or expectations. Help them see that they
   matter and that people depend on them.

KEY MESSAGE

Being responsible isn't just about rules—it's about showing others they can count on
you. Your actions matter. People notice. And people need you.

CLOSING THOUGHT

Children thrive when they feel useful and valued. This page helps shift the mindset
from "I forgot again" to "I'm someone who follows through because others are counting on me." Responsibility becomes something they own—not something they avoid.

RESEARCH REFERENCE

Diamond, A. (2013). Executive functions. *Annual Review of Psychology, 64,* 135–168.

Activity 5.1: GrowNOW Video Journals

1. Record a video at the beginning of the day. Answer these questions:
   - What are my goals for today?
   - What would my perfect day look like?
   - What do I want to avoid?
   - How do I want to feel at the end of the day?
2. Record another video at the end of the day. Answer these questions:
   - What went well today?
   - What didn't go well?
   - What are my goals for tomorrow?

Activity 5.2: Who Gets Which Version of Me?

1. Mom
Gets:

_____

Needs:

_____

2. Dad
Gets:

_____

Needs:

_____

3. Siblings
Gets:

_____

Needs:

_____

4. Teachers
Gets:

_____

Needs:

_____

5. Friends
Gets:

_____

Needs:

_____

6. Classmates
Gets:

_____

Needs:

_____

Activity 5.3: Cause and Effect

If I do this now: Later, I can:

_____ → _____

_____ → _____

_____ → _____

_____ → _____

_____ → _____

Activity 5.4: What Do the Distractions Do for Me?

Distraction/stimulus	What do I like about this distraction?	What happens after I do it?
School laptop games	_____	_____
Talking in class	_____	_____
Making others laugh	_____	_____
Scrolling on a phone	_____	_____
Daydreaming	_____	_____
Passing notes	_____	_____
Wandering the classroom	_____	_____

Activity 5.5: Yesterday Was a Learning Experience

Yesterday I

_____

_____

_____

It gave me

_____

_____

_____

Today I will

_____

_____

_____

Activity 5.6: Who Am I Becoming?

Who I want to be:

_____

_____

Steps Forward   Steps Backward

_____   _____

_____   _____

_____   _____

_____   _____

Activity 5.7: People Need Me

My responsibilities toward others:	When I get it done:	When I do not get it done:
_____	_____	_____
_____	_____	_____
_____	_____	_____

CHAPTER 6

Playbook Parenting

*Building Leadership, Consistency, and
Calm Authority in the Home*

Parenting a child with ADHD and executive function challenges is uniquely demanding. It requires patience, clarity, structure, and a level of emotional regulation that can feel almost impossible in the face of daily meltdowns, defiance, avoidance, or power struggles. It's easy to feel like nothing works, or worse—that you're failing.

This chapter is for you—the parent, the caregiver, the adult who's in the trenches day after day.

In *The Executive Function Playbook*, we emphasize that executive function development doesn't begin with the child—it begins with the environment around the child. Specifically, with the adults who provide clarity, consistency, and calm leadership. Without a structured environment and emotionally regulated caregivers, even the best interventions fall apart.

This chapter includes a collection of worksheets and reflection tools designed specifically for adults. These pages will help you:

- ◆ Identify and stop patterns of permissive parenting
- ◆ Set boundaries without guilt
- ◆ Unplug your child's brain from negative attention cycles
- ◆ Reclaim your role as a calm, confident authority
- ◆ End the exhausting cycle of negotiating, arguing, and over-explaining
- ◆ Realign with your parenting partner—so you're leading from the same page

While you'll often see the terms "mom" and "dad" used throughout these pages, please know this workbook was written with all families in mind—regardless of structure, gender, or roles. Every family deserves love, consistency, and clarity. Whether you are a single parent, stepparent, grandparent, foster caregiver, or any other version of a caregiving team, your leadership matters. Your presence matters. Your ability to step into calm, regulated authority is a powerful intervention in itself.

This chapter builds on the foundational message in *The Executive Function Playbook*: that kids do not grow from chaos, inconsistency, or permissiveness. They grow from predictable boundaries, emotionally neutral feedback, and steady adult presence. These worksheets are here to help you build exactly that—even when it's hard.

You'll find tools to help you:

◆ Reflect on your parenting patterns
◆ Rebalance roles and responsibilities
◆ Set weekend limits, tech boundaries, and consistent expectations
◆ Create unified plans with your parenting partner
◆ Step away from rescuing or entertaining, and step into leading

These pages are honest, practical, and sometimes uncomfortable—because parenting growth often begins with self-awareness. But you'll find that the more consistent you become, the more your child begins to regulate, initiate, and grow. It may not happen overnight, but every step you take toward strong leadership lays the foundation your child has been craving.

Let's help you parent with purpose, calm, and clarity—so your child can stop testing the boundary and start trusting it.

Activity 6.1: Setting Boundaries

Executive function skills strengthened: Self-regulation, self-motivation, self-awareness

This workbook page is designed specifically for parents and caregivers who are learning to set consistent, healthy, and effective boundaries with their child. ADHD parenting often comes with a unique emotional toll: guilt, exhaustion, and the sense that every day is a negotiation. This page helps eliminate that cycle by bringing clarity and structure to your responses as a parent.

When boundaries are predetermined, communicated in advance, and upheld consistently, children with ADHD feel safer, more secure, and ultimately more in control.

They learn that actions have consequences—not as a punishment but as a predictable outcome. This is how we foster true emotional growth and internal accountability.

INSTRUCTIONS FOR PARENTS

Use this sentence structure to create clear, non-negotiable boundaries:

When *(child's name)* **does** _____,

I will _____ **until** _____.

Here are a few examples:

◆ When *Liam* refuses to turn off the video game, **I will** unplug the system and store it away **until** homework is completed and turned in.

◆ When *Ava* begins yelling or using disrespectful language, **I will** leave the room without engaging **until** she is calm and ready to communicate respectfully.

◆ When *Noah* throws his backpack and refuses to start homework, **I will** stop offering help or reminders **until** he asks calmly and respectfully.

◆ When *Emma* starts demanding her phone back aggressively, **I will** hold onto it **until** we complete our evening routine peacefully together.

This format is empowering for both parent and child. It removes the emotional reactivity and keeps parenting decisions grounded in logic, structure, and fairness.

WHY THIS MATTERS

Children with ADHD often thrive on structure but resist it in the moment. Your consistent response becomes the boundary that helps them grow.

Most importantly, this worksheet supports authoritative parenting—where warmth meets firmness. When children know exactly what will happen and when, it reduces anxiety, power struggles, and behavioral flare-ups.

This is not about punishment—it's about predictable consequences.

KEY MESSAGE

Consistency is kindness. Boundaries protect your energy, reduce conflict, and help your child grow.

CLOSING THOUGHT

You are not being mean—you are being clear. And clarity builds trust. When boundaries are consistent, your child learns what to expect, how to regulate themselves, and how to grow into a more independent and resilient version of themselves.

Activity 6.2: Home Safe Space

Executive function skills strengthened: Self-regulation

In moments of dysregulation, many children and teens with ADHD struggle to access their internal coping strategies. They may act impulsively, lash out, or escalate behaviors—simply because their brain is in a state of emotional hijack. This workbook page supports the creation of a designated, structured, non-negotiable *home safe space* where the child can go to regain regulation.

The goal here is to develop internal skills for emotional reset, not to punish or isolate. The child (with adult guidance) will identify a specific location in the home that feels comforting, private, and secure—a consistent place to cool down, recalibrate, and return to baseline.

Once identified, the rules for the space must be clear:

- **No technology is permitted.** Screens provide external dopamine but do not build self-regulation.
- **No interruptions unless requested.** This is a "reset zone," not a time for lecturing or continued talking.
- **Safety and comfort are prioritized.** It may include soft items, drawing materials, books, or calming visuals, but not overstimulating or avoidant distractions.

This exercise is designed for parents and children to do together. Many families lack a system for de-escalation at home, resulting in power struggles and emotional blowups. By pre-establishing a safe space and reinforcing its purpose, the child is learning the executive function skill of pause-and-reset—a critical foundation for emotional control and long-term behavioral growth.

KEY MESSAGE

Regulation cannot be forced in the heat of the moment. A consistent, screen-free safe space gives children a tool to practice self-soothing and to re-enter challenges with greater emotional control.

CLOSING THOUGHT

We don't want children to learn that others must calm them down. We want them to develop the internal strategies that allow them to calm themselves. This is how we build emotional independence and resilience.

Activity 6.3: Family Grit

Executive function skills strengthened: Grit, resilience, self-regulation, self-motivation

Based on the groundbreaking research of psychologist Angela Duckworth, grit is defined as passion and perseverance toward long-term goals—continuing to work hard despite challenges, setbacks, boredom, or the urge to quit. Families today, especially those navigating ADHD, are often trapped in cycles of instant gratification, over-accommodation, and tech dependency. This workbook page offers a powerful reset.

Each member of the family must commit to a grit-building challenge:

◆ Choose one activity or hobby they will stick with for at least three months.
◆ The activity must follow **three core rules**:
  1. **No quitting before the three-month minimum.** Frustration and boredom are part of the process.
  2. **No technology involved.** No esports, social media, phones, YouTube, coding, or screen-based tools.
  3. **Must take place outside the home.** This is to foster real-world engagement, reduce isolation, and promote executive functioning through scheduling, initiation, and perseverance.

Examples may include joining a sports team, taking a weekly art or music class, attending a volunteer group, enrolling in martial arts, participating in a community choir or theater, or committing to weekly hikes or fitness classes.

Each family member will fill in:

◆ My chosen activity: _____
◆ Why I chose this: _____
◆ What I will do when I feel like quitting: _____
◆ What I hope to feel or gain after three months: _____

This page is a contract of commitment—not for perfection, but for progress.

This task teaches that growth comes from doing hard things, not from seeking comfort. When children see their parents following through with grit and consistency, they internalize that same resilience.

KEY MESSAGE

Real growth doesn't happen through comfort. It happens when we stick with things, even when we don't feel like it. Grit is grown through commitment and consistency.

CLOSING THOUGHT

Every member of the family benefits when the culture of the home shifts from immediate gratification to long-term perseverance. This is how we build character and resilience—together.

REFERENCE

Duckworth, A. L. (2016). *Grit: The Power of Passion and Perseverance.* Scribner.

Activity 6.4: Partner Tag-In

Executive function skills strengthened: Self-regulation

In homes raising children with ADHD, parenting can feel like a constant state of alert. One parent often carries the majority of the emotional and mental labor—most commonly, the mother. Over time, this imbalance leads to chronic stress, burnout, and dysregulation. Children, especially those with ADHD, are highly sensitive to the emotional climate of the home. They model what they see.

This workbook page introduces a "Partner Tag-In System"—a proactive, respectful, and clear plan that allows one caregiver to step in when the other begins to show signs of burnout, dysregulation, or emotional fatigue. The goal is to maintain a calm and supportive environment for the child, while also supporting the adults' mental health.

STEP 1: DEFINE THE SIGNS

These are the signs that I (Parent A) am becoming dysregulated:
These are the signs that I (Parent B) am becoming dysregulated:

STEP 2: DEFINE THE SIGNAL

When I notice my partner is becoming dysregulated, I will say or do:

_____ (e.g., "I got this," or a physical tap on the shoulder)
This is the cue that I'm tagging in and taking over parenting responsibilities for now.

STEP 3: WHAT HAPPENS NEXT

The dysregulated parent will take a break by:

- Going for a walk
- Listening to music
- Going into another room to decompress
- Doing breathing or mindfulness exercises
- Journaling or texting a friend

IMPORTANT PRINCIPLE

The child does not need to witness parental conflict or dysregulation. When one parent calmly tags in and the other calmly steps out, the child experiences a stable and consistent adult presence, which builds emotional safety and trust.

KEY MESSAGE

Regulated adults raise regulated kids. Your calm is contagious. By creating a system to support one another, you show your child what teamwork, empathy, and healthy emotional regulation truly look like.

CLOSING THOUGHT

Your ADHD child doesn't need perfection. They need to see emotional maturity in action. With the Partner Tag-In system, you are modeling balance, respect, and self-care—all vital life skills they will carry into adulthood.

Activity 6.5: Family Events

Executive function skills strengthened: Self-regulation, mental flexibility

In ADHD households, daily life can become overly focused on managing behavior, completing tasks, and surviving routines. What often gets lost is the *family identity*—the joyful, shared experiences that make being together meaningful. This worksheet helps bring that back.

The goal is simple but powerful: Each member of the family takes a turn choosing a specific event that the whole family will do together. These experiences create structure, encourage compromise, strengthen family bonds, and develop vital executive function skills like flexibility, cooperation, and follow-through.

When a child or teen has ADHD, flexibility doesn't come easily. They may struggle to engage in nonpreferred activities or tolerate group plans. But with repeated practice, and the feeling of being heard and included, they develop the ability to regulate their emotions, shift their thinking, and enjoy time with others—even when things aren't fully on their terms.

Instructions:

Each family member picks one event to do as a family. It must:

◆ Be something everyone is willing to try
◆ Involve *no screens*
◆ Take place outside of the home when possible
◆ Be fun, safe, and reasonable in cost and time

Each person writes their chosen activity, along with the date it will take place.

Examples of Family Activities:

◆ Go to a nature trail or hiking path together
◆ Visit a new playground or park
◆ Play board games together (everyone gets to pick one round)
◆ Go out for ice cream after dinner
◆ Build something together (like a birdhouse, Lego set, puzzle, etc.)
◆ Attend a local event (library activity, food truck night, art fair)
◆ Go bowling, mini-golfing, or roller skating
◆ Try a new sport or class together (tennis, rock climbing, yoga)
◆ Do a service project (volunteer together at an animal shelter or food drive)
◆ Have a "fancy dinner" at home where everyone dresses up and helps cook

Guiding Rules:

◆ No complaining about another person's pick
◆ Every person's choice is equally valued
◆ The family must follow through with each event
◆ No phones or screens during the family event

KEY MESSAGE

Shared experiences build stronger families. Kids with ADHD thrive when they feel emotionally connected and when their lives include joyful routines—not just corrections and consequences.

CLOSING THOUGHT

A child's favorite memories won't come from a screen—they come from real moments spent with people who love them. Make time for those moments, and their behavior—and your family connection—will transform.

Activity 6.6: Goals for Everyone

Executive function skills strengthened: Perspective-taking skills, mental flexibility, self-motivation

Families thrive when everyone feels seen, valued, and supported. This workbook page encourages each family member—Mom, Dad, Son, and Daughter—to create one meaningful goal for each of the other members. These goals should be kind, hopeful, and rooted in growth.

For example:

- *"I want Dad to take more breaks and play with me outside."*
- *"I hope my sister feels more confident talking to friends."*
- *"I want my mom to have more time to relax."*

This activity helps build empathy and awareness by encouraging family members to *look beyond themselves* and think about the needs, strengths, and struggles of others. It also promotes mental flexibility by helping each member consider different perspectives—a critical executive function skill.

Instructions:
1. Each family member fills out one goal for each of the others.
2. Share the goals out loud as a group.
3. Reflect on how these goals make you feel—and how they show support and care.

KEY MESSAGE
Perspective-taking is one of the most advanced executive function skills—and it's the glue that holds families together. When we slow down and think about others, we become better communicators, better partners, better parents, and better siblings.

CLOSING THOUGHT
Empathy is a skill, not a trait. Practicing it regularly in the home builds emotional resilience, mutual respect, and long-term connection.

RESEARCH REFERENCE
Schonert-Reichl, K. A., & Lawlor, M. S. (2010). The effects of a mindfulness-based education program on pre- and early adolescents' well-being and social and emotional competence. *Mindfulness, 1*(3), 137–151. https://doi.org/10.1007/s12671-010-0011-8

This study shows that explicitly teaching perspective-taking and emotional understanding in structured activities improves empathy, emotional regulation, and social competence—especially when done within meaningful relationships.

Activity 6.7: Specific Responses
This workbook page provides parents with specific responses to use when their child displays common ADHD-related behaviors such as:

- Self-defeating comments
- Complaining

♦ Learned helplessness
♦ Lying

In emotionally charged moments, parents often struggle to say the right thing or let their own dysregulation make the moment worse. This page offers clear, prewritten scripts that equip caregivers to respond with calm, confidence, and consistency—reinforcing long-term executive function skills rather than fueling cycles of negativity.

Parents are encouraged to rehearse and internalize the following responses:

1. SELF-DEFEATING COMMENTS

Example Behavior: "I'm so stupid. I can't do anything right."
Scripted Response:

"I can tell you're feeling frustrated. Everyone struggles sometimes. This is a moment to pause, breathe, and try again. Let's talk about your next step forward."

2. COMPLAINING

Example Behavior: "This is so unfair. Why do I have to do this?"
Scripted Response:

"You don't have to like it, but it still needs to get done. Complaining won't change the rule. You've done hard things before, and you can do this too."

3. LEARNED HELPLESSNESS

Example Behavior: "I don't know how to do this. You do it for me."
Scripted Response:

"I know this is hard, but I'm not going to do it for you. I'll sit next to you, and we can figure out the first step together. You are capable."

4. LYING

Example Behavior: "I didn't do that!" (when clearly they did)
Scripted Response:

"I care more about you being honest than being perfect. If you made a mistake, let's fix it together. Telling the truth is always the first step toward solving the problem."

KEY MESSAGE

Scripted parenting doesn't mean robotic parenting—it means being prepared. When we pre-plan our words, we stay calm in chaos and teach our kids emotional steadiness by modeling it ourselves.

CLOSING THOUGHT

Every emotional moment with your child is a chance to either reinforce their dysregulation or teach them how to rise above it. The more regulated the parent, the more regulated the home.

RESEARCH REFERENCE

Barkley, R. A. (2013). *Defiant Children: A Clinician's Manual for Assessment and Parent Training* (3rd ed.). Guilford Press.

Activity 6.8: The Prompt Hierarchy

DESCRIPTION

One of the most important goals in raising a child with ADHD and executive dysfunction is to shift them away from *prompt dependence* and toward true *independence*. This workbook page introduces and explains the Prompt Hierarchy—a visual framework that illustrates levels of prompting from most to least intrusive, helping adults strategically fade support over time.

The Prompt Hierarchy includes:

1. **Full physical prompt:** The adult physically guides the child's body through the task (e.g., guiding their hand to start writing).
2. **Partial physical prompt:** The adult provides a physical cue, but not full assistance (e.g., touching their hand lightly to initiate movement).
3. **Modeling:** The adult shows the child what to do by completing the task first while the child watches.
4. **Verbal prompt (direct):** The adult tells the child exactly what to do (e.g., "Put your shoes on now").
5. **Verbal prompt (indirect):** The adult uses a less direct verbal cue (e.g., "What do you need to put on your feet before we leave?").
6. **Visual prompt:** The child is provided with a checklist, schedule, or visual card instead of being told.
7. **Gestural prompt:** The adult points or gestures to the materials or location to initiate action.
8. **Natural cue:** The child responds to natural environmental cues (e.g., hearing the school bell and packing up independently).

Alongside the image, this worksheet includes space for adults to list examples of how they currently prompt their child in common routines (e.g., morning routine, homework, chores) and how they can begin fading those prompts. The goal is to reduce verbal prompting over time, replacing it with visuals, gestures, or natural cues that strengthen the child's executive function system.

KEY MESSAGE

Executive function growth happens when adults strategically reduce their support. Fading prompts teaches children how to initiate, follow through, and complete tasks on their own—one of the foundational components of independence.

CLOSING THOUGHT

If you always step in, they never step up. The longer we provide high-level prompts, the longer our children stay reliant on us to get through the day. Prompt fading isn't just a strategy—it's a mindset shift toward long-term success.

RESEARCH REFERENCE

Cooper, J. O., Heron, T. E., & Heward, W. L. (2020). *Applied Behavior Analysis* (3rd ed.). Pearson.

Activity 6.9: Use Less Language
DESCRIPTION

One of the most important and often overlooked strategies in ADHD parenting is the *intentional reduction of language*. As emphasized in *The Executive Function Playbook*, the ADHD brain is highly sensitive to verbal overload. Long-winded explanations, repeated lectures, and emotional monologues often escalate dysregulation rather than reduce it. Children with ADHD frequently miss or misinterpret lengthy verbal input due to their deficits in working memory and self-regulation.

This workbook page provides a concrete tool for parents: a set of brief, clear, and emotionally neutral scripts to use during the most common high-stress parenting moments. These scripts are designed to regulate the parent first, eliminate the "verbal tornado," and offer the child clear, consistent direction with minimal words.

Examples of Situations and Minimal Language Scripts:
1. **Child is refusing to complete a chore.**
   → Instead of: "How many times do I have to tell you? You said you'd help me with the dishes and you haven't moved. I'm getting really tired of this."
   → Say: "Dish time. Now."

2. **Child is dysregulated and yelling.**
   → Instead of: "You need to calm down. This is not how we act. What's going on with you?"
   → Say: "I'm here. Not safe to talk. Take space."

3. **Child says, "I hate school; I'm not going."**
   → Instead of: "That's ridiculous. School is your job. You don't have a choice, and this attitude is unacceptable."
   → Say: "I hear you. Still going."

4. **Child is procrastinating on homework.**
   → Instead of: "If you don't get started soon, it'll be too late. Then you'll complain, and I won't be able to help. Why do we go through this every night?"
   → Say: "Start now. One thing. I'll check in."

5. **Child says, "This is too hard, I can't do it!"**
   → Instead of: "You always say that. You can do it. Just try your best and stop giving up so easily."
   → Say: "You've done hard things. Try one part."

This page also includes a customizable space for parents to write their own frequent high-conflict situations and practice scripting low-language responses.

KEY MESSAGE

The less you say, the more your child can regulate. Use your presence, tone, and consistency more than words. Language overload overwhelms the dysregulated brain.

CLOSING THOUGHT

Parenting an ADHD child is not about saying more—it's about saying *less*, with clarity and calm. When your words are few, your message becomes stronger.

RESEARCH REFERENCE

Barkley, R. A. (2013). *Taking Charge of ADHD: The Complete, Authoritative Guide for Parents* (3rd ed.). Guilford Press.

Activity 6.10: A Different Time-Out!

DESCRIPTION

One of the most effective executive function-based parenting strategies is the *parent-initiated time-out*. Unlike a punitive "go sit in the corner" time-out, this version is about adult regulation and boundary setting. This page builds on the core concept from *The*

Executive Function Playbook—that structure, clarity, and emotional containment are essential for helping a child with ADHD learn to self-regulate.

In emotionally escalated moments, many parents find themselves stuck in the trap of over-explaining, negotiating, and arguing with their dysregulated child. This only fuels the conflict. When the parent calls a time-out, it signals that the conversation or behavior has escalated past the point of productivity, and it must stop immediately.

Here's the rule:

Once a parent calls "time-out," the topic is done for 24 hours—no discussion, no negotiation, no circling back. At the exact same time the following day, the parent can decide to revisit it, but not before. This boundary communicates to the child: "I will not reward dysregulation with attention. We are done. It's time to move on."

This page includes a customizable worksheet with:

- A space to list common triggers or topics that frequently escalate (e.g., screen time, bedtime, social plans).
- A Time-Out Log to record:
  - The date/time the time-out was called
  - The topic that escalated
  - The child's reaction
  - What the parent did to stay calm
  - Whether the topic was revisited 24 hours later—and if so, how

Parents are also guided to rehearse and internalize key phrases like:

- "Time-out. We'll talk again at 7 p.m. tomorrow. Not before."
- "This conversation is over for 24 hours."
- "I care too much to argue. I'll see you at 7 p.m. tomorrow."

KEY MESSAGE

Time-outs are not punishments—they are boundaries. They signal strength, consistency, and a parent's commitment to staying emotionally calm, even in chaos.

CLOSING THOUGHT

Your calm is your child's roadmap. By stepping away and sticking to a firm time-out rule, you model executive functioning in action—and give your child space to regulate on their own.

RESEARCH REFERENCE

Greene, R. W. (2016). *Raising Human Beings: Creating a Collaborative Partnership with Your Child*. Scribner.

Activity 6.11: The Child Is *Not* the Parent

Executive function skills strengthened: Self-regulation, verbal working memory

OVERVIEW

Many children with ADHD and executive function challenges struggle with limits, authority, and emotional regulation when they don't get their way. Their brains are wired to seek novelty, control, and instant gratification—making boundaries feel frustrating or even intolerable. At the same time, many well-meaning parents, hoping to avoid conflict or emotional outbursts, unintentionally relinquish their authority, leading to role confusion where the child believes they are the one in control.

This workbook page is a powerful reset. It draws a clear, visual boundary between adult decisions and child choices, helping both the parent and child understand and respect their roles. It strengthens verbal working memory by giving the child a structured language framework for understanding what is and isn't negotiable. It also fosters self-regulation by reducing the uncertainty and power struggles that often fuel emotional dysregulation.

INSTRUCTIONS FOR THE ADULT

Use this page proactively—before a power struggle occurs. This is not a reactive tool to be used mid-meltdown, but a calm, collaborative conversation that helps establish family structure and expectations. Sit down with your child and explain that everyone in the family has responsibilities, and it's your job as the adult to keep things fair, safe, and healthy.

Together, complete the two sections:

1. **Decisions Parents Make with No Negotiation**
2. **Decisions My Child Makes**

Keep the tone firm but warm—this is about clarity and consistency, not control or punishment.

STEP-BY-STEP GUIDANCE

1. **Set the tone.**

   Begin with: "Every family works best when everyone knows their role. My job is to be the parent. Your job is to be the child. Let's talk about what that means."

2. **Complete the first column: adult decisions.**

   "Decisions Parents Make with No Negotiations"

   Fill in three to five non-negotiable decisions that parents control. These may include:

   • Bedtime
   • What's for dinner
   • Screen time limits
   • Safety rules
   • Morning routine

3. Explain that these decisions are final—not because the child doesn't matter, but because parents are responsible for the big picture.

4. **Complete the second column: child choices.**

   "Decisions My Child Makes"

   Identify three to five areas where the child does have control or input. These may include:

   • What to wear from a pre-approved set of clothes
   • Which book to read before bed
   • What toy to play with after homework
   • How to organize their school supplies

5. Emphasize that healthy independence means having some choices, not all choices.

6. **Review together.**

   Ask: "How does it feel to know what you get to choose?" and "Why do you think parents make some decisions without asking?"

   Use this as an opportunity to explain why structure creates safety, and that parents set limits because they care.

7. **Revisit often.**

   Post this page somewhere visible. Return to it when challenges arise: "Remember, this is something I decide as the parent."

KEY MESSAGE

Children feel more secure—not less—when they know someone is confidently in charge. Boundaries aren't about control; they're about safety, structure, and love.

CLOSING THOUGHT

Kids with ADHD thrive with clear expectations and consistent roles. When adults step fully into their authority with warmth and calmness, they help children build the self-regulation skills they desperately need. Empowering the parent doesn't disempower the child—it frees them to be a child.

RESEARCH REFERENCE

Baumrind, D. (1991). The influence of parenting style on adolescent competence and substance use. *The Journal of Early Adolescence, 11*(1), 56–95.

Activity 6.12: Sibling Fighting

Executive function skills strengthened: Self-regulation

OVERVIEW

Sibling conflict is one of the most common—and emotionally draining—challenges in households with children who struggle with self-regulation. For children with ADHD and executive function delays, sibling fighting often becomes a predictable emotional script: an impulsive reaction to boredom, frustration, or overstimulation, with one or both children using conflict as a way to seek attention or control. Unfortunately, when parents repeatedly intervene, referee, or take sides, they may unintentionally reinforce the very behavior they're trying to stop.

This workbook page is designed to interrupt the emotional payoff of sibling fighting. It helps children identify the situations and triggers that commonly lead to conflict, while clearly outlining how parents will respond when it occurs. The goal is to reduce parental reactivity and make it known—upfront and in writing—that fighting will not be rewarded with attention, negotiation, or emotional energy.

This approach strengthens self-regulation by shifting responsibility for de-escalation back onto the children, while supporting parents in staying consistent, calm, and in control of their own emotional responses.

INSTRUCTIONS FOR THE ADULT

Before conflict arises, sit down with both (or all) siblings and complete this page together. Treat it as a family agreement—not a punishment or a lecture. Your role is to help your children:

- ◆ Recognize the patterns that lead to conflict.
- ◆ Understand that parent involvement is no longer guaranteed.
- ◆ See that resolving conflict is a skill they must begin to practice on their own.

Be firm and clear in explaining that sibling fighting is not a tool for getting attention and will not result in a reward or reaction.

STEP-BY-STEP GUIDANCE

1. **Identify common triggers.**

   Complete the first prompt: *"Sibling fighting tends to happen when. . ."*

   Brainstorm with your children and write down three recurring situations that usually lead to conflict. Examples may include:
   - When we're bored
   - When we share a toy or device
   - When someone feels ignored or jealous

2. Emphasize that recognizing patterns is the first step to breaking them.

3. **Establish parental responses.**

   Fill in: *"When there is sibling fighting, parents will. . ."*

   This section is for the adults to define clear, calm, and non-negotiable responses. The goal is to stop feeding the conflict cycle with attention.

   Sample responses might include:
   - "We will not get involved or take sides."
   - "We will walk away and give no reaction."
   - "We will not speak to either child until there is calm."

4. Make sure all responses are actionable, consistent, and realistic for you to follow through with.

5. **Clarify the why.**

   Briefly explain to the children:

   "When you fight, it's easy to pull us in. But from now on, we're trusting you to solve it yourselves or take a break. We will not reward fighting with attention."

6. **Reinforce self-regulation goals.**

   Remind your children that this plan is not about punishment but about growing up, learning to stay calm, and solving problems independently.

KEY MESSAGE

Sibling fighting often continues because it works. When parents step back and children take ownership of solving their own problems, self-regulation grows—and the fighting loses its power.

CLOSING THOUGHT

Children learn self-regulation by being allowed—and expected—to practice it. When parents stop reacting to every argument and instead create predictable, non-reactive systems, they create space for true growth, maturity, and sibling connection.

RESEARCH REFERENCE
Patterson, G. R. (1982). *Coercive Family Process*. Eugene, OR: Castalia Publishing.

Activity 6.13: Every Single Day Expectations
Executive function skills strengthened: Self-motivation

OVERVIEW
Self-motivation thrives in predictability, clarity, and consistency—especially for children with ADHD and executive function challenges. These children often wake up each day without a clear internal roadmap for what's expected, leading to power struggles, avoidant behaviors, or emotional dysregulation. When routines and values change depending on the mood of the day or which parent is present, the result is confusion, inconsistency, and eroded motivation.

This page helps families align on non-negotiable daily expectations—a set of agreed-upon values, routines, and behaviors that are reinforced every single day. It creates a shared foundation for the child and both caregivers, reducing tension and restoring family-wide clarity and structure. These expectations become part of the child's mental "anchor," reducing the daily executive burden of decision-making and promoting a stable environment for internal motivation to grow.

INSTRUCTIONS FOR THE ADULT
This page should be completed as a united front between caregivers—ideally with both parents or guardians present. Begin by discussing what values and routines are most important for your household. These should reflect your shared goals: structure, wellness, connection, respect, and consistency.

Next, work with your child to introduce these as daily family expectations, not just rules. Emphasize that this is what the entire family does each day—not as a punishment but as a commitment to a healthy, supportive, and predictable home environment.

STEP-BY-STEP GUIDANCE
1. **Align as caregivers first.**
   Before involving the child, parents should privately decide on four to six daily expectations they both agree to uphold. These should be realistic, clear, and measurable, such as:
   - Go outside for fresh air or movement.
   - Sit together for dinner (even briefly).

- Speak to each other with kindness.
- Prioritize people over screens.
- Get to school on time without yelling.
- Start winding down by 8:30 p.m. for a 9 p.m. bedtime.

2. **Introduce the concept to the child.**

   Frame the page as a way for the family to "work as a team" and help everyone succeed. Say something like:

   "In our family, there are some things we will do *every single day* because they help us grow, stay calm, and feel connected."

3. **Complete the statement together.**

   Read and fill in: *"In this family, every single day, we will. . ."*
   List the agreed-upon expectations in the space provided. Let your child contribute where appropriate, and read the list aloud to reinforce understanding.

4. **Explain the purpose behind each expectation.**

   For each item, briefly discuss *why* it matters. This builds **buy-in** and helps the child see the bigger picture.

5. **Display and revisit often.**

   Post this page in a central location (e.g., refrigerator, hallway). Revisit it during family meetings or when routines begin to slip. Use it as a reminder—not a threat—and stay consistent.

KEY MESSAGE

Consistency builds motivation. When expectations are the same every day—regardless of which parent is present—children feel more secure, less confused, and more capable of rising to meet them.

CLOSING THOUGHT

For children with ADHD, inconsistency is kryptonite. Unified, predictable parenting—grounded in daily expectations—not only supports emotional regulation and motivation but restores peace and clarity to the entire family system. Clarity isn't controlling—it's compassionate.

RESEARCH REFERENCE

Chronis-Tuscano, A., et al. (2016). Parenting practices and treatment outcomes in children with ADHD: A review and implications for intervention. *Clinical Child and Family Psychology Review, 19*(3), 170–180.

Activity 6.14: Parents Are *Not* Entertainers

Executive function skills strengthened: Self-regulation, self-motivation

OVERVIEW

In today's fast-paced, overstimulating world, many children—especially those with ADHD—have developed a low tolerance for boredom. They expect constant entertainment, instant gratification, and external stimulation. As a result, when boredom sets in, they often turn to parents not out of need, but habit—expecting the adult to become a source of novelty, distraction, or entertainment.

This page teaches a foundational executive function lesson: boredom is not a problem to be solved by others—it is a developmental opportunity. Boredom gives children the space to build creativity, initiative, emotional regulation, and problem-solving. When a child is taught that their boredom is theirs to manage, they begin to activate their internal executive system: setting goals, starting tasks, and engaging their imagination—all essential components of self-regulation and self-motivation.

This page helps shift the emotional burden off parents and onto the child in a healthy and empowering way.

INSTRUCTIONS FOR THE ADULT

Use this page preventively—before the child is bored. Sit down together and explain the difference between being ignored and being independent. Let your child know that it is not your job to constantly provide stimulation. It is not a rejection—it is a signal of trust: "You are capable of managing your own time and feelings."

Read the page together out loud, emphasizing the key messages:

◆ Boredom is good.
◆ You are strong enough to figure it out.
◆ Mom and dad will not fix it for you.

This page serves as a boundary and a mindset shift for both parent and child.

STEP-BY-STEP GUIDANCE

1. **Introduce the idea of healthy boredom.**
   Ask: "Have you ever felt bored and not known what to do?"
   Explain: "That's actually a good thing—it means your brain is ready to grow."
2. **Read the page aloud together.**
   Slowly read the key message:

   "Boredom is good. Boredom is healthy. When you are bored, Mom and Dad cannot cure your boredom for you. That is your responsibility. You are strong, you are creative, you are resilient. If you come to us when you are bored, know that we cannot help you—you must figure it out yourself."

3. **Discuss what this means.**

   Ask:
   - "What does it feel like to be bored?"
   - "What are some things you can do with your time when you're bored?"
   - "Why do you think we're not going to fix it for you anymore?"

4. **Build a boredom toolbox (optional).**

   Help the child brainstorm a list of independent activities they can turn to when boredom strikes. Include a mix of physical, creative, and quiet options.

5. **Set the boundary and stick to it.**

   When the child comes to you complaining of boredom, calmly refer back to the page. Say, "This is something you're strong enough to figure out. I trust you."

KEY MESSAGE

Boredom is not something to avoid—it's something to embrace. It's where creativity lives and motivation begins. The more a child learns to sit in their boredom, the more they grow.

CLOSING THOUGHT

When parents stop entertaining their children, they stop robbing them of the chance to build internal skills. Learning to manage boredom is not just about passing time—it's about learning to trust oneself, tolerate discomfort, and take initiative. That's executive function in action.

RESEARCH REFERENCE

Hunter, A. E., & Eastwood, J. D. (2021). Boredom and self-regulation: A motivational perspective. *Personality and Individual Differences, 168*, 110305.

Activity 6.15: Utilize Your Tribe
Executive function skills strengthened: Self-regulation

OVERVIEW

Children with ADHD often demonstrate a dramatic contrast in behavior between school and home. This is not accidental—it's a function of how executive dysfunction and emotional dysregulation interact with the nature of relationships. As explained in *The Executive Function Playbook*, children with ADHD typically save their most intense behaviors—outbursts, aggression, defiance, and even destruction—for the only relationships they know to be truly unconditional: mom and dad.

As these behaviors escalate, many parents begin to feel isolated, ashamed, and overwhelmed, often keeping the severity of the situation a secret. But secrecy fuels the cycle. When extreme behaviors go unchecked and unshared, the child's power increases—and the parent's confidence and clarity decrease. Silence is the enemy of support.

This workbook page guides parents and caregivers to break the cycle of isolation by actively building a behavioral support team, or "tribe." It normalizes the need for outside accountability and helps parents identify trusted individuals they can call on when behaviors become severe. It teaches the child that there are multiple adults in their life who care, who will step in, and who will reinforce the same standards and boundaries—helping restore both structure and safety in the home.

INSTRUCTIONS FOR THE ADULT

Sit down as a parenting team (or individually if applicable) and complete this page in a quiet moment—not during or directly after a behavioral incident. The purpose is to plan proactively and reduce future overwhelm.

In the center of the page, identify your child's core support system—people who:

- ◆ Share your values and standards
- ◆ Are calm under pressure
- ◆ Will reinforce your parenting choices
- ◆ Will not rescue or excuse your child's behavior

These could include:

- ◆ A trusted aunt or uncle
- ◆ A family friend or neighbor
- ◆ A coach or extracurricular leader
- ◆ A guidance counselor, social worker, or teacher
- ◆ A spiritual mentor, youth leader, or clinician

Make sure to choose adults who are emotionally regulated, reliable, and have the capacity to engage when needed.

STEP-BY-STEP GUIDANCE
  1. Read the core message aloud.

      Remind yourselves: "We do not have to handle this alone. Silence helps no one. We will not allow our home to become a place where harmful behavior is hidden."

2. **Identify members of your tribe.**

   In the space provided, write down three to five people who:
   - Know and care about your child
   - Would be willing to support your family during escalated behaviors
   - Will align with your goals for your child's growth

3. **Assign supportive roles.**

   For each person, briefly note *how* they might help. Examples:
   - "Uncle Jay can come over and speak firmly with him after an incident."
   - "Coach Lisa can hold him accountable for behavior at practice."
   - "Mr. Alvarez (guidance counselor) can check in weekly."

4. **Communicate proactively.**

   Once your list is complete, consider reaching out to each person and sharing:
   - That you're working on supporting your child's growth
   - That you're naming a "tribe" of trusted adults to call on
   - That you value their help and want to keep them in the loop

5. **Introduce the concept to your child.**

   Depending on age and readiness, explain to your child that more adults will be helping hold them accountable—not to punish, but to help them grow. Say something like:

   "We love you too much to keep these behaviors a secret. You're part of a team, and we're all here to help you succeed."

KEY MESSAGE

The more regulated adults involved in a child's life, the safer and more supported that child becomes. There is no shame in asking for help—it's a sign of strength, not failure.

CLOSING THOUGHT

Behavioral intensity behind closed doors should never become a family's burden to carry alone. When parents step out of isolation and into community, they take back control, reinforce expectations, and model emotional courage. The child learns: "I'm not just accountable to Mom and Dad. I'm accountable to my tribe."

RESEARCH REFERENCE

Hoza, B., et al. (2005). What aspects of peer relationships are impaired in children with attention-deficit/hyperactivity disorder? *Journal of Consulting and Clinical Psychology, 73*(3), 411–423.

Activity 6.16: Complaining Does Not Equal Cannot
Executive function skills strengthened: Self-regulation, self-motivation

OVERVIEW
Children and teens with ADHD often develop highly predictable avoidance patterns. When faced with nonpreferred tasks—schoolwork, chores, transitions, or responsibilities—they frequently rely on a familiar set of complaints to delay, resist, or escape. These complaints may sound like:

- "I can't do this."
- "It's too hard."
- "This is boring."
- "You never help me."
- "Why do I have to?"

While these statements can sound like genuine distress, they're often tactical and rehearsed, used to trigger parent involvement, gain control of the situation, or be let off the hook. Over time, this pattern can undermine the development of self-motivation and erode the parent's confidence in setting firm expectations.

This page brings the pattern into the light. It helps parents and children identify common complaints used as manipulation and teaches the child that just because they don't like something doesn't mean they can't do it. Writing these phrases down makes the behavior conscious, reducing its power and empowering parents to respond consistently and calmly.

INSTRUCTIONS FOR THE ADULT
Use this page as a proactive, calm conversation tool—not in the middle of an argument or after a meltdown. Sit with your child and say:

"We've noticed you tend to say some of the same things when you don't want to do something. It's okay to not love every task, but we're not going to let those complaints get in your way anymore."

Then, together, write down the top three to five complaints your child frequently uses to avoid tasks. Next, use the second section to identify how you (as parents) will consistently respond to each one moving forward. This gives both child and adult a clear, rehearsed script for staying on track.

STEP-BY-STEP GUIDANCE

1. **Identify the avoidance phrases.**

   Fill in: *"Common complaints from (child's name) include:"*

   Write three to five specific phrases the child uses when resisting. Let them help list them if appropriate—it helps increase awareness and buy-in.

2. **Debunk the complaints.**

   Briefly discuss each one:

   - "Is this always true?"
   - "What really happens after you say this?"
   - "What's your brain trying to avoid when you say this?"

3. **Develop calm, firm parental responses.**

   Fill in: *"How parents will effectively handle these complaints:"*

   For each complaint, list a specific response the parents will use.

   Examples:

   - Complaint: "I can't do it."
     Response: "You don't have to finish it all right now—just start with step one."
   - Complaint: "This is stupid."
     Response: "You're allowed to feel that way, but it still needs to get done."

4. Focus on responses that are non-reactive, consistent, and emotionally neutral.

5. **Share the plan with the child.**

   Clearly explain: "From now on, when we hear one of these complaints, we're not going to get pulled in. We're going to stick to the plan. That complaint doesn't work anymore."

6. **Post the page as a visual reminder.**

   Keep the page somewhere visible so both adults and the child can refer to it. Repetition strengthens the boundary and builds internal motivation over time.

KEY MESSAGE

Just because you don't like it doesn't mean you can't do it. Complaining is not a reason to stop. You are capable—and we're not falling for the same tricks anymore.

CLOSING THOUGHT

When children with ADHD learn that avoidance and complaining no longer provide an escape route, they begin to build real frustration tolerance, independence, and self-motivation. Repetition creates patterns—but so does breaking them. This page gives families the language and structure to do just that.

RESEARCH REFERENCE

Barkley, R. A. (2013). *Taking Charge of ADHD: The Complete Authoritative Guide for Parents.* New York, NY: Guilford Press.

Activity 6.17: Permissive Parenting
Executive function skills strengthened: Self-regulation

OVERVIEW

At the core of executive function development is the consistent presence of structure, boundaries, and calm authority from adults. Children with ADHD, in particular, thrive when they are surrounded by caregivers who provide predictable expectations and follow-through. But in the face of emotional outbursts, defiance, or fatigue, even the most well-intentioned parents may begin to slide into permissive parenting—giving in, overindulging, or avoiding conflict altogether just to keep the peace.

Permissive parenting feels easier in the moment, but it teaches children the wrong lessons: that rules are flexible, boundaries are negotiable, and persistence pays off—not in effort, but in protest. Over time, this dynamic erodes a child's ability to self-regulate, because the external world becomes inconsistent and unpredictable.

This workbook page gently brings awareness to the unintentional ways both parents may have adopted permissive habits, and invites them to reflect on how those patterns might be unintentionally reinforcing negative behaviors. By making this a collaborative, judgment-free exercise, parents strengthen their own consistency—and offer their child the firm, calm foundation they need to grow.

INSTRUCTIONS FOR THE ADULT

This page is designed to be completed by both caregivers—separately but side-by-side. Each partner reflects on the other's parenting patterns, not to criticize, but to identify and address blind spots. The goal is team alignment, not blame.

Before completing the page, read the following statement aloud together:

"Permissive parenting is when we overindulge or avoid enforcing rules to keep the peace. It often feels helpful or loving in the moment—but over time, it makes it harder for our child to learn how to regulate, accept limits, and take responsibility."

Then, each partner fills out the assigned section honestly and respectfully.

STEP-BY-STEP GUIDANCE

1. **Create a shared understanding.**

   Discuss what permissive parenting looks like in your home. Common signs include:
   - Giving in when the child complains or protests
   - Letting rules slide "just this once"
   - Avoiding hard conversations to prevent meltdowns
   - Doing tasks for the child to avoid resistance
   - Allowing screen time or treats after defiant behavior

2. **Complete the reflection sections.**
   - *"Examples of how Mom has unintentionally become permissive"* (completed by Dad)
   - *"Examples of how Dad has unintentionally become permissive"* (completed by Mom)

3. Each partner should write two to three specific patterns they've observed. Use gentle, specific language.

   Examples:
   - "You tend to say yes to more screen time when he whines."
   - "You often clean up her messes instead of asking her to do it."
   - "You don't enforce bedtime when she resists."

4. **Share and reflect.**

   Exchange answers respectfully. Discuss how these patterns may have developed, and how they could be shifted to provide more consistent structure for your child.

5. **Recommit to unified boundaries.**

   Together, decide on two to three small parenting boundaries or routines that both caregivers will uphold moving forward. Consider writing them on a follow-up page or family expectations chart.

KEY MESSAGE

Permissiveness may feel like kindness, but it teaches inconsistency. When parents gently hold the line—together—they teach their child how to hold themselves together, too.

CLOSING THOUGHT

Parenting a child with ADHD is a challenge that requires intentional teamwork. This page is not about blame—it's about returning to alignment. A united front provides the emotional container your child needs to thrive. Firmness is love. Consistency is compassion.

RESEARCH REFERENCE

Baumrind, D. (1966). Effects of authoritative parental control on child behavior. *Child Development, 37*(4), 887–907.

Activity 6.18: Parenting Same Page
Executive function skills strengthened: Self-regulation, self-motivation

OVERVIEW

One of the most powerful supports a child with ADHD can receive is a unified, consistent parenting approach. When parents operate with different expectations, consequences, and emotional tones, the child often experiences confusion, frustration, and—most commonly—learns to manipulate the divide. This isn't because the child is inherently deceitful, but because inconsistency naturally invites testing, avoidance, and control-seeking behavior, especially for children with underdeveloped executive function skills.

This workbook page brings both caregivers into alignment by having each parent separately define their true personal goals for their child—emotional, academic, behavioral, and relational. Then, together, they reflect on how to synchronize their parenting strategies to work toward those goals as a team. This process strengthens the child's self-regulation by creating a predictable home environment and reinforces their self-motivation by removing inconsistent messages and divided authority.

When parents parent from the same page, the child no longer wastes energy navigating a moving target. Instead, that energy is redirected toward learning, growth, and emotional security.

INSTRUCTIONS FOR THE ADULT

Complete this page together in a quiet, reflective moment—not during or after a conflict. The goal is not to debate or correct one another, but to gain insight and alignment.

First, each parent independently writes down what they want most for their child—goals related to character, resilience, success, happiness, emotional development, etc. Then, use the second section to determine how you can bridge any differences and create a unified parenting approach to help your child reach those goals.

This is not about perfect agreement on every detail—it's about shared vision, consistent messages, and predictable boundaries.

STEP-BY-STEP GUIDANCE

1. **Reflect on personal goals.**

    Complete the prompts:
    - *"What are my true goals for (child's name)?"*
    - Mom writes in one section, Dad in the other.

2. Encourage each caregiver to think beyond behavior. What kind of person do you hope your child becomes? What life skills do you want them to develop?

3. **Compare and highlight overlaps.**

    Share your goals with each other. Circle or highlight where you overlap. This helps identify your shared vision and reveals common ground.

4. **Address gaps respectfully.**

    If differences emerge (e.g., one prioritizes emotional growth, the other discipline), discuss how those differences can complement each other, rather than compete.

5. **Create a unified plan.**

    In the space provided (or on a follow-up sheet), write down two to four action steps for how you will parent from the same page. These may include:
    - Using the same language around boundaries
    - Responding to meltdowns or disrespect the same way
    - Reinforcing daily routines with consistency
    - Backing each other up in front of the child

6. **Make it visible.**

    Keep this page somewhere private but accessible. Revisit it during moments of doubt or disagreement to re-anchor in your shared goals.

KEY MESSAGE

When parents are aligned, children feel safer, more secure, and more motivated. Unity builds trust, clarity, and growth—while division builds confusion and control-seeking.

CLOSING THOUGHT

Parenting on the same page doesn't mean agreeing on everything—it means agreeing on what matters most and working as a team to get there. When children with ADHD see their parents as a unified, calm, and consistent team, they develop the very skills we hope to build in them: resilience, emotional control, and internal motivation.

RESEARCH REFERENCE

Loe, I. M., & Feldman, H. M. (2007). Academic and behavioral outcomes of children with ADHD. *Journal of Pediatric Psychology, 32*(6), 643–654.

Activity 6.19: Different Parenting Roles—One Team

Executive function skills strengthened: Self-regulation, self-motivation

OVERVIEW

Children with ADHD thrive in homes where routines are clear, boundaries are consistent, and the emotional climate is calm. But behind the scenes, many parenting teams operate with unspoken imbalance—where one parent carries a disproportionate share of the mental, emotional, and logistical labor of raising the child. When this imbalance goes unaddressed, it can lead to resentment, miscommunication, inconsistent parenting, and disjointed expectations—all of which undermine the child's ability to self-regulate and stay motivated.

This workbook page offers parents a safe and structured way to step back and assess who is doing what and how each caregiver defines their role in the parenting partnership. It's not about blame—it's about building a stronger team. By having both parents reflect and write down their current contributions, the exercise fosters mutual understanding, increases empathy, and highlights areas that may need rebalancing.

When children see their parents working together, not in conflict or burnout, it models teamwork, collaboration, and emotional responsibility—core values that contribute to their own executive function development.

INSTRUCTIONS FOR THE ADULT

Complete this page together, but fill in your respective sections individually and honestly. The goal is to identify:

- ◆ What roles or responsibilities each parent takes on most often
- ◆ Where there may be imbalance
- ◆ How you can move closer to a 50-50 distribution of parenting duties—both physical and emotional

This is not about assigning equal tasks each day, but about ensuring both partners feel respected, supported, and aligned in raising your child.

STEP-BY-STEP GUIDANCE

1. Clarify the purpose.

Read this statement aloud together:

"We may have different parenting roles, but we are one team. The more balanced we are, the more stability, calm, and consistency we offer our child."

2. **Complete the role reflections.**
   - *"Mom's Parenting Roles"* (completed by Mom)
   - *"Dad's Parenting Roles"* (completed by Dad)
3. Encourage each parent to include physical tasks (e.g., making lunches, helping with homework, bedtime routines) and mental/emotional tasks (e.g., noticing mood shifts, organizing playdates, planning therapy sessions, setting boundaries).
4. **Compare and reflect.**
   Once completed, share and review your answers together. Ask:
   - Are there any surprises?
   - Are there roles one of us is taking on silently?
   - Are there any responsibilities that feel unfairly weighted?
5. **Discuss opportunities to rebalance.**
   Highlight any patterns of imbalance, then create a short list of two to three small changes you can implement to bring the team into better balance.
   Examples:
   - "Dad will take over school emails and bedtime three nights per week."
   - "Mom will step back during homework time to allow for more independence."
   - "We'll alternate who handles morning routine prep."
6. **Reaffirm your team identity.**
   End with a commitment: *"We're in this together. When we support each other, we support our child."*

KEY MESSAGE

Even when roles are different, the goal is the same. The strongest families are built not on perfection, but on partnership.

CLOSING THOUGHT

Parenting a child with ADHD is demanding—emotionally, mentally, and physically. The more evenly the weight is shared, the more likely each parent is to stay regulated, clear, and connected. When parents work as one team, their child learns not just structure, but love in action.

RESEARCH REFERENCE

Cabrera, N. J., Shannon, J. D., & Tamis-LeMonda, C. S. (2007). Fathers' influence on their children's cognitive and emotional development: From toddlers to pre-K. *Applied Development Science, 11*(4), 208–213.

Activity 6.20: The Weekend

Executive function skills strengthened: Self-regulation, self-motivation

OVERVIEW

For children with ADHD and executive function challenges, weekends often become a free-for-all—a time where routines disappear, boundaries blur, and excessive screen use, late nights, and power struggles become the norm. Without the external structure of school, these children are at higher risk of dysregulation, low motivation, and behavioral escalation.

This workbook page empowers parents to reclaim the weekend by creating a written agreement that defines—clearly and without discussion—what is off-limits and what is allowed. By establishing limits in writing and offering healthy, structured choices, parents shift the weekend from a reactive environment into a predictable and purposeful space.

This practice builds self-regulation by setting consistent boundaries, and promotes self-motivation by encouraging the child to choose from a curated menu of meaningful activities that don't rely on screens or external entertainment.

INSTRUCTIONS FOR THE ADULT

Complete this page with your parenting partner first, then introduce it to your child as a clear, confident, and non-negotiable weekend plan. Use calm and neutral language to set expectations, and focus on the opportunity to explore alternatives rather than emphasizing restriction.

This is not a punishment—this is a parenting boundary rooted in executive function growth. Present it as a plan to support your child's brain, not to take away fun.

STEP-BY-STEP GUIDANCE

1. **Define what's off-limits.**

   In the first section, write down what your child cannot access or do on weekends. Be specific. Examples might include:
   - No iPads or tablets
   - No personal smartphones
   - No access to Wi-Fi
   - No YouTube or video games
   - No staying in pajamas past 10 a.m.
   - No screens before chores are done

2. Use language like: "These are not options this weekend."

3. **List approved weekend activities.**

In the next section, brainstorm with your partner (or child, if appropriate) a list of healthy, screen-free options they can choose from. Include:

- Outdoor activities: bike rides, walks, playground, nature hikes
- Creative projects: Legos, crafts, puzzles, baking
- Social engagement: playdates, family games, calling a grandparent
- Physical movement: trampoline, sports, obstacle courses
- Productive tasks: helping with a project, reorganizing toys, reading

4. Phrase it as: "This is your menu of awesome things you *can* do this weekend."

5. **Post and stick to the plan.**

Keep the page visible and refer to it rather than re-explaining or re-debating when resistance arises. Use firm, calm responses like:

- "That's not part of the weekend plan."
- "You're free to choose from the list."
- "We already agreed—this isn't a discussion."

6. **Follow through consistently.**

Self-regulation is built when boundaries are predictable. If the page says it's off-limits, it's off-limits. If a child resists or complains, hold the boundary without engaging in power struggles.

KEY MESSAGE

Weekends don't need to feel chaotic or out of control. With clear expectations and meaningful alternatives, they can become a space for creativity, connection, and growth—without needing screens to survive.

CLOSING THOUGHT

The ADHD brain doesn't take weekends off—and neither should boundaries. But when structure and freedom are balanced, children learn to manage their time, regulate their impulses, and make better choices. This page gives them a map—and the freedom to move within it.

RESEARCH REFERENCE

Christakis, D. A., et al. (2018). The effects of screen time on executive function in children and adolescents. *Pediatrics, 142*(6), e20183663.

Activity 6.1: Setting Boundaries

When _____ (child's name) does _____

I will _____

until _____.

Activity 6.2: Home Safe Space

Where is your child's safe space in the home? Remember, no technology is permitted here, and interruptions from parents are not allowed.

_____

_____

_____

What items are in the safe space to make it feel safe and comforting? For example: soft items, drawing materials, books, or calming visuals.

_____

_____

_____

Activity 6.3: Family Grit

Each member of the family will pick one activity/hobby that they will do each week for three months. The activity cannot involve tech, and it must take place outside the home.

_____'s Activity

◆ My chosen activity: _____	◆ Why I chose this: _____
◆ What I will do when I feel like quitting: _____	◆ What I hope to feel or gain after three months: _____

Activity 6.4: Partner Tag-In

Parent A

These are the signs that Parent A is becoming dysregulated:

_____

_____

When Parent B notices Parent A is becoming dysregulated, Partner B will say or do:

_____

_____

After Parent B tags in, Parent A will self-regulate by:

_____

_____

Parent B

These are the signs that Parent B is becoming dysregulated:

_____

_____

When Parent A notices Parent B is becoming dysregulated, Parent A will say or do:

_____

_____

After Parent A tags in, Parent B will self-regulate by:

_____

_____

Activity 6.5: Family Events

Each member of the family picks one event or activity that the whole family must do together. Include the date that the event will take place.

Family member #1:

_____

_____

Family member #2:

_____

_____

Family member #3:

_____

_____

Family member #4:

_____

_____

Activity 6.6: Goals for Everyone

Each member of the family chooses a goal for the other family members.

Parent A Goal for Parent B: _____ Goal for _____ (child's name): _____ Goal for _____ (child's name): _____	Parent B Goal for Parent A: _____ Goal for _____ (child's name): _____ Goal for _____ (child's name): _____
_____ (child's name): Goal for Parent A: _____ Goal for Parent B: _____ Goal for sibling: _____	_____ (child's name): Goal for Parent A: _____ Goal for Parent B: _____ Goal for sibling: _____

Activity 6.7: Specific Responses

Come up with a scripted response for when your child displays each of the following behaviors:

1. Self-defeating comments (e.g., "I can't do anything right.")
Response:

_____

_____

2. Complaining (e.g., "This is so unfair.")
Response:

_____

_____

3. Learned helplessness or emotional manipulation (e.g., "I don't know how. You do it for me.")
Response:

_____

_____

4. Lying (e.g., "That wasn't me!")
Response:

_____

_____

Activity 6.8: The Prompt Hierarchy

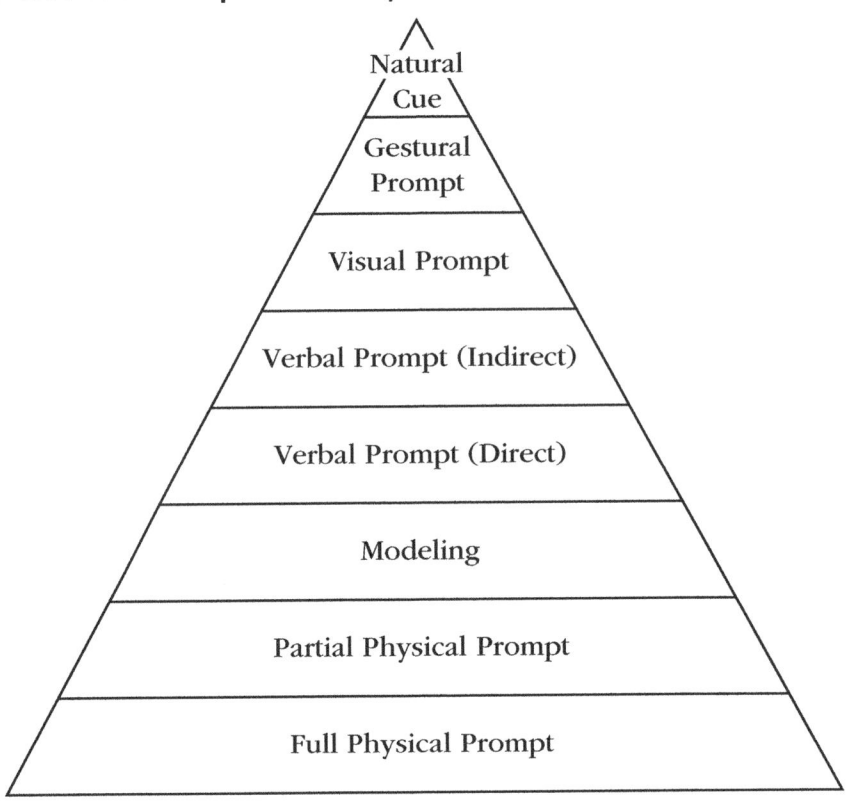

Natural Cue

Gestural Prompt

Visual Prompt

Verbal Prompt (Indirect)

Verbal Prompt (Direct)

Modeling

Partial Physical Prompt

Full Physical Prompt

<u>Morning Routine</u>

How I currently provide prompts:

_____

How I can start to fade these prompts:

_____

<u>Homework</u>

How I currently provide prompts:

_____

How I can start to fade these prompts:

_____

<u>Chores</u>

How I currently provide prompts:

_____

How I can start to fade these prompts:

_____

Activity 6.9: Use Less Language

Use scripted responses to reduce verbal overload.

What are some high-stress moments where you can use less language with your child?

1. If my child says/does: _____

Instead of saying: _____

_____

I'll say: _____

2. If my child says/does: _____

Instead of saying: _____

_____

I'll say: _____

3. If my child says/does: _____

Instead of saying: _____

_____

I'll say: _____

4. If my child says/does: _____

Instead of saying: _____

_____

I'll say: _____

Activity 6.10: A Different Time-Out!

<u>Common Triggers for Escalation</u>

_____

_____

_____

_____

_____

<u>Time-Out Log</u>

Date/time the time-out was called	Topic	Child's reaction	What I did to stay calm	Revisited after 24 hours? How?

<u>How do I call a time-out?</u>
Practice using phrases like:

- "Time-out. We'll talk again at 7 p.m. tomorrow. Not before."

- _____

- _____

Activity 6.11: The Child Is *Not* the Parent

Decisions Parents Make with No Negotiations	Decisions _____ (*child's name*) Makes

Activity 6.12: Sibling Fighting

Sibling fighting tends to happen when:

1. _____

_____

_____

2. _____

_____

_____

3. _____

_____

_____

When there is sibling fighting, parents will:

1. _____

_____

_____

2. _____

_____

_____

3. _____

_____

_____

Activity 6.13: Every Single Day Expectations

In the _____ family, every single day, we will:

_____

_____

_____

_____

_____

_____

Activity 6.14: Parents Are *Not* Entertainers

Boredom is good. Boredom is healthy. When you are bored, your parents cannot cure your boredom for you. That is your responsibility. You are strong, you are creative, you are resilient. If you come to us when you are bored, know that we cannot help you—you must figure it out yourself.

<u>Build Your Boredom Toolbox</u>
When boredom strikes, what can you do? Try to think of some physical, creative, and quiet activities that you can do independently.

Activity 6.15: Utilize Your Tribe

We do not have to handle this alone. Silence helps no one. We will not allow our home to become a place where harmful behavior is hidden.

Who can help?   What can they do?

◆ _____ → _____

◆ _____ → _____

◆ _____ → _____

◆ _____ → _____

◆ _____ → _____

Activity 6.16: Complaining Does Not Equal Cannot

Complaint from _____ (child's name):   How parents will respond:

1. _____ → _____

2. _____ → _____

3. _____ → _____

4. _____ → _____

5. _____ → _____

Activity 6.17: Permissive Parenting

Permissive parenting is when we overindulge or avoid enforcing rules to keep the peace. It often feels helpful or loving in the moment—but over time, it makes it harder for our child to learn how to regulate, accept limits, and take responsibility.

Examples of how Parent A has unintentionally become permissive (completed by Parent B):

1. _____

2. _____

3. _____

Examples of how Parent B has unintentionally become permissive (completed by Parent A):

1. _____

2. _____

3. _____

Activity 6.18: Parenting Same Page

Parent A: What are my true goals for
_____ (child's name)?

1. _____

2. _____

3. _____

Parent B: What are my true goals for
_____ (child's name)?

1. _____

2. _____

3. _____

Our Unified Plan

Write down two to four action steps for how you two will parent from the same page.

_____

_____

_____

_____

Activity 6.19: Different Parenting Roles—One Team

We may have different parenting roles, but we are one team. The more balanced we are, the more stability, calm, and consistency we offer our child.

My Parenting Roles (completed by Parent A)

My Parenting Roles (completed by Parent B)

_____   _____

_____   _____

_____   _____

_____   _____

How can we have a better balance?

_____

_____

_____

We're in this together. When we support each other, we support our child.

_____

_____

_____

_____

Activity 6.20: The Weekend

Off-limits activities during the weekend:

_____

_____

_____

_____

_____

Awesome things you can do during the weekend:

_____

_____

_____

_____

_____

_____

_____

CHAPTER 7

Home Executive Functioning

Creating Structure, Boundaries, and Predictability
Where It Matters Most

Executive function skills are not just for the classroom—they are deeply tied to how a child functions within the four walls of their home. In fact, it's often at home—where the environment is looser, expectations are fuzzier, and emotions run higher—that a child's executive function challenges are most visible.

This chapter is about building the kind of structure, consistency, and clarity that children with ADHD *need*—and crave—in the home setting.

In *The Executive Function Playbook*, we highlight that many kids with ADHD perform better at school than at home. This is not because they're more compliant or more motivated in a classroom—it's because school is naturally structured. The day is segmented. The expectations are clear. There are boundaries, transitions, and routines that are followed every single day. That structure becomes a kind of scaffolding for the child's underdeveloped executive system.

But at home, that scaffolding often disappears.

This chapter provides parents with the tools to build that same executive structure at home—not with rigid rules or power struggles, but with clarity, confidence, and consistency. The worksheets in this section will help you put expectations down in writing, create predictable routines, and establish boundaries that are no longer up for debate. When the structure is written, posted, and repeated, children begin to internalize it—and that is when true executive functioning begins to take root.

These worksheets will help you:

◆ Establish daily routines and non-negotiables
◆ Set tech and screen boundaries that are clear and enforceable
◆ Create weekend expectations and family norms
◆ Define responsibilities and consequences without emotional reactivity
◆ Reduce negotiating, reminding, and repeating
◆ Turn vague hopes ("I wish they would get ready on time") into actionable plans

Each page is a practical tool to reduce chaos and increase follow-through. You'll notice that many of the activities include space for both the adult and the child to participate—because buy-in happens when expectations are clear, not when they're shouted in frustration.

In *The Executive Function Playbook*, we talk about the importance of a "predictable environment" as the foundation for skill development. This chapter is where that environment is built—one page, one rule, one routine at a time.

No more guessing. No more negotiating. No more wondering why your child can stay regulated in one setting but falls apart in another. These pages will give you everything you need to make home life more structured, more peaceful, and more predictable—for everyone.

Let's bring executive functioning home.

Activity 7.1: Morning Routine: Visual Timeline
Executive function skills strengthened: Self-awareness, self-regulation, self-motivation

OVERVIEW
For children and teens with ADHD, mornings are often chaotic, emotionally charged, and full of missed steps and rushed transitions. This is not due to a lack of intelligence or effort—it's the result of underdeveloped executive functioning, especially in the areas of time awareness, task initiation, planning, and emotional regulation.

In *The Executive Function Playbook*, we emphasize that one of the most effective strategies for managing complex transitions is the use of visual structure. Children with ADHD benefit from seeing information in a concrete, externalized format, rather than having to rely on internal memory or vague verbal reminders. This is especially true during high-pressure times like the morning routine, where multiple steps must happen in sequence and on a time limit.

This worksheet helps the adult and child co-create a visual morning timeline—a simple, personalized flow of what needs to happen, in what order, and by what time. Creating this visual timeline strengthens self-awareness (by mapping out daily needs), self-regulation (by helping the child anticipate transitions), and self-motivation (by giving them a clear, achievable plan).

INSTRUCTIONS FOR THE ADULT (PARENT, TEACHER, OR CLINICIAN)

Use this page to build a visual timeline *together* with the child. Instead of telling them what their morning "should" look like, guide them through the process of owning the routine by helping to create it step-by-step.

Explain that the goal of this worksheet is to give the morning routine a *visual shape*—like a map or timeline they can follow every day. This increases predictability, reduces anxiety, and improves follow-through.

STEP-BY-STEP GUIDANCE

1. **List the core morning tasks.**

   Brainstorm all the necessary steps in the child's morning—from waking up to getting out the door. Keep the list specific, observable, and in the child's own words when possible.

   Example task list:
   - Wake up
   - Turn off alarm
   - Get dressed
   - Eat breakfast
   - Brush teeth
   - Comb or style hair
   - Pack lunch/snack (or confirm it's packed)
   - Prepare backpack
   - Set a goal for the day
   - Put on shoes/coat
   - Be at the door ready to leave by 7:30 a.m.

2. **Add time estimates (optional but helpful).**

   Next to each task, help the child assign an approximate time or duration:
   - Wake up—6:30 a.m.
   - Get dressed—by 6:40 a.m.
   - Breakfast—6:40–6:55 a.m.
   - Out the door—by 7:30 a.m.

3. This helps develop time awareness and improves pacing. You can use clocks, icons, or visual timers for reinforcement.

4. **Create the visual timeline.**

   Use the page's blank timeline template or draw boxes, arrows, or icons to create a left-to-right or top-to-bottom visual flow. Include clocks or illustrations if that helps the child stay engaged.

   This timeline becomes the *blueprint* for how their morning should feel and flow.

5. **Display it and use it.**

   Once completed, consider displaying the visual timeline near where the child gets ready in the morning. Refer to it consistently. Encourage the child to self-check their progress rather than relying solely on verbal prompts.

   Optional tools:
   - Laminate the timeline and check off with dry-erase markers.
   - Use icons or drawings for younger students.
   - Add a "done" column for task completion.

WHY THIS MATTERS

Children with ADHD often know what they're *supposed* to do—but they struggle to do it *in the right order, in the right amount of time*, and *without adult reminders*. Creating a visual timeline removes ambiguity and gives them a tool for independence.

It also reduces the emotional burden on parents, who often feel stuck in the role of "morning manager." When children begin to reference and use their own routine map, they begin to build internal scaffolding for self-starting and follow-through—two of the most vital executive function skills.

KEY MESSAGE

Routines don't have to be overwhelming. When students create a clear, visual plan and refer to it consistently, they become more independent, more confident, and more capable of managing time and transitions without constant reminders.

CLOSING THOUGHT

When a child can *see* the path, they're more likely to walk it. This visual timeline transforms mornings from a rushed blur into a manageable rhythm—one they can eventually follow with calm, confidence, and pride.

Activity 7.2: My Morning Routine: Independent vs. Help

Executive function skills strengthened: Self-awareness, self-motivation

OVERVIEW

Morning routines can quickly become a battleground for families—especially when ADHD is involved. What should be a predictable, low-stress part of the day often turns into a cycle of reminders, arguments, resistance, and emotional escalation. In *The Executive Function Playbook*, we examine how this pattern is frequently fueled by a lack of clarity, control, and independence on the child's part—and over-prompting and stress on the adult's part.

This worksheet is designed to disrupt that cycle by helping both child and adult identify two important things:

1. What the child is truly capable of doing on their own, even if they're not doing it yet
2. What still requires adult help, based on developmental readiness and current skill level

By separating tasks into these two categories, this activity increases self-awareness in the child and helps them begin to take greater ownership over their morning. At the same time, it supports self-motivation by helping them build toward more independence—and supports adults in reducing unnecessary prompting, which often leads to power struggles and dysregulation.

INSTRUCTIONS FOR THE ADULT (PARENT, TEACHER, OR CLINICIAN)

This worksheet is best completed through a collaborative conversation. The child and adult will work together to fill out two lists:

- Five tasks the child can do independently (no help needed)
- Five tasks the child still needs help with

This is not about what the child is currently doing—but what they are capable of doing based on age, maturity, and skill level. The goal is to identify realistic opportunities for increased independence, while also acknowledging where support is still needed.

This exercise also helps adults examine where over-prompting may be unintentionally reinforcing negative behavior cycles, especially in ADHD-driven conflict loops.

STEP-BY-STEP GUIDANCE

1. **Frame the conversation.**

   Begin by saying:

   "Everyone has some things they can do on their own and some things they still need help with—especially in the morning. Today, we're going to figure out which parts of your morning you're ready to own all by yourself, and which parts we'll still do as a team."

2. **List five tasks the child can do independently.**

   On the left side of the worksheet, help the child identify five things they are fully capable of doing on their own in the morning—even if they don't always follow through yet.

   Be honest and developmental in your assessment. You might say:
   - "Do you *know how* to do this without help?"
   - "Have you done it by yourself before?"
   - "If I wasn't reminding you every day, could you still do this?"

3. **Look at these examples:**
   - Brush teeth
   - Pack backpack
   - Get dressed
   - Eat breakfast
   - Tie shoes

4. **Label this section clearly:** "I Can Do These on My Own."

5. **List five tasks the child still needs help with.**

   On the right side, work together to identify five tasks that still require adult support, guidance, or co-regulation. This could include tasks that are too complex, emotionally triggering, or inconsistently completed without reminders.

   Examples:
   - Waking up on time
   - Managing time while eating breakfast
   - Remembering all belongings
   - Staying focused during transitions
   - Regulating emotions after a setback

6. **Label this section:** "I Still Need Help with These."

7. **Talk about the why.**

   For each item on both lists, reflect together:
   - "Why do you think this one is easy for you?"
   - "What makes this one harder right now?"
   - "What would help you feel more confident doing this on your own?"

8. **Review patterns and set intentions.**
   Once the lists are complete, zoom out and discuss:
   • "Are there any things on the 'Help' list you'd like to work toward doing on your own soon?"
   • "How can I remind you less and help you take more ownership?"
   • "What's one thing you want to do completely by yourself tomorrow morning?"

WHY THIS MATTERS

Children with ADHD are often caught in negative attention loops during morning routines. They may resist tasks not because they can't do them, but because conflict and chasing behaviors activate dopamine—while routine tasks feel boring and nonstimulating. Unfortunately, adult prompting often feeds this cycle, creating a daily "cat and mouse game" that reinforces oppositional behavior and leaves everyone dysregulated.

This worksheet breaks that cycle by giving the child a clear inventory of ownership, while helping the adult step back and reduce unnecessary engagement. With consistent use, this tool promotes smoother mornings, increased independence, and a stronger sense of competence for the child.

KEY MESSAGE

Kids are capable of more than we realize—but only if we give them space to try, fail, and grow. When children learn to take ownership of what they can do, and when adults stop doing it *for* them, the whole morning becomes calmer, clearer, and more collaborative.

CLOSING THOUGHT

When we hand children the map instead of dragging them through the route, they learn to guide themselves. This page helps them begin that journey—task by task, one morning at a time.

Activity 7.3: My Morning Routine: Natural Consequences

Executive function skills strengthened: Self-awareness, self-motivation, self-evaluation

OVERVIEW

One of the most common struggles for parents of children with ADHD is managing morning behavior without constant conflict. When students are late, forgetful, or uncooperative, it can disrupt the entire household—causing missed buses, late arrivals to school and work, and high emotional stress for everyone involved.

As described in *The Executive Function Playbook*, children with ADHD often do not learn from abstract consequences like lectures, threats, or punishment. What works best is when consequences are natural, predictable, and clearly connected to the child's actions. Even more effective? When those consequences are *agreed upon in advance*—removing the need for daily negotiations or emotional decision-making in the moment.

This page helps the adult and child work together to predetermine natural consequences for specific morning-related behaviors. By doing this ahead of time, both sides have a shared understanding of what will happen if the routine breaks down. It increases self-awareness (the child understands the impact of their behavior), self-motivation (they know what's at stake), and self-evaluation (they begin to connect cause and effect on their own).

INSTRUCTIONS FOR THE ADULT (PARENT, TEACHER, OR CLINICIAN)

This worksheet should be completed *proactively*, not in response to a problem. Use it to create **structure and clarity** so that mornings feel less reactive and more predictable for both the adult and the child.

On this page, you and the child will work together to answer two key prompts:

◆ If I am late to school because of my actions. . .
◆ If I cause my parent to be late to work. . .

Under each, you will write the natural consequence that will occur. The consequence should be:

◆ Directly related to the behavior
◆ Pre-agreed upon and not emotionally charged
◆ Reasonable and enforceable
◆ Framed as a *learning opportunity*, not punishment

STEP-BY-STEP GUIDANCE

1. **Start with a calm conversation.**

   Say something like:

   "Sometimes mornings get stressful, and we all end up feeling frustrated. Let's work together to figure out what should happen if things go off track. That way, we don't have to argue or figure it out in the moment. Everyone knows the plan."

2. Discuss the two scenarios.

Talk about:

- What happens if the child's actions cause them to be late to school
- What happens if the child's behavior causes the adult to be late to work

3. Emphasize that these are natural consequences—not punishments, but the logical result of certain actions.

4. Determine the consequences.

Brainstorm consequences that are directly tied to the behavior and appropriate for the child's age.

Examples for being late to school:

- "I have to walk into the school office and sign myself in."
- "I miss part of free time/recess and have to make up missed work."
- "No special privileges (screen time, etc.) that evening."
- "I have to write down what I will do differently tomorrow."

5. Examples for causing a parent to be late to work:

- "I help with evening prep to make up for the lost time."
- "I lose a choice-based privilege that afternoon."
- "I write an apology note to my parent."
- "I lose my screen time for the evening and have to reflect with a journal prompt."

6. Write it down clearly.

Use the worksheet space to write:

- The situation/behavior (e.g., late to school due to not getting dressed on time)
- The pre-agreed consequence

  Use simple, clear language. Consider adding visual icons or checkboxes for younger students.

7. Reinforce the agreement.

Post the page somewhere visible during the morning routine (e.g., fridge or bedroom door). Refer to it if needed—but avoid re-discussing or renegotiating once the consequence is in motion.

WHY THIS MATTERS

ADHD brains thrive on clarity and consistency. When consequences are unpredictable or emotionally reactive, children either escalate behaviors or tune them out completely. But when the consequences are logical, preset, and respectfully enforced, children begin to understand the power of their own choices—and take more responsibility for the outcome of their actions.

This practice also reduces the emotional load on parents, who often feel trapped in morning battles that repeat endlessly. With a plan in place, parents can step back and allow the consequence to do the teaching.

KEY MESSAGE

Clear expectations + natural consequences = a more peaceful and productive morning. When children know what will happen—and why—they're more likely to stay motivated, focused, and accountable.

CLOSING THOUGHT

The goal is not to control your child. The goal is to teach them to control *themselves*. This worksheet gives them the structure, awareness, and predictability they need to do just that—one morning at a time.

Activity 7.4: My Morning Routine: Distractions

Executive function skills strengthened: Self-awareness, self-evaluation, self-regulation

OVERVIEW

One of the greatest barriers to smooth and successful mornings for children and teens with ADHD is distraction. While many students struggle with attention in general, the morning routine presents a uniquely vulnerable moment: multiple tasks, high expectations, short timelines, and minimal internal motivation. Distractions—no matter how small—can quickly derail the entire process.

In *The Executive Function Playbook*, we emphasize that children with ADHD do not simply need to "try harder" or "pay attention more." The neurological differences in ADHD impact their time awareness, task shifting, and inhibitory control—making them especially vulnerable to distractions without even realizing they've become off-task. This is due in part to time blindness, where the child cannot feel the urgency or understand how much time is passing until it's too late.

This worksheet helps both the adult and child identify three major distractions that interfere with getting out the door in the morning—and more importantly, create a plan to eliminate those distractions completely, rather than attempting to manage or "balance" them.

Children with ADHD often don't yet have the regulation skills to set limits on stimulating distractions, and exposure to these items (especially screens or playful interactions) triggers immediate dopamine release, making it nearly impossible to return to nonstimulating tasks like brushing teeth or packing a backpack.

The solution isn't more willpower. The solution is eliminating distractions until the child has developed enough self-regulation and foresight to manage them independently—which may take years.

INSTRUCTIONS FOR THE ADULT (PARENT, TEACHER, OR CLINICIAN)

This activity is best done before the start of a new school week or at the end of a rough morning, when reflection can lead to insight. The adult and child should work together to identify specific distractions and develop realistic solutions that can be implemented immediately.

Use the worksheet to complete two columns:

1. **"What distracts me in the morning?"**
   - List three specific distractions that regularly cause the child to become off-task, dysregulated, or delayed.
2. **"How can we eliminate this distraction completely?"**
   - For each distraction, write a clear plan to remove or limit access to that item, activity, or trigger during the morning routine.

EXAMPLES:

What distracts me in the morning?	How can we eliminate this distraction completely?
Watching YouTube or scrolling phone	Phone stays on kitchen counter until after school.
Playing with toys or Legos	Toys are put away each night before bed.
Talking to sibling instead of getting dressed	Everyone gets ready in separate rooms with quiet music playing.
Drawing or coloring before school	Art supplies are off-limits until after school hours.

Be specific and firm, but also collaborative. Make sure the child understands *why* this plan is being made—not as a punishment but as a tool to help their brain stay on track and avoid rushed, stressful mornings.

KEY CONCEPTS TO REINFORCE WITH THE CHILD

- ◆ "Your brain is easily pulled toward fun or interesting things. That's not your fault—it's how ADHD works."
- ◆ "Right now, it's not about learning to balance distractions—it's about removing them completely so you can focus on what needs to be done."
- ◆ "You'll build the skills over time to bring these things back, but first we have to set you up for success."

WHY THIS MATTERS

ADHD is a regulation disorder, not a knowledge disorder. Children often know what they're supposed to do—but they can't do it consistently when competing stimuli are present. That's why waiting for them to "grow out of it" or "figure it out" only leads to repeated frustration for both the child and the parent.

By identifying and removing distractions proactively, this worksheet helps the child develop insight into their patterns and gives the adult the structure to support without nagging. It shifts the dynamic from punishment to partnership.

KEY MESSAGE

ADHD brains are wired for stimulation, not structure. To create peaceful, successful mornings, we don't need to fight that wiring—we need to work with it by removing the distractions that keep kids stuck and helping them succeed one step at a time.

CLOSING THOUGHT

You can't regulate what you don't recognize. But when a child becomes aware of their distractions—and when adults help remove them without shame—they begin to build the muscle of true executive function: the power to choose what matters over what's tempting.

Activity 7.5: My Morning Routine: My Perfect Morning

Executive function skills strengthened: Nonverbal working memory

OVERVIEW

Nonverbal working memory—the ability to create and hold mental images—is at the core of planning, preparation, and follow-through. For students with ADHD, this skill is often underdeveloped. They may have difficulty imagining the future, visualizing successful outcomes, and drawing on past experiences to shape their behavior. Without this internal "mental movie," the morning routine becomes a series of disjointed tasks rather than a cohesive flow.

In *The Executive Function Playbook*, we discuss how the development of nonverbal working memory allows students to begin using future thinking to guide present behavior. This worksheet gives both the adult and the child an opportunity to pause, imagine, and articulate what a "perfect morning" looks and feels like—both from a logistical and emotional perspective.

It encourages the child to practice mental visualization, and the parent to begin stepping back from over-functioning. A successful morning is not about control—it's about shared expectations, independence, and reducing the daily dance of over-prompting and resistance.

INSTRUCTIONS FOR THE ADULT (PARENT, TEACHER, OR CLINICIAN)

Start by explaining to the child that this activity will help them build an important executive function skill: the ability to imagine the future and use that image to guide their actions.

Use a calm voice and an unrushed tone. Let the child know that you're going to help them create a mental movie—a detailed picture in their mind of what a successful morning looks and feels like.

STEP-BY-STEP GUIDANCE

1. **Set the stage.**

   Have the child sit comfortably. Ask them to close their eyes, put their head down if helpful, and take a few deep breaths.

   Say:

   "Let's imagine your perfect morning. Not just what happens, but how it feels. Let's walk through it together, like a movie in your mind."

2. **Guide the mental movie.**

   Prompt the child to visualize each part of the morning in detail:

   - What time do you wake up?
   - How do you feel when you open your eyes?
   - What happens first? Next?
   - What are you doing? How are you moving?
   - How do you talk to your parent? What are they saying to you?
   - What do you do with your time?
   - How do you feel as you're getting ready?
   - How do you feel when you walk out the door?

3. Encourage rich sensory details: sounds, sights, emotions, and pace.

4. **Document the visualization.**

   Once the visualization is complete, open the worksheet.

   Child's Section:

   - **"What does my perfect morning look like?"**

     Help them describe the visual details of their mental movie.

   - **"How does it feel to have a perfect morning?"**

     Guide them to articulate the emotional tone: calm, focused, proud, energized, etc.

5. **Parent's Section:**

   - **"How do I feel when my child has a perfect morning?"**

     This reflection gives the adult a chance to describe their ideal morning—not in terms of controlling behavior, but in terms of emotional tone, independence, and peace.

6. **Reinforce the partnership.**

Emphasize that **perfect mornings are a shared effort**. It's not the child's job alone—and it's not the adult's job to constantly step in. A successful routine happens when:

- The **child takes ownership** of their actions and avoids seeking negative attention
- The **parent resists over-prompting**, micromanaging, or adopting the mindset: "If I don't step in, nothing gets done"

WHY THIS MATTERS

Students with ADHD often lack the internal visualization and foresight to imagine what success looks like. Instead, they live in the "now" and respond reactively to each moment. Teaching them to mentally rehearse the future is not just a calming practice—it builds the muscle of internal guidance that replaces the need for constant adult intervention.

Likewise, many well-meaning parents fall into the pattern of over-prompting, believing that their constant supervision is the only path to a successful morning. In reality, this removes responsibility from the child and leads to power struggles and burnout. When both adult and child reflect on what success looks like, they begin to realign their roles toward collaboration, not control.

KEY MESSAGE

The ability to *visualize success* is the foundation of achieving it. When children mentally rehearse their perfect morning and adults reflect on what true independence looks like, both begin to build a healthier, more sustainable morning routine.

CLOSING THOUGHT

Don't just manage mornings—*envision* them. And then, together, build the habits that turn that vision into reality.

Activity 7.6: My Morning Routine: Preparation

Executive function skills strengthened: Self-motivation, future thinking

OVERVIEW

For students with ADHD, mornings often feel rushed, disorganized, and chaotic. But the root of those struggles rarely begins in the morning—it often begins the night before. In *The Executive Function Playbook*, we emphasize the importance of building future thinking: the ability to mentally project yourself forward in time, anticipate needs, and take action now to set yourself up for later success.

This page is designed to help both the adult and the child reflect on how evening preparation can dramatically reduce morning stress, increase independence, and help students feel more successful. It promotes the development of essential executive function skills, including planning, prioritization, time management, problem-solving, and self-motivation.

When children take ownership of their routine the night before, they begin to shift from reactive behaviors to proactive habits. This reduces the need for excessive adult prompting and creates a calmer, more cooperative household dynamic.

INSTRUCTIONS FOR THE ADULT (PARENT, TEACHER, OR CLINICIAN)

This activity should be done collaboratively and calmly, ideally during the evening or weekend when there's time to think without pressure. Your role is to guide your child in identifying three to five specific things they can do before bed to prepare for a smoother morning. These should be realistic, age-appropriate, and tailored to your household's needs.

Help your child understand that these are not just tasks—they are tools that protect their morning from stress and distraction.

STEP-BY-STEP GUIDANCE

1. **Explain the purpose.**
   Say:

   "Sometimes mornings feel rushed and stressful. But we can actually make mornings much easier by doing a few things the night before. That way, we're not scrambling, forgetting things, or getting upset with each other. Let's figure out what you can do before bed to help tomorrow morning go well."

2. **Reflect on current pain points.**
   Together, think about what parts of the morning usually lead to conflict, rushing, or forgetfulness. Use this to guide your preparation list.

3. **List evening preparation tasks.**
   Use the worksheet to list three to five things the child can do before bed to help create a calm, successful morning. Encourage them to think in terms of both physical tasks and mental/emotional preparation.

   Examples:
   • Lay out clothes for the next day.
   • Pack backpack with homework and materials.
   • Make or pack lunch.
   • Charge devices or put them in a designated location.

- Review tomorrow's schedule and set a goal.
- Put all school items near the front door.
- Visualize the morning and go to bed on time.

4. Add a motivation element.

Consider adding a small reflection space:

"Why do I want to do this?"
Help your child link these preparations to positive outcomes, like having more free time, avoiding stress, or feeling proud of being ready.

5. Make it a routine.

Post this list in a visible place and refer to it each evening. Treat it as a predictable habit, not a one-time exercise.

WHY THIS MATTERS

Children with ADHD often struggle to connect present actions with future consequences—a core deficit in executive functioning. They live in the "now," and as a result, they tend to put off or avoid preparatory tasks that don't offer immediate gratification. But building the skill of future thinking—and making preparation part of their identity—is a crucial step toward long-term independence.

This worksheet also helps adults begin to step back. Many parents carry the emotional and logistical load of the morning routine, leading to exhaustion and burnout. By shifting some of that responsibility to the evening before—and involving the child in the planning—parents are less likely to fall into the trap of over-functioning and over-prompting.

KEY MESSAGE

A successful morning starts the night before. When students learn to plan ahead and take ownership of their routine, they build the muscle of future thinking—one of the most powerful executive function skills for lifelong success.

CLOSING THOUGHT

Preparation is not about perfection—it's about empowerment. When children feel capable of shaping their own success, even small steps become big victories. Give them the tools, trust the process, and watch them rise.

Activity 7.7: Evening Routine

Executive function skills strengthened: Future thinking skills

This workbook page establishes a clear, non-negotiable structure around the evening routine to strengthen future thinking—the ability to anticipate, visualize, and plan for what's coming next. Children and teens with ADHD typically struggle with this due to deficits in nonverbal working memory and time management. This difficulty in imagining future consequences leads to poor transitions, resistance, and chronic bedtime battles.

This worksheet is designed to help families draw a firm boundary at a designated time each night, communicating it in advance and in writing to reduce dysregulation, power struggles, and repeated negotiation.

The adult fills out the worksheet and goes over it with the child in a calm moment—not during or after a conflict. It should be read aloud together and posted visibly in the home. The adult writes:

"In the **(last name)** family, the evening routine begins at _____ **p.m.**
Starting at this time, the following items will no longer be available to you:"

Below this, the adult lists any and all devices or distractions that must be turned off at that designated time:

- Wi-Fi (router is shut off)
- Cell phone
- iPad/tablet
- Video game console
- Laptop/Chromebook
- TV
- Group chats or FaceTime

The message is clear: this is not a punishment, but a boundary. It reinforces the idea that routines are family-based structures rooted in values, not individual preferences. And most importantly, when it's written down, it becomes "law." This decreases the executive function load on both the adult and child—there is no longer a need for verbal reminders, last-minute debates, or escalating arguments.

Evening routines are essential for preparing the ADHD brain for sleep. Stimulation from screens disrupts melatonin production, delays sleep onset, and increases anxiety. When devices are turned off at a predictable time every night, the child begins to learn that nighttime is a calm, consistent, low-stimulation part of the day—and that transitions can be smooth and successful when there are clear expectations.

KEY MESSAGE

Structure is not control; it's safety. Predictable evening boundaries reduce conflict, promote better sleep, and support healthy brain development.

CLOSING THOUGHT

When routines are visible and agreed upon in advance, children learn that limits are not personal—they're part of growing up. This helps foster security, reduce anxiety, and strengthen independence.

Activity 7.8: Evening Routine, Part 2: The Visual Timeline

Executive function skills strengthened: Self-regulation, self-motivation, nonverbal working memory, future thinking skills

This workbook page is designed to help parents and caregivers create a visual timeline of the evening routine using real-world photos of the actual child completing the routine tasks. This is not a generic checklist or abstract series of clipart images. Instead, it is a powerful and personalized executive function tool that uses the child's own body and lived experience to strengthen nonverbal working memory—the internal skill of visual imagery that allows us to "see" the future in our mind's eye.

Children with ADHD often struggle with time blindness and weak visualization skills. They cannot mentally picture what the rest of the evening should look like or how long it will take. This lack of foresight makes them far more vulnerable to avoidance, distractions, and dysregulation. By using real photos of themselves completing each task in sequence, the adult is helping them build a concrete visual roadmap they can actually follow.

INSTRUCTIONS FOR ADULTS

1. Work with your child to break down the evening routine into specific steps.
2. Take real photos of your child doing each task in order.
3. Print or display these images in a timeline layout—either on paper, a poster, or digitally.
4. Go over the timeline together daily to reinforce it as a routine and not a one-time activity.

EXAMPLE TIMELINE STEPS (PHOTOS SHOULD BE OF YOUR CHILD DOING EACH)

◆ Double-check that all homework is turned in and submitted online
◆ Place school laptop in designated area
◆ Turn in phone and other devices to parent
◆ Take a shower
◆ Brush and floss teeth
◆ Change into pajamas
◆ Say goodnight to each family member
◆ Lay in bed with a book or magazine (nondigital)
◆ Lights out and go to sleep

WHY REAL-WORLD PHOTOS MATTER

According to research on visual learning and working memory, children retain and process real images of themselves more effectively than abstract icons or cartoon clip art. The brain treats personal photos as memory cues, which can more reliably activate nonverbal working memory, the foundation for all future planning and task completion.

This timeline is also deeply tied to self-motivation. When a child can see what success looks like—step-by-step, in their own environment—they are far more likely to internalize the routine, complete it independently, and reduce prompt dependence on the adult.

KEY MESSAGE

A visual timeline made from your own photos builds powerful internal memory systems that support independence, consistency, and bedtime success.

CLOSING THOUGHT

The goal isn't perfection. It's predictability. When children can picture success, they are more likely to live it.

Activity 7.9: Evening Routine, Part 3: My Tasks

Executive function skills strengthened: Self-regulation

Establishing an effective evening routine is one of the most powerful ways to support children and teens with ADHD in building healthy sleep habits, reducing family conflict, and improving emotional regulation. This page helps students take responsibility for their own transition into nighttime by making the tasks leading up to sleep explicit and time-bound.

This worksheet begins with a clear boundary:

"Starting at _____ p.m., I will stop what I am doing and ensure I complete the following steps before laying in bed:"

From that starting point, the adult helps the child list each step required to wind down and complete their evening responsibilities. This typically includes turning off all screens, putting away school materials, finishing hygiene routines (such as brushing teeth, washing face, or taking medication), and transitioning into bed.

One of the core executive function challenges this targets is *transitioning from a preferred activity to a nonpreferred task*, a major difficulty for those with ADHD. Because preferred tasks (like screens or play) offer instant dopamine, stopping them often leads to resistance or dysregulation. That's why this worksheet helps pre-commit to a specific time for stopping, which supports time awareness and future thinking, and eliminates negotiation or conflict.

When the child writes down these steps themselves, it activates their internal planning and prioritization systems. As outlined in *The Executive Function Playbook*, this also reinforces the *Stop, Think, Act* cycle, especially when transitions are predictable and consistent. Over time, this builds stronger self-monitoring and internal structure, replacing the need for adult prompting with internal ownership.

KEY MESSAGE

Children with ADHD benefit from clearly defined routines and visual cues. Evening transitions are one of the hardest times for families, and pre-committing to a stop time and listing steps can prevent last-minute battles and promote independent regulation.

CLOSING THOUGHT

When a child learns to identify what needs to get done and when to do it—especially during times when they are tired, dysregulated, or overstimulated—they are beginning to build the real-world skills of follow-through, accountability, and independence.

Activity 7.10: Evening Routine, Part 4: Successful Feeling

Executive function skills strengthened: Self-awareness, self-motivation, perspective-taking

This workbook page invites the child or teen to reflect on the emotional outcomes of their evening routine decisions, encouraging deep connections between behavior, emotion, and motivation. By identifying how their actions the night before affect both their own mood and the feelings of those around them the next morning, they begin to build powerful internal insight.

The page asks the following prompts:

1. *When I have a successful evening routine, in the morning I feel _____.*
2. *When I do NOT have a successful evening routine, in the morning I feel _____.*
3. *When I do have a successful evening routine, my parents feel _____.*

This activity helps children make the essential link between evening behavior and morning outcomes. It reinforces the understanding that regulation and preparation are not isolated acts—they ripple forward, shaping how a person feels, how others respond, and how the next day unfolds. These reflections also build perspective-taking skills, which are often underdeveloped in children with ADHD, especially in relation to how their actions impact others emotionally.

This is not about blame or guilt—it's about awareness and connection. The goal is to help children begin to internalize *why* routines matter: not just because an adult says so, but because they personally experience the benefits of regulation and consistency, and because they start to recognize how their behavior impacts their family system.

As emphasized in *The Executive Function Playbook*, emotions are powerful drivers of behavior. When we help a child reflect on how they want to feel and how they want others to feel, we shift them from being externally managed to internally motivated.

KEY MESSAGE

Emotions shape motivation. Helping children understand how evening routines affect how they feel the next morning—and how their actions impact others—builds intrinsic motivation and emotional intelligence.

CLOSING THOUGHT

Children are more likely to engage in new behaviors when they understand the emotional "why" behind them. By reflecting on how routines shape feelings, we equip them to take more ownership of their day—and their relationships.

Activity 7.11: Evening Routine, Part 5: "I'm Not Tired!"

Executive function skills strengthened: Self-regulation, self-evaluation, self-awareness

This workbook page addresses one of the most common evening struggles for children and teens with ADHD—the inability or refusal to wind down at bedtime. While parents often find themselves in power struggles around sleep, it's important to shift the focus from *forcing sleep* to *creating a predictable environment for winding down*. This helps avoid the conflict-driven dysregulation that commonly emerges at the end of the day.

The page begins by stating:

"If the evening routine begins at _____ p.m., and I do not feel tired, I can do the following things in my room all by myself:"

Together, the adult and the child list three specific, calming, screen-free activities the child can do independently in their room during this time. Examples may include:

◆ Reading a book or magazine
◆ Drawing or coloring
◆ Listening to soft music or calming sounds

- Writing or doodling in a paper journal
- Playing quietly with fidget toys or puzzles

This clear boundary sends the message:

"You don't need to be asleep, but you do need to be winding down."

This avoids unnecessary battles and also builds the essential executive function skill of self-regulation in a low-stimulation environment. The child is given autonomy within clear limits, and the adult avoids constant prompting and arguing. By creating a designated time and space to calm their body and mind without the stimulation of screens or conflict, the child begins to practice internal regulation—a foundational building block for emotional maturity.

For many children with ADHD, this is also an opportunity to identify nonscreen sources of dopamine that are sustainable and restorative. Over time, they begin to recognize how these activities help them feel calmer, more focused, and better prepared for the next day.

KEY MESSAGE
The goal of bedtime isn't instant sleep—it's creating the internal and external conditions that allow the brain and body to calm down and rest. Kids need predictable routines and low-stimulation choices, not conflict or control.

CLOSING THOUGHT
When we give children with ADHD a structured, screen-free environment to wind down independently, we aren't just improving bedtime—we're building lifelong self-regulation skills that empower them far beyond the evening routine.

Activity 7.12: Evening Routine, Part 6: Parent Safety
Executive function skills strengthened: Self-awareness, social perspective-taking

This workbook page is designed to set clear nighttime boundaries and reduce patterns of conflict and negative attention-seeking that often arise during the evening routine for children and teens with ADHD. Many of these children have difficulty transitioning to sleep because their brains crave stimulation, conflict, or engagement. One of the most common behaviors seen is the child escalating emotionally or behaviorally at night to pull the parent back into interaction—often unconsciously—to delay the evening routine and avoid sleep.

To address this, this page includes the following statement:

"When the clock turns to ___ p.m., and (child's name) shows the following behaviors, parents are NOT able to help, talk to, or do anything for them. All they can do is focus on themselves and go to sleep."

Below this statement, the adult and child work together to identify and list three specific behaviors that will signal the need for parent disengagement. These may include:

◆ Yelling or screaming
◆ Repeatedly getting out of bed
◆ Making demands or trying to negotiate
◆ Slamming doors
◆ Interrupting the parent's own routine

By listing these behaviors ahead of time and writing them down as family expectations, the adult is no longer caught off guard, and the child is no longer confused about boundaries. This removes the temptation for power struggles and attention-seeking by creating a predictable, written plan.

The parent is now empowered to disengage without guilt, knowing that the boundary has been pre-established. At the same time, the child becomes more aware of their own behavior, how it affects others, and what is expected at night. It is not a punishment—it is a necessary shift in responsibility. The child learns that when they are dysregulated or resisting boundaries, others cannot and should not intervene until regulation returns.

KEY MESSAGE
Parents cannot help when the child is dysregulated or attempting to manipulate the evening routine through negative behaviors. Calm, predictable disengagement creates safety and accountability for both the parent and child.

CLOSING THOUGHT
By naming the behaviors that disrupt the evening routine and defining when the adult must stop engaging, we teach children with ADHD that structure, not control or conflict, is what helps everyone feel safe, respected, and ready to rest.

Activity 7.1: Morning Routine: Visual Timeline

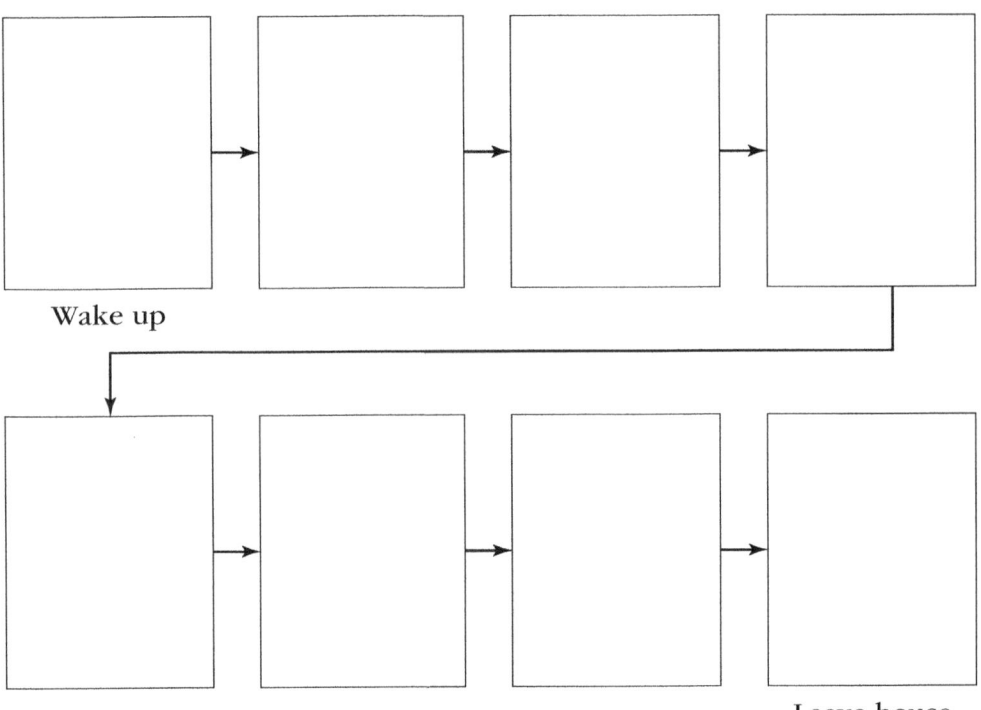

Wake up

Leave house

Activity 7.2: My Morning Routine: Independent vs. Help

What I can do independently: What I need help with:

1. _____   1. _____

2. _____   2. _____

3. _____   3. _____

4. _____   4. _____

5. _____   5. _____

Activity 7.3: My Morning Routine: Natural Consequences

If I am late to school, these are the consequences:

_____

_____

_____

_____

If my behavior causes my parent to be late to work, these are the consequences:

_____

_____

_____

_____

Activity 7.4: My Morning Routine: Distractions

What distracts me in the morning?   How can we eliminate this distraction?

1. _____ → _____

2. _____ → _____

3. _____ → _____

Activity 7.5: My Morning Routine: My Perfect Morning

The Perfect Morning for _____
(*child's name*)

What does my perfect morning look like?

_____

_____

_____

The Perfect Morning for Parents
How does it feel to have a
perfect morning?

_____

_____

_____

How do I feel when my child has a perfect morning?

_____

_____

_____

Activity 7.6: My Morning Routine: Preparation

What can I do before bed to prepare for a successful morning routine?

_____

_____

_____

_____

_____

_____

_____

Why do I want to do this?

_____

_____

_____

_____

_____

_____

Activity 7.7: Evening Routine

In the _____ family, the evening routine begins at _____ p.m.

Starting at this time, the following things will no longer be available to you:

_____

_____

_____

_____

_____

Activity 7.8: Evening Routine, Part 2: Visual Timeline

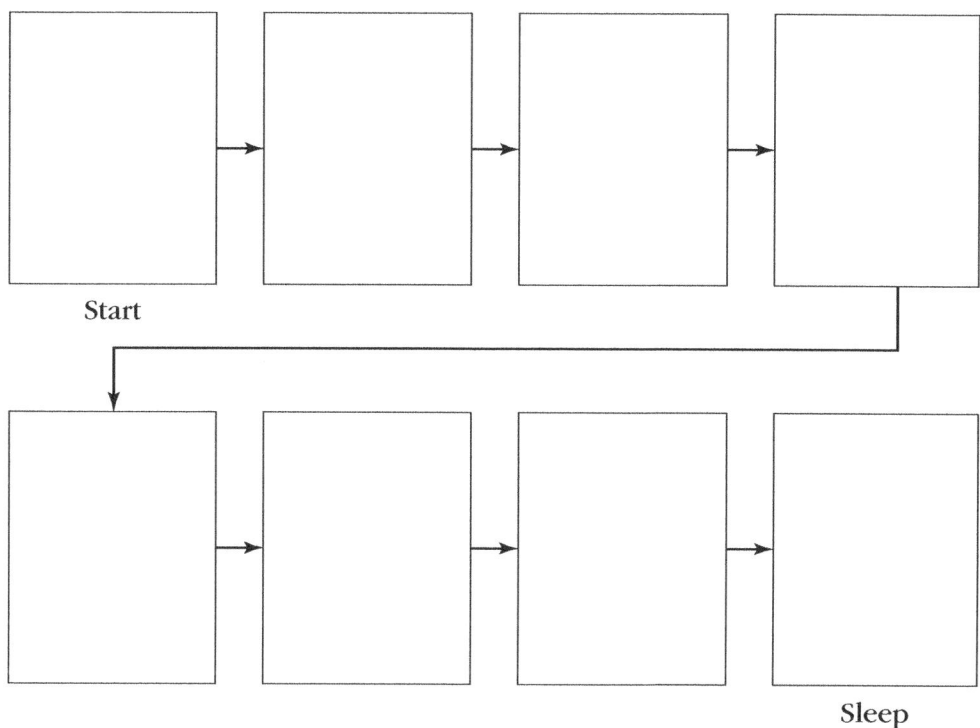

Start

Sleep

Activity 7.9: Evening Routine, Part 3: My Tasks

Starting at _____ p.m. I will stop what I am doing and ensure I complete the following steps before laying in bed:

_____

_____

_____

_____

_____

Activity 7.10: Evening Routine Part 4: Successful Feeling

1. When I have a successful evening routine, in the morning I feel:

_____

_____

_____

_____

2. When I do NOT have a successful evening routine, in the morning I feel:

_____

_____

_____

_____

3. When I do have a successful evening routine, my parents feel:

_____

_____

_____

_____

Activity 7.11: Evening Routine, Part 5: "I'm Not Tired!"

If the evening routine begins at _____ p.m., and I do not feel tired, I can do the following things in my room all by myself:

1. _____

2. _____

3. _____

Activity 7.12: Evening Routine, Part 6: Parent Safety

When the clock turns to ___ p.m., and _____ *(child's name)* shows the following behaviors, parents are *not* able to help, talk to, or do anything for them. All they can do is focus on themselves and go to sleep.

1. _____

2. _____

3. _____

CHAPTER 8

Homework

Ending the Daily Battles and Building Independent Work Habits

For many families of children with ADHD, homework is not just a task—it's a daily nightmare. It's the time of day when emotions run high, power struggles emerge, and parents are pulled into an exhausting cycle of reminding, negotiating, and managing meltdowns. What should take 20 minutes often takes two hours—and no one leaves the table feeling successful.

This chapter exists to change that.

In *The Executive Function Playbook*, we address the reality that most children with ADHD are not struggling with ability—they're struggling with initiation, persistence, and completion. Homework highlights this more than almost anything else. It requires a child to stop what they're doing, start something nonstimulating, stay with it despite boredom, and finish it without constant external support. These are executive function tasks—and they must be taught, not expected.

The worksheets in this chapter are designed to help families finally break the cycle. They provide a concrete structure for approaching homework with clarity, predictability, and internalized ownership. These are not just systems for getting the work done—they are tools to reduce prompt dependence, increase task initiation, and promote follow-through without emotional exhaustion.

These worksheets will help you:

- ◆ Create consistent homework routines and expectations
- ◆ Identify the time of day and environment most suited for focused work
- ◆ Reduce screen-based distractions before they start

- Establish pre-work rituals to help the brain "shift into gear"
- Promote self-starting, even when the task is hard or boring
- Prevent parents from doing all the heavy lifting, coaching, or correcting

In *The Executive Function Playbook*, we talk about the dangers of over-functioning parents—those who step in too often, too loudly, or too emotionally. These worksheets are designed to support parents in stepping back and allowing the child to step up, while still maintaining calm leadership and consistency.

If your child has ever said "I don't know what to do," or "This is stupid," or simply refused to even start, these tools are for you. They don't rely on rewards, threats, or long lectures. They rely on structure, internal reflection, and executive function modeling—the real ingredients of sustainable change.

Let's end the nightly arguments. Let's take the pressure off both you and your child. Let's build a homework routine that works—not just for school success, but for life skills.

Activity 8.1: Homework Success: Setup and Organization
Executive function skills strengthened: Self-awareness, self-motivation

OVERVIEW
Homework can become one of the most emotionally charged daily tasks for children and teens with ADHD—and for their parents. While the actual assignments may be achievable, the setup, transition, and environment are often where the real problems begin. Executive functioning challenges such as task initiation, planning, emotional regulation, and self-monitoring make it difficult for students to get started, stay on track, and complete work independently.

In *The Executive Function Playbook*, we describe the concept of "external structure before internal habits." That means before a child can reliably manage homework on their own, they must be surrounded by the right external scaffolding—an intentional and strategic setup that makes it easier for the brain to stay regulated and focused.

This worksheet is designed to build that structure by guiding both the adult and the child through a five-part reflective planning process: Who, What, When, Where, and Why. Each question helps increase the child's ownership and awareness of their homework habits, while giving the adult insight into where breakdowns are likely to occur and how to prevent them.

INSTRUCTIONS FOR THE ADULT (PARENT, TEACHER, OR CLINICIAN)
This worksheet is meant to be filled out together. It is not a quiz or test but rather a shared conversation to create a consistent, predictable homework routine. Use it as a

guide to build a plan that fits the child's unique needs, while protecting against common ADHD pitfalls like isolation, distraction, and poor time awareness.

Step-by-Step Planning Prompts

1. **WHO—Who is involved?**

   "Do I want to do my homework completely alone or with someone checking in on me occasionally?"

   "Do I need someone nearby to help me stay on track or assist when I'm confused?"

   Encourage honest reflection. Many ADHD students say they want to work alone but actually benefit from quiet co-working or check-ins. Help them think beyond pride or independence and instead reflect on what actually works for them.

2. **WHAT—What needs to get done?**

   "Do I know what my homework is?"

   "Is it written down somewhere?"

   "Do I understand the directions for each assignment?"

   Clarify that before work begins, the child should *always* know what the full workload is. Encourage use of planners, homework portals, or daily checklists to increase clarity.

3. **WHEN—When is homework done?**

   "Do I do homework right after school, or do I need a break first?"

   "If I take a break, how long is it, and what will I do during that break?"

   "What time will I start, and what time will I be finished?"

   Avoid vague goals like "later" or "after dinner." ADHD brains struggle with open-ended time windows. Instead, set specific start times and boundaries. If a break is needed, make it short (15–30 minutes) and nonscreen-based to avoid hyperfocus and transition issues.

4. **WHERE—Where is homework done?**

   "Is my homework done in a place where I can focus?"

   "Is it in public view so someone can check in on me if I get stuck or distracted?"

   Do not allow homework to be done in the child's bedroom. Bedrooms often contain the most distractions and the least accountability. Instead, choose a designated homework zone in a public area—kitchen table, dining room, home office—with as few distractions as possible. Quiet music, a timer, and necessary supplies can all help.

5. **WHY—Why does it need to get done?**

   "Why is it important for me to complete my homework?"

   "What happens when I don't do it?"

"How does doing my homework help me get closer to my goals?"
Connect homework to a meaningful purpose. Rather than framing it as an obligation, help the child link it to pride, independence, and long-term goals like earning privileges, getting good grades, or being ready for the next stage of life.

Why This Matters

For children with ADHD, homework is rarely about the assignment itself. The breakdown happens in the setup—knowing when, where, how, and why to begin. By walking through these five strategic questions together, the adult helps the child build mental scripts for success. Over time, these scripts become internalized, improving the child's ability to initiate tasks, evaluate needs, and self-direct.

This page also supports parents in avoiding the common pitfall of hovering or arguing every evening. With a consistent plan in place, emotional energy can be preserved, and students are more likely to rise to expectations without constant reminders.

KEY MESSAGE

Homework success begins long before the first pencil is picked up. When students with ADHD are guided through *who*, *what*, *when*, *where*, and *why*—they gain the structure and clarity their brain needs to succeed.

CLOSING THOUGHT

Support creates independence. When we slow down to plan and prepare, we build not just better homework habits—but stronger, more confident learners.

Activity 8.2 Homework Success: The Time Period
Executive function skills strengthened: Self-motivation

OVERVIEW

Children and teens with ADHD often struggle with starting, sustaining, and finishing tasks that are not inherently stimulating—especially homework. Add in school-issued technology, and you've created a perfect storm for distraction, dysregulation, and daily conflict.

In *The Executive Function Playbook*, we emphasize that structure precedes success. Students cannot build internal motivation or discipline without first having a consistent, predictable external framework that reduces ambiguity and temptation. This worksheet provides just that—a clear, collaborative agreement between the adult and child about the start and end time for homework, as well as firm guidelines about when the school-issued laptop or tablet is turned in.

The goal of this activity is not to punish or control but to protect the child's executive functioning system from overstimulation, poor habits, and the long-term consequences of unstructured digital access. When expectations are clear and non-negotiable, students are more likely to follow through—and adults are less likely to fall into power struggles.

INSTRUCTIONS FOR THE ADULT (PARENT, TEACHER, OR CLINICIAN)

Use this worksheet as a structured contract—not a threat, ultimatum, or punishment. Explain that this is a family routine designed to support the child's success and reduce stress for everyone involved. The goal is to help the child build healthy habits and complete their work during a focused, protected time window each day.

You may say:

"Homework doesn't have to be a daily battle. Together, we're going to create a clear time each day for homework, and then hand in your school laptop so your brain can take a break and you can reset. We're doing this not as a punishment—but to make sure your brain is getting what it needs to stay sharp and grow stronger."

How to Use the Worksheet

Fill in the following structured sections together with your child or teen:

- **Homework is done from _____ p.m. to _____ p.m.**
  Choose a consistent daily time window that works with your family's schedule. Homework should not bleed into the entire evening or fluctuate day to day.
- **At _____ p.m., the school laptop is given to:**
  This is the most important part of the agreement. Technology **must be turned in at a firm time**—no bargaining, "I'm almost done," or last-minute requests. The device is given to the named adult, no matter what.
- **Laptop will be returned to you after you successfully complete the morning routine tomorrow.**
  This connects the privilege of technology to follow-through and effort, not completion or perfection. If the morning routine is carried out responsibly, the device is returned at the appropriate time the next day.

Why This Matters

This worksheet is grounded in neuroscience and developmental research. The adolescent brain is still developing the prefrontal cortex, which governs self-regulation, attention, time management, and inhibition. The idea that students "just need to learn to resist distractions" on their own is both scientifically inaccurate and developmentally unfair.

Students with ADHD are especially vulnerable to tech-based distractions. Educational technology (EdTech)—while well-intentioned—has created a silent epidemic of dysregulation. Unmonitored access leads not just to avoidance of schoolwork, but to dopamine-seeking behaviors, exposure to harmful content, and the deterioration of executive function habits.

If you've already taken the difficult but powerful step of limiting screens in your home, school-issued laptops can undo your progress. This worksheet puts the power back in your hands. Remember, that device is funded by your tax dollars. It is not a toy, a private device, or a free pass to the internet. It is a tool for schoolwork only—and your child is not developmentally equipped to self-monitor their use of it without external structure.

KEY MESSAGE

Consistent tech boundaries are not restrictive—they are **protective**. They help ADHD students stay focused, preserve their mental health, and build the internal habits they need for long-term success.

CLOSING THOUGHT

Structure is not about control—it's about care. When we remove the overwhelming burden of temptation, we make room for progress, peace, and real learning. Your child deserves that. And so do you.

Activity 8.3 Homework Success: Checklist—Did You Turn It In?
Executive function skills strengthened: Self-evaluation

OVERVIEW

In today's academic environment, it's becoming increasingly common for students—especially those with ADHD and executive functioning challenges—to complete an assignment but forget the final and most important step: turning it in.

This may seem like a minor slip to adults, but it's actually a reflection of core executive function deficits: specifically, task completion, memory retrieval, attention shifting, and self-monitoring. In *The Executive Function Playbook*, we stress the importance of building self-evaluation routines into daily tasks—not just to finish them, but to ensure the brain is tracking the task through to completion.

This checklist-based worksheet is a simple yet powerful tool to help students internalize that "done" doesn't mean *done until it's delivered*. With support and consistency, this routine can help reduce late work, missed credit, and the demoralizing cycle of "I did it, but I still got a zero."

INSTRUCTIONS FOR THE ADULT (PARENT, TEACHER, OR CLINICIAN)

This checklist should be used daily, preferably right after the designated homework period (as set in Workbook page 29). Guide the student in checking off each box only after the action has been completed, not when they *plan* to do it.

This sheet builds both accountability and clarity—two areas where ADHD learners often struggle.

How to Use the Checklist

Help the child or teen go through each item in order. Read each step aloud if needed, and encourage honest self-reflection.

This worksheet helps build awareness of specific executive function breakdowns. Use this insight to plan supports for next time.

Why This Matters

Many adults assume that if a child did the homework, it will naturally get submitted. But for students with ADHD, the executive function chain is fragile—especially at the end of a task when the brain is most tired. Even after expending the mental effort to complete an assignment, they often lose track of the final step.

Repeatedly forgetting to turn in work can be discouraging and emotionally damaging for students who are trying their best. Over time, they begin to internalize failure and lose motivation. This checklist helps interrupt that pattern by making the final step visible, intentional, and achievable.

When paired with calm adult guidance and consistent use, this worksheet can transform an overlooked habit into a non-negotiable success behavior.

KEY MESSAGE

Finishing your homework isn't the last step—turning it in is. Self-evaluation ensures that effort turns into outcomes, and helps students build lasting habits of independence.

CLOSING THOUGHT

Students with ADHD don't fail to turn things in because they're lazy—they fail because their brain isn't wired to track invisible steps. But when we make those steps visible and structured, we build the bridge to follow-through—and self-confidence.

Activity 8.4 Homework Success: Natural Consequences
Executive function skills strengthened: Self-motivation

OVERVIEW

For children and teens with ADHD, consequences—when applied correctly—are not punishments. They are teaching tools. And one of the most effective ways to build self-motivation is to allow children to experience the real-world outcomes of their choices in a clear, predictable, and emotionally neutral way. This page is designed to help parents and children collaboratively predetermine natural consequences related to homework completion—removing the emotional charge and ambiguity that often surrounds schoolwork at home.

As described in *The Executive Function Playbook*, motivation in ADHD is highly externalized and reactive. These students are less likely to be internally driven by deadlines or future goals and more likely to respond to immediate feedback—especially when it's structured and consistent. Yet, because homework is assigned by teachers but expected to be supported at home, parents are often caught in a gray zone: unsure how much to enforce, when to back off, and how to discipline without damaging the relationship.

This worksheet provides clarity for everyone involved. By establishing natural consequences ahead of time, students gain accountability, parents reduce stress, and arguments are replaced with expectations that feel fair and firm.

INSTRUCTIONS FOR THE ADULT (PARENT, TEACHER, OR CLINICIAN)

Guide the child in thinking through the following question:

"What happens when you don't complete your homework on time?"

Emphasize that this is not about punishment or yelling. It's about making agreements in advance, so there are no surprises and no debates in the moment. When consequences are known ahead of time, the child learns to take greater ownership of their choices—and is more likely to follow through.

You might say:

"Just like in the real world—if we miss a flight, show up late to work, or don't pay a bill—there's a consequence. That doesn't mean we're bad people. It just means we need to plan better next time. That's what we're practicing here."

How to Use This Worksheet

Fill in the following with the child or teen. These consequences should be realistic, related, and reasonable. They should not shame the child, but they should encourage responsibility. Avoid vague punishments like "you'll be in trouble" and instead opt for clear, meaningful actions.

If I do not complete my homework on time. . .

1. **Natural consequence #1:**
   Example: I lose access to my video games for the night.
2. **Natural consequence #2:**
   Example: I must complete homework the next morning before I can do anything else.
3. **Natural consequence #3:**
   Example: I need to email my teacher and explain that I didn't turn it in on time.

Be sure to review these consequences regularly and refer back to this page if conflicts arise. The key is follow-through—not punishment.

Why This Matters

Without consistent accountability, ADHD students don't learn the essential connection between actions and outcomes. While many schools offer accommodation plans with extended deadlines or no penalties for late work, these well-intentioned adjustments can unintentionally weaken the development of executive function skills like task initiation, future planning, and motivation.

Dr. Russell Barkley, one of the leading experts in ADHD, has warned:

"If you want to see an ADHD person fail, create an environment where there are no consequences."

That doesn't mean being harsh or rigid—but it does mean creating a realistic learning environment where effort, time, and responsibility are rewarded—and where avoidance has natural, predictable outcomes.

When consequences are clear, consistent, and collaboratively designed, students with ADHD are more likely to develop the intrinsic motivation that is often under-developed in their brains.

KEY MESSAGE

Predictable, natural consequences don't hurt children with ADHD—they help them grow. They bridge the gap between impulse and reflection, and they teach follow-through in a way lectures and reminders never will.

CLOSING THOUGHT

Empowerment doesn't come from rescuing children from failure. It comes from giving them the tools—and accountability—to face it, learn from it, and move forward stronger.

Activity 8.5 Homework Success: Parents

Executive function skills strengthened: Self-advocacy, self-awareness, self-regulation, self-motivation

OVERVIEW

Few parts of the daily routine create as much friction, frustration, and emotional fallout in ADHD households as homework time. For many parents, this is the moment when anxiety, guilt, and the fear of failure collide. For children, it becomes an arena for conflict, avoidance, and stimulation—not learning. This workbook page is designed to interrupt that destructive cycle by prompting both the child and the adult to reflect on the emotional and behavioral patterns that surface when parents get involved in homework.

In *The Executive Function Playbook*, we highlight how emotional regulation—not intelligence or effort—is often the core executive function skill lacking during homework time. The ADHD brain thrives on novelty, excitement, and stimulation. Homework, by contrast, is predictable, repetitive, and often frustrating. Conflict with parents offers the ADHD brain something homework does not: a dopamine rush. The arguing, the power struggle, the raised voices—it's all highly stimulating, and for many kids, it becomes a subconscious reward system that reinforces the very behaviors families are trying to extinguish.

At the same time, parents of children with ADHD often carry deep-seated worries. Many of them also have ADHD themselves and struggle with emotional regulation. They fear that their child's struggles reflect their own inadequacies as parents. They believe that if they don't step in, the homework won't get done. And while their intentions are good, the result is often overstepping, power struggles, and a collapse in the child's autonomy.

This worksheet brings those unspoken dynamics into the open and invites a collaborative reset.

INSTRUCTIONS FOR THE ADULT (PARENT, TEACHER, OR CLINICIAN)

Walk your child through each reflection prompt. These are open-ended questions that invite emotional insight and promote honest discussion. The goal is not to criticize, blame, or justify—but to name patterns, understand motivations, and foster emotional safety during homework time.

Introduce the worksheet by saying something like:

"Homework is hard for a lot of kids. And sometimes, it becomes even harder when we argue about it. Today, we're going to look at what happens when I step in too much, and what we can both do to make this go better. I want to help, but I also want you to grow."

You may need to model responses or share your own feelings as a parent to create safety.

Worksheet Prompts

Ask the child or teen to respond in their own words:

1. **When my parents step in and get involved in my homework, it makes me feel:**
2. **When I get into an argument with my parents over homework, and it keeps me from having to do this boring homework, it makes me feel:**
3. **If I actually need help, I will say:**
4. **When I see my child struggling with homework, I feel:**
5. **Instead of stepping in right away, I can remind myself:**

Why This Matters

Homework is not just an academic task—it's a mirror for a family's emotional regulation patterns. When a child becomes dependent on a parent's constant involvement, they miss out on learning how to initiate, sustain, and complete tasks independently. Even worse, they learn that frustration or conflict is a ticket out of effort.

For the ADHD brain, conflict is reinforcing. It is fast-paced, emotional, and stimulating—all things that a worksheet is not. Therefore, if a child can provoke a parent into arguing, they've just replaced boredom with dopamine—and the homework becomes secondary. Over time, this creates a feedback loop where conflict is unconsciously sought.

Meanwhile, many parents internalize their child's homework output as a direct reflection of their own worth or parenting skills. But as we stress in *The Executive*

Function Playbook, your child's independence will not grow if you're doing the work for them, fighting them through it, or rescuing them from the discomfort of trying.

By establishing boundaries, reducing emotional involvement, and coaching children on when and how to ask for help, you shift from being a manager to being a mentor. You give your child the space—and the discomfort—they need to grow.

KEY MESSAGE
When parents become over-involved in homework, the child's growth stalls. Reducing conflict and stepping back allows the child to develop true ownership and internal motivation.

CLOSING THOUGHT
You are not your child's executive function system. You are their guide. Trust that stepping back at the right times is not neglect—it's an act of love that gives your child room to rise.

Activity 8.6 Homework Success: WHERE
Executive function skills strengthened: Self-regulation

OVERVIEW
One of the most underestimated factors in ADHD homework success is location. Students with ADHD and executive function challenges often struggle not because they're incapable of doing the work, but because they're placed in environments full of high-stimulation distractions—especially at home. These distractions are often emotional (arguments, negative attention seeking), or digital (phones, video games, social media), and the ADHD brain naturally gravitates toward both.

In *The Executive Function Playbook*, we explore how setting up the right environment is not about forcing productivity—it's about reducing barriers. The brain with ADHD craves novelty and stimulation, and will do anything to avoid low-stimulation tasks like homework. That's why location matters more than we think. A change in where work is done often changes how the brain engages with it.

This page is designed to help adults and children collaboratively establish a structured, distraction-free location for homework—one that prevents emotional and digital interference, and instead promotes task initiation, focus, and follow-through.

INSTRUCTIONS FOR THE ADULT (PARENT, TEACHER, OR CLINICIAN)
Start by explaining to the child that where homework is done plays a huge role in how well it gets done. It's not a punishment to change locations—it's a strategy for success.

Make it clear that this is an expectation, not a negotiation. That said, children are still given the chance to have input and feel a sense of autonomy within boundaries.

For children who resist choosing or push back entirely, you may say:

"These are the three places that will help your brain do your best work. You get to pick one. If you choose not to pick, I'll choose for you. And if homework doesn't happen in that space, then none of the screens (phone, TV, games, etc.) will happen either. That's the deal."

How to Use This Worksheet

Fill out the following with the child, offering suggestions or guiding them if needed. If they refuse to participate or give input, complete it yourself and present the options as firm expectations.

Homework Location Planning Sheet **Instructions:** Choose three locations where homework can be done successfully. These should be:

- ◆ Free of screens (unless required for school use, and even then, monitored)
- ◆ Outside the bedroom
- ◆ Free from siblings, pets, and other major distractions

My 3 Possible Homework Locations:
(e.g., Kitchen table from 4 to 5 p.m., with phone in a different room, Local library study carrel, with headphones Quiet corner of parent's home office, with supervision)

→ If the student refuses to choose, the parent writes:

"I have chosen location ____ for my child. This will be the homework location until further notice."

Why This Matters

For the ADHD brain, environmental structure often takes the place of internal self-regulation. Most children with ADHD are not developmentally able to consistently regulate themselves amidst high-stimulation triggers like screens and sibling conflict. When homework is done in the bedroom, on the bed, or near a device, it's nearly impossible for the child to resist the temptation—and each failure further chips away at motivation and confidence.

By designating a physical space for productivity, parents are not being controlling—they're removing the child's greatest obstacles and providing them with a clear path to success. This physical boundary often becomes the foundation for future habits of independence and self-discipline.

KEY MESSAGE

Structure is not punishment—it's protection. When children with ADHD are placed in low-distraction environments, their brains are better able to work, focus, and finish what they start.

CLOSING THOUGHT

You don't need to fight your child's brain—you need to design for it. Where they do their work may matter more than how they feel about it. Give their brain the best chance to succeed by setting the scene for success.

Activity 8.7 Homework Success: Studying

Executive function skills strengthened: Self-awareness,   self-regulation, self-motivation

OVERVIEW

Studying is one of the most misunderstood and under-supported academic tasks for students with ADHD and executive function challenges. In *The Executive Function Playbook*, we explain that studying is not a single action—it's a multistep executive function process that requires self-initiation, sustained attention, working memory, self-monitoring, and delayed gratification. This makes it one of the most taxing academic activities a student can engage in—especially for the ADHD brain, which is built for stimulation, not long-term planning.

While many parents report that their child "just doesn't know *how* to study," the deeper truth is this: studying feels unbearable because it is effortful, unstimulating, and often unrewarding in the moment. It lacks structure, has unclear endpoints, and offers no instant feedback. Unlike completing a worksheet or turning in an assignment, the "success" of studying isn't felt until days later—if at all. That delay between effort and outcome is one of the hardest things for a developing executive function system to manage.

This worksheet is designed to help students build a predictable structure around studying, starting with planning and preparation before the studying begins. When students take time to identify what subject they need to study for—and then name a specific strategy that fits that subject—they begin to build the internal habits of organization, prioritization, and motivation.

INSTRUCTIONS FOR THE ADULT (PARENT, TEACHER, OR CLINICIAN)

Use this worksheet to help the student prepare for an upcoming quiz, test, or project that requires studying. It is most effective when completed in advance of the test—ideally several days ahead of time.

Begin with a supportive and collaborative tone:

"Studying isn't just about knowing what to do—it's about figuring out a plan that actually works for your brain. Let's come up with the best way to study *your* way for each subject. This will help you feel more confident and less overwhelmed."

This is also an opportunity to teach the difference between active studying (quizzing, flashcards, teaching someone else, writing from memory) and passive studying (rereading notes, scanning a study guide, highlighting)—which is less effective, especially for ADHD learners.

Worksheet Structure

Repeat the following for multiple subjects (at least two to three if applicable). This can be printed multiple times or extended on additional pages.

Subject/Topic I Have a Test or Quiz In:
(e.g., Social Studies—American Revolution)

Best Way(s) for Me to Study This Subject:
(Check or describe below)

☐ Review flashcards
☐ Teach it out loud to someone else
☐ Use Quizlet or digital study tools
☐ Draw pictures or diagrams
☐ Write down what I remember and then check notes
☐ Have someone quiz me
☐ Break it into small parts across two to three days
☐ Other:

Where will I study?
When will I start studying?
How will I know I'm finished?

Why This Matters

Students with ADHD often fail tests not because they didn't study—but because the act of studying was never initiated or the strategy used was ineffective. Planning before studying starts reduces emotional resistance and gives the brain a clear starting point. When students know what to expect, they're more likely to engage.

Additionally, students with ADHD often experience intense emotional responses to the idea of failure. Avoiding studying becomes a way to protect their self-esteem. By turning studying into a collaborative, structured task, we remove ambiguity, reduce overwhelm, and help students take control of their own learning.

KEY MESSAGE

Studying is not just about effort—it's about structure. The clearer and more specific the plan, the more likely the brain is to follow through.

CLOSING THOUGHT

Don't wait for motivation—build a routine. When students learn how to prepare for studying, they begin to see themselves not just as students, but as independent learners.

Activity 8.8 Homework Success: Being Proactive

Executive function skills strengthened: Self-regulation, self-motivation

OVERVIEW

Homework is more than just an academic task for students with ADHD—it is often an emotionally charged experience. For many families, homework time is the single most stressful part of the day. In *The Executive Function Playbook*, we explain how this stress is often rooted not in the work itself, but in the emotional and neurological load that homework places on the ADHD brain.

Students with ADHD often dread homework, not because they lack the ability but because it consistently overwhelms their executive functioning system. It requires them to start a task that feels boring, sustain attention over time, regulate emotions and distractions, manage frustration, and persist without immediate reward. These demands, compounded daily, lead to avoidance, resistance, and conflict.

This worksheet is designed to give students a proactive voice. Instead of reacting negatively every day when homework comes up, this activity helps the student and adult identify what exactly makes homework feel so difficult—and what concrete strategies can be used to address those challenges before they spiral. The act of naming the struggle and planning for it builds emotional resilience, grit, and a sense of internal control.

INSTRUCTIONS FOR THE ADULT (PARENT, TEACHER, OR CLINICIAN)

Sit down with the student during a calm moment—not during or right before homework—and introduce the idea of proactive planning.

You might say:

"We know that homework isn't fun, and we've seen it cause stress. But instead of letting those feelings take over every time, let's figure out what exactly makes it feel so hard—and how we can get ready for it. That way, when homework shows up, we're already prepared."

The goal is not to eliminate frustration but to develop self-awareness and coping strategies. Help the student answer the following questions honestly and without judgment. Reassure them that this isn't about criticizing them—it's about supporting them.

Worksheet Structure

Question 1: What do I hate the most about homework?

(Be specific—is it the writing, the reading, the sitting still, the time it takes, the fear of not doing well, the pressure from parents?)

Question 2: How does homework make me feel?

(Examples: frustrated, nervous, angry, bored, embarrassed, hopeless.)

Question 3: What do I usually do when these feelings come up?

(Examples: argue, avoid, pretend to do it, rush through it, cry, shut down.)

Question 4: What can I do instead, to help myself when homework feels hard?

(Examples: take a break, talk to someone, use a checklist, set a timer, use a fidget, change location.)

Question 5: What can the adult do to help me stay calm and on track?

(Be clear about what's helpful vs. what makes it worse.)

Why This Matters

Homework resistance is not laziness—it is often a coping mechanism for feeling overwhelmed, helpless, or anxious. When students are not taught how to anticipate and manage these emotions, they default to avoidance and argument. Over time, this leads to damaged parent child relationships, lower confidence, and a growing fear of failure.

By giving students a space to talk honestly about their struggles and by validating their emotions while introducing clear strategies, we help them shift from a reactive mindset to a proactive one. This is the foundation of executive function development.

KEY MESSAGE

When students are taught to expect challenges—and plan for them—they begin to replace resistance with resilience.

CLOSING THOUGHT

Avoiding the task won't make it easier. But understanding *why* it's hard—and *what to do about it*—can transform homework from a daily battle into a manageable part of the day.

Activity 8.9 Homework Success: Taking a Break First
Executive function skills strengthened: Self-evaluation, self-regulation

OVERVIEW

For students with ADHD, one of the most common friction points at home is the moment they walk in the door after school and are told, "Time to do your homework." After a full day of structured demands, emotional regulation, and social expectations, the ADHD brain is depleted—and the desire to "take a break first" is not only understandable, it's biologically and psychologically valid.

In *The Executive Function Playbook*, we highlight the importance of honoring the child's need for decompression while simultaneously avoiding the trap of overstimulation. The danger lies not in the break itself—but in what the break consists of.

Many parents mistakenly believe that any break is a good break, but for ADHD learners, the wrong kind of break can sabotage the entire evening. High-dopamine activities like video games, YouTube, or scrolling social media hijack the brain's reward system. Once the child's brain is flooded with stimulation, it becomes nearly impossible to pivot to a low-stimulation task like homework. The only transition mechanism many children have left at that point is to create conflict—a behavior that, ironically, provides another form of dopamine.

This worksheet helps both the adult and the child co-create a plan for healthy breaks—ones that truly recharge the brain without derailing the evening. It introduces the idea of *intentional breaks* and builds executive functioning through anticipation, planning, self-awareness, and transition readiness.

INSTRUCTIONS FOR THE ADULT (PARENT, TEACHER, OR CLINICIAN)

Before homework time arrives, use this page with the child to build a consistent after-school plan. Do this collaboratively and during a nonstressful moment (e.g., weekend, morning, or after dinner the day before).

Explain:

"It makes total sense that you want a break after school—we all do. But certain breaks actually make it harder for your brain to get back on track. Let's come up with a few healthy breaks that really help you recharge, and make it easier to start your homework afterward."

The goal is to shift from reactive breaks ("I just want to do this now") to planned, productive breaks that are time-limited, manageable, and don't hijack the brain.

Worksheet Structure

Part 1: What I Usually Do When I Get Home
(Help the child reflect on their current routine.)

Part 2: How These Breaks Usually Make Me Feel Afterward
(Help the child identify emotional states like sluggish, irritable, energized, calm, etc.)

Part 3: What Kinds of Breaks Actually Help Me Recharge Without Making It Harder to Start Homework
(Pick two to three options. Good examples include reading, drawing, music, stretching, short walk, journaling, quiet LEGO play, snack time, etc.)

Part 4: What Time Should the Break End and Homework Begin?
(Set a consistent transition time. Use visual timers or alarm reminders if needed.)
Break Ends At: _____   Homework Starts At: _____

Part 5: What the Adult Will Do to Help the Transition Be Smooth (Without Arguing or Nagging)
(Examples: gentle five-minute warning, visual timer, positive encouragement, silent transition cue)

Why This Matters
ADHD brains struggle with transitioning between tasks, especially when going from high-interest to low-interest activities. This page is not about denying the need for rest—it's about teaching self-awareness and intentional decision-making. When breaks are chosen thoughtfully and boundaries are clear, children learn to self-regulate and prepare their brains for success, rather than delay and derail the entire evening.

This is also a major opportunity for parental modeling. Just like we all want a few minutes to reset after work, children need a similar grace period—but it must be handled wisely.

KEY MESSAGE

It's not about whether a child takes a break—it's about *what kind* of break they take. The right kind of break prepares the brain. The wrong kind of break hijacks it.

CLOSING THOUGHT

Planning the after-school transition is one of the most powerful things you can do to reduce conflict, protect your evening, and set your child up for long-term executive function success.

Activity 8.1: Homework Success: Setup and Organization

WHO—Who is involved?

_____

_____

WHAT—What needs to get done?

_____

_____

WHEN—What time period is homework done?

_____

_____

WHERE—Where is homework done?

_____

_____

WHY—Why does it need to get done?

_____

_____

Activity 8.2: Homework Success: The Time Period

Homework is done from _____ p.m. to _____ p.m.

At _____ p.m., the school laptop is given to _____. This happens *no matter what*, whether you say you are done or not.

The laptop will be returned to you after you successfully complete the morning routine tomorrow.

Activity 8.3: Homework Success: Checklist—Did You Turn It In?

EARN YOUR SCREEN TIME

HAVE YOU? CHECK IT OFF WHEN IT'S DONE	M	T	W	T	F
MADE YOUR BED					
GOTTEN DRESSED					
PUT AWAY DIRTY CLOTHES					
EATEN BREAKFAST					
BRUSHED YOUR TEETH					
COMBED YOUR HAIR					
DONE SOMETHING CREATIVE					
READ FOR 20 MINUTES					
DONE SOMETHING KIND					
PLAYED OUTSIDE FOR 30 MINUTES					
CLEANED UP YOUR ROOM/PLAY AREA					
WRITTEN A STORY OR COLORED					
DONE SOMETHING HELPFUL					

YOU CAN EARN SCREEN TIME!

Activity 8.4: Homework Success: Natural Consequences

If homework is not completed on time, the following natural consequences will take place:

1. _____

2. _____

3. _____

Activity 8.5: Homework Success: Parents

1. When my parents step in and get involved in my homework, it makes me feel:

   _____

   _____

2. When I get into an argument with my parents over homework, and it keeps me from having to do this boring task, it makes me feel:

   _____

   _____

3. If I actually need help, I will say:

   _____

   _____

Activity 8.6: Homework Success: "Where" Options

Doing homework at home *isn't working*.
Homework can be done in these places instead. *Pick one:*

1. _____

2. _____

3. _____

Activity 8.7: Homework Success: Studying

1. Subject/topic that I have a test or quiz in: _____

What's the best way for me to study for this?

_____

Where will I study?

_____

When will I start studying?

_____

How will I know I'm finished?

_____

2. Subject/topic that I have a test or quiz in: _____

What's the best way for me to study for this?

_____

Where will I study?

_____

When will I start studying?

_____

How will I know I'm finished?

_____

3. Subject/topic that I have a test or quiz in: _____

What's the best way for me to study for this?

_____

Where will I study?

_____

When will I start studying?

_____

How will I know I'm finished?

_____

Activity 8.8: Homework Success: Being Proactive

1. What do I hate the most about homework?

_____

_____

2. How does homework make me feel?

_____

_____

3. What do I usually do when these feelings come up?

_____

_____

4. What can I do instead, to help myself when homework feels hard?

_____

_____

5. What can an adult do to help me stay calm and on track?

_____

_____

Activity 8.9: Homework Success: Taking a Break First

1. What do I usually do when I get home from school?

_____

_____

2. How do these breaks usually make me feel afterward?

_____

3. What kinds of breaks actually help me recharge without making it harder to start homework?

_____

_____

4. What time should the break end and homework begin?

_____

5. What will my adult do to help the transition be smooth (without arguing or nagging)?

_____

_____

CHAPTER 9

Academic Executive Functioning

Empowering Teachers and School Staff to Build Executive Function Skills in the Classroom

Executive function is the invisible skill set that determines whether students succeed or struggle—not just academically but behaviorally, socially, and emotionally. In the classroom, students with executive function challenges may appear disorganized, inattentive, impulsive, avoidant, or disengaged. But beneath those behaviors is often a lagging skill, not a lack of effort.

This chapter is designed specifically for teachers, special educators, school counselors, and support staff—the professionals on the front lines of student development. These worksheets will help you bring executive functioning directly into your classroom culture and routines, without needing to overhaul your entire curriculum.

In *The Executive Function Playbook*, we emphasize that executive functioning is not a subject to be taught—it is a system to be supported. The school environment plays a major role in shaping and reinforcing executive skills like time management, self-monitoring, task initiation, and working memory. When schools embed EF practices into daily instruction, students gain not only academic confidence but real-world readiness.

The worksheets in this chapter are built to:

- Help students set realistic, measurable academic goals
- Support transitions and routine-building for students who struggle with follow-through
- Provide teachers with prompts to develop metacognitive reflection in students

241

◆ Create opportunities for student ownership over assignments, deadlines, and organization

◆ Encourage accountability and self-direction without over-accommodation or learned helplessness

These tools are grounded in the principles outlined in *The Executive Function Playbook*, particularly the need to shift from external reminders to internal language and reflection. When students are given the right structure, space, and language to think through their own process—not just their performance—they begin to develop the internal systems they've been missing.

Whether you're working with one student, a small group, or an entire class, these pages can be used flexibly. They are not only interventions—they are conversation starters, classroom routines, and executive functioning supports that can be embedded into the day in practical, accessible ways.

Students with ADHD and executive function challenges don't need more reminders. They need adults who understand how executive systems work and who are willing to teach, model, and reinforce those skills consistently.

This chapter is here to help you do exactly that—one worksheet, one conversation, one moment at a time.

Let's bring executive function into the classroom—so students can succeed far beyond it.

Activity 9.1: Calling Out in Class

Executive function skills strengthened: Self-awareness, self-evaluation, self-regulation, perspective-taking

This workbook page is designed to help children and teens with ADHD reflect on the impulsive classroom behavior of calling out or interrupting during lessons—one of the most common academic executive functioning challenges. Many students engage in this behavior without realizing the emotional or neurological drivers behind it and without understanding its broader impact on their learning environment and social relationships.

The page begins with the self-reflective prompt:

"During class I often feel _____."

This helps the student connect the emotion (e.g., boredom, excitement, anxiety, frustration, eagerness) to the action of blurting out.

Next, the student completes:

"This feeling makes me want to interrupt and call out. I like to do this because _____."
This gets to the motivation behind the action. Often, it may be because calling out is stimulating, gets a reaction from peers, or provides a quick dopamine boost.

The next section explores the social and academic consequences with the following:

♦ "When I interrupt and blurt out, my teacher feels _____."
♦ "My classmates feel _____."

This cultivates perspective-taking, helping students become more aware of how their impulsive behaviors affect others—often creating frustration for teachers and causing peers to feel annoyed, distracted, or even embarrassed on their behalf.
Finally, the adult and student can discuss the ultimate question:

"Does this strategy actually work for you? Does it help you reach your Best Self Goals?"
This ties the behavior back to long-term goals and the internal motivation to become a more effective learner, teammate, and friend.

KEY MESSAGE
Calling out in class often begins with a feeling—usually boredom, anxiety, or a desire for stimulation. Understanding this emotion and how it fuels impulsive behavior is the first step in changing it. Executive function growth means developing the ability to pause, reflect, and regulate.

CLOSING THOUGHT
Self-awareness is the foundation of behavioral change. When students recognize why they act a certain way and how it impacts those around them, they build the internal skills to pause, reflect, and choose more productive behaviors—without losing who they are.

Activity 9.2: Self-Advocacy
Executive function skills strengthened: Self-awareness, self-regulation, self-evaluation, self-advocacy

This workbook page is designed to help children and teens with ADHD identify uncomfortable emotional states at school and learn how to safely and appropriately express their needs. Students with executive function challenges often internalize stress, confusion, or embarrassment, and instead of asking for help, they may act out, shut down, or avoid the task altogether. Self-advocacy is not intuitive for many—it's a learned executive function skill that must be taught, modeled, and practiced.

The first prompts guide the student to acknowledge how they feel at school:

- "I do not like feeling _____ at school."
- "Doing _____ makes me feel _____."

These help the student name emotions (e.g., overwhelmed, confused, rushed) and connect them to triggering academic activities like reading aloud, timed math tests, or writing assignments.

Next, the student reflects on the barrier to self-advocacy:

"I need help, but I do not know how to ask or get it."
This validates a common experience and sets the stage for skill-building.

The final section gives a framework for planning actionable steps with this prompt:

"Acceptable ways to self-advocate in (teacher's name) class is to do these three things:"
Three lines follow to list concrete, respectful, and feasible ways to ask for support—such as raising a hand with a specific signal, writing a note, or quietly requesting a break card.

Students can work with the adult to generate strategies that are developmentally appropriate and aligned with classroom norms. Once practiced, these self-advocacy skills empower students to communicate early, before dysregulation sets in.

KEY MESSAGE
Asking for help is not a weakness—it's a strength. When students can recognize their needs and communicate them respectfully, they build independence, emotional regulation, and resilience.

CLOSING THOUGHT
Self-advocacy transforms school from a place of anxiety to a place of support. When students are taught that it's okay to speak up for what they need, they become more confident, capable, and connected in their learning environment.

Activity 9.3: Resources

Executive function skills strengthened: Self-awareness, self-evaluation, self-motivation

This workbook page is designed to help students build stronger internal awareness of the supports around them and how those supports can foster academic success. Too often, students with ADHD either don't know what school-based resources are available to them or don't use them consistently—whether due to forgetfulness, embarrassment, or lack of clarity on when and how to use them.

This page provides a space for the student and school staff to collaborate and list *all available academic resources* within the school environment. Examples might include:

- Resource room or learning support
- Teacher office hours
- Test center for extended time
- Peer tutoring
- Break passes
- Writing or math lab
- Graphic organizers or outlines
- Use of a fidget or seating choice

Prompt 1:
"The following resources are available to me at my school:"

_____

_____

Then, the worksheet transitions to real-time reflection, giving the student a place to track the *use and impact* of a chosen resource:

Prompt 2:
"On (date), I used (resource) for (task). It helped me with _____, and made me feel _____."

This turns the page into a flexible academic journal that serves several key purposes:

- **Self-monitoring:** The student tracks how often they are accessing supports.
- **Data for school staff:** This provides real-world feedback on whether the supports are effective, appropriate, or need to be modified or phased out.
- **Positive reinforcement:** Reflecting on how the resource helped and how it made the student feel can increase their willingness to use supports proactively.

◆ **Ownership:** Completing this reflection builds self-motivation by helping the student see themselves as an active participant in their own learning journey.

KEY MESSAGE

Your school offers tools to help you succeed, but *you* are the one who makes them work. By using the resources around you and noticing how they help, you're becoming more independent and empowered.

CLOSING THOUGHT

You don't need to do everything alone. Success starts with recognizing the support that's already there—and knowing when to reach for it.

Activity 9.4: School Work Becomes Homework

Executive function skills strengthened: Self-evaluation

This page is designed as a structured teacher-parent communication tool to ensure clarity and accountability when school assignments are not completed during the school day and subsequently become homework. In today's digital age of EdTech platforms, communication between school and home can often become inconsistent, fragmented, or overly reliant on technology that parents may not be familiar with. Further complicating matters, each teacher may use different platforms or communication styles, making it difficult for parents to track expectations, due dates, or incomplete assignments.

Children and teens with ADHD typically struggle with working memory and task initiation and are frequently unreliable when it comes to reporting homework assignments. They may unintentionally forget, or they may tell their caregivers they have no homework as a way of avoiding an overwhelming or boring task. Relying on them as the sole source of communication is often ineffective and leads to frustration on all sides.

This worksheet eliminates guesswork. Teachers can quickly complete it when a student fails to finish a classwork assignment and it needs to be continued at home. It includes simple fields for:

◆ **Date**
◆ **Subject**
◆ **Assignment Name**
◆ **Was this originally classwork?** Yes / No
◆ **Reason for Incompletion:** (Distracted/Needed more time/Absent/Other)
◆ **Now becomes homework?** Yes / No
◆ **Due Date**
◆ **Teacher Comments (if any)**

The form can be printed, emailed, or uploaded to a digital folder to ensure that all parties—student, teacher, and parent—are informed and aligned.

KEY MESSAGE

Executive function challenges make it hard for ADHD students to independently track and report their assignments. A consistent communication system between home and school builds accountability, reduces stress, and allows adults to step in appropriately without relying on a faulty reporting system.

CLOSING THOUGHT

The less we rely on memory and verbal communication from the child, the more likely we are to reduce tension, increase follow-through, and help the student grow into a self-sufficient learner with strong executive functioning skills.

Activity 9.5: Study Hall/Work Tracker

Executive function skills strengthened: Self-evaluation, self-motivation

Many students with ADHD are granted structured or unstructured study hall periods, academic support blocks, or free time throughout the school day intended for independent work completion. In theory, these blocks are opportunities for students to catch up on missing assignments, begin homework, or seek help. In practice, however, they often become one of the most unproductive parts of the school day.

Students with ADHD frequently lack the internal self-monitoring and motivation systems to regulate their behavior during unstructured time. These periods are rarely closely supervised, and school-issued technology provides an abundance of off-task temptations—from games to chat threads to unrelated websites. Without intentional structure, these windows of academic opportunity are frequently wasted, leading to more homework, more stress, and increased frustration for both the student and parent at home.

This worksheet is designed to serve as a daily accountability form, completed by a school staff member, to reinforce awareness of how time was used—or misused—and what the academic consequences are. It reads:

Today during (study hall/free time), (student name) was expected to:

Instead, (student name) spent their time:

The following is incomplete work that must now be completed by:

Teacher/staff initials: _____

Student initials (optional): _____

This tracking form builds an essential bridge between school and home, ensuring that adults know what was supposed to happen and what actually occurred. It helps students develop metacognition by reflecting on how they use their time and what changes might be necessary in the future.

KEY MESSAGE

Unstructured school time is a privilege—but for students with ADHD, it must be earned and structured intentionally. Without support, these periods often go to waste, compounding executive function struggles later in the day.

CLOSING THOUGHT

With consistent use of this tracker, students begin to recognize the link between their in-school choices and their after-school stress. The goal is not punishment—it's awareness, accountability, and the slow, steady development of independence and ownership.

Activity 9.6: School Likes and Dislikes

Executive function skills strengthened: Self-evaluation, self-advocacy, self-awareness

This workbook page is designed to provide students with a structured opportunity to reflect on their personal experience at school—what parts of the school day feel successful, meaningful, or enjoyable, and what parts feel frustrating, boring, or stressful.

For many students with ADHD and executive dysfunction, school becomes a place they associate with constant correction, negative feedback, and internal feelings of failure or comparison. These students often don't feel heard, and their individual preferences and strengths can be overlooked. This worksheet invites them to express both their positive and negative feelings about school in a safe, guided, and constructive format—supported by a caring adult.

On this page, students will complete the following:

Three things I enjoy about school:

Three things I do *not* enjoy about school:

This exercise not only strengthens self-evaluation skills but also encourages self-advocacy. If a child states that they dislike a particular subject, environment, or routine, this opens the door for school staff to explore why—and what supports or accommodations may help. Similarly, identifying what a student enjoys allows parents and teachers to build on those moments of engagement and motivation.

KEY MESSAGE

Empowering students to voice their likes and dislikes builds trust, improves communication, and provides adults with key insight into how to better support learning and motivation.

CLOSING THOUGHT

All students want to feel seen, heard, and supported. When we give children the space to reflect honestly on their school experience, we lay the foundation for a stronger adult-student relationship—and create opportunities for meaningful change.

Activity 9.7: Natural Consequences

Executive function skills strengthened: Self-awareness, self-evaluation, self-regulation

This worksheet is designed to help students and school staff work collaboratively to identify and clearly define natural consequences for common school-based behaviors—*before* they happen. When students with ADHD engage in impulsive or unexpected behaviors, the response from adults is often reactive, inconsistent, or inappropriate. One of the most common but misguided consequences given is the removal of recess—something that is not only developmentally harmful but counterproductive for students who need movement and stimulation to regulate and succeed.

This workbook page creates a proactive plan that fosters structure, clarity, and accountability for both the student and the adult. It removes the guesswork and emotional reactivity by assigning logical, natural consequences in advance. The goal is not punishment—it is learning, self-monitoring, and consistency.

On this worksheet, the adult and child will complete:

1. When I _____, the natural consequence is _____

Each consequence should be reasonable, related to the behavior, and focused on helping the student build awareness and internal regulation. Removing access to movement, social interaction, or outdoor play is *never* appropriate for students with ADHD, and this page reinforces that stance by modeling better alternatives rooted in executive functioning skill-building.

KEY MESSAGE

Proactively assigning natural consequences builds trust, prevents power struggles, and helps students take ownership of their choices in a structured, supportive environment.

CLOSING THOUGHT

When students know what to expect, and consequences are fair and predictable, they are far more likely to reflect, grow, and regulate their behavior over time. Predictability is not a crutch—it is a tool for emotional safety and long-term independence.

Activity 9.8: Where and Why?

Executive function skills strengthened: Self-awareness, self-evaluation, self-regulation

This worksheet gives students the opportunity to reflect on specific academic or behavioral challenges they face during the school day, while also helping them make sense of *why* these challenges occur. For students with ADHD, executive dysfunction—especially in the form of poor working memory—often means they struggle to identify patterns in their behavior or understand how their choices affect themselves and others. As a result, they may repeat the same mistakes without ever stopping to ask "why."

This workbook page helps break that cycle. By directly prompting the student to reflect on one specific area of difficulty and then walk through the *why* behind that struggle, it sets the stage for meaningful insight and change. Working alongside a school staff member, the student is then guided to proactively problem-solve and create a realistic improvement plan.

> **Prompts on the worksheet:**
> 1. **Sometimes in school, I struggle with:**
>   (*e.g., staying in my seat, starting my work, raising my hand instead of calling out*)
> 2. **Why do I struggle with this?**
>   (*e.g., I feel anxious, it's boring, I forget what I'm supposed to do, I get distracted easily*)
> 3. **To be proactive, we can improve this by:**
>   (*e.g., taking short breaks, using a visual checklist, sitting closer to the teacher, having a silent signal with the teacher*)

This activity not only promotes a growth mindset by identifying areas of development but also helps build metacognition—the ability to think about one's own thinking. With adult scaffolding and guidance, the student can identify internal and external triggers and co-create strategies that are practical and tailored to their needs.

KEY MESSAGE

Understanding *why* a struggle is happening is the first step in changing it. By naming it, explaining it, and planning for it, students develop the internal skills needed for long-term growth.

CLOSING THOUGHT

Awareness breeds empowerment. When students feel heard and supported in identifying their challenges, they are far more likely to take responsibility and rise to the occasion. This is how we build self-regulated, motivated learners who believe in their ability to grow.

Activity 9.9: "I Can't Wait!"

Executive function skills strengthened: Time management, nonverbal working memory, verbal working memory, self-regulation, self-motivation

This workbook page introduces students to the powerful executive function skill of *delayed gratification*. For children and teens with ADHD, time can feel abstract, distant, and irrelevant. They are often "time blind"—unable to feel the passage of time or hold future rewards in mind. As a result, they struggle to persist through boring or nonpreferred academic tasks, even when something fun or meaningful is just around the corner.

This worksheet aims to reframe that experience. By giving students a space to clearly identify what they're looking forward to after school and by helping them *visualize* it and talk themselves through it, they strengthen both nonverbal and verbal working memory. The goal is to help them "hold the future in mind" while they do hard things now.

> **Prompts on the worksheet:**
> 1. **At school, I have to work hard through difficult, challenging, and boring things I do not want to do.**
>   (*e.g., long reading passages, group work, math problems, long lectures*)
> 2. **I can't wait for school to be over, so I can:**
>   (*e.g., ride my bike, play with my dog, go to baseball practice, have a snack, play a game*)

This structured reflection builds a practical mindset: "The faster and more focused I am now, the sooner I get to what I love." It can also serve as a cue for educators to build in visual reminders of upcoming rewards or breaks, helping students manage their emotional regulation during long academic periods.

KEY MESSAGE

Visualizing what's coming next helps you push through what's hard right now. Motivation grows when the future feels real and reachable.

CLOSING THOUGHT

Big goals start with small actions. By keeping a fun future activity in mind, students learn to regulate their attention and effort in the present—and that's the heart of executive functioning.

Activity 9.10: School Laptop Monitoring

Executive function skills strengthened: Self-evaluation, self-awareness, self-regulation

This workbook page is designed to increase accountability, self-monitoring, and digital responsibility in students with ADHD who struggle to use school-issued technology appropriately. The ADHD brain is driven by stimulation-seeking, novelty, and instant gratification, making unsupervised access to Internet-connected laptops a recipe for distraction.

This worksheet serves as both a *behavior tracker* for the teacher and a *self-reflection tool* for the student. It includes the following sections:

1. **Time Off Task**
   - Teachers log the approximate time the student became distracted.
   - This helps identify patterns (e.g., always off-task during independent work, after lunch, or mid-morning).
2. **Websites Accessed**
   - The student is asked to list the noneducational websites they visited (e.g., YouTube, Google Docs used for chatting, online games, shopping sites).
3. **Why Did I Go There?**
   - The student reflects on what prompted the behavior: boredom, anxiety, avoidance, need for stimulation, conflict with a peer, etc.
   - This promotes insight into the emotional or situational triggers behind the distraction.
4. **What Did I Miss While Off Task?**
   - Teachers note specific classwork, instructions, or group work the student missed during the distraction period.
   - This reinforces the real-world impact of being off-task and helps the student understand cause and effect.

5. How Will This Affect Me?

- The student completes this final section by reflecting on how the missed material will affect their homework, grades, or understanding of the topic.

This page is also designed to be shared with administration and IT staff as data for school-wide digital safety decisions. Many schools make the mistake of placing the burden of self-regulation on the student without acknowledging the neurodevelopmental reality that most children with ADHD cannot resist the temptations of unmonitored internet access. This worksheet creates data that empowers teachers and parents to advocate for site-blocking and structured supervision during tech-based learning.

KEY MESSAGE

If we want students with ADHD to succeed, we must remove temptation and help them learn *why* they go off task—not just punish them for it.

CLOSING THOUGHT

Technology should support learning, not sabotage it. With the right tools and insight, students can learn to take control of their attention—and schools can help them get there.

Activity 9.11: Resources Available

Executive function skills strengthened: Self-awareness, self-motivation

This workbook page helps students with ADHD identify, understand, and take ownership of the academic and emotional supports available to them throughout the school day. Students with executive dysfunction often miss out on crucial opportunities for support—not because they are lazy or unmotivated but because they struggle with working memory, time awareness, and self-advocacy.

This worksheet aims to reframe the school day for the student—not as something being done *to* them but as something filled with *built-in support* if they learn how and when to access it.

The page includes three columns for completion alongside a supportive adult:

1. **Resource Name**
   - Examples might include: Study Hall, Resource Room, After-School Help, Peer Tutoring, Counselor Check-In, Advisory Period, or Homework Club.
2. **When and Where Is This Available?**
   - Clearly outlines the time of day and location of each resource.
   - Helps the student build future thinking skills and visualize their school day more clearly.

3. **How Can This Help Me?**
   - The student reflects (with adult guidance) on the specific benefits of the resource.
   - This may include: "I'll get homework started early," "I'll have a quiet place to work," "I'll feel less overwhelmed," or "I'll have someone to check my work."

By filling this out, students become more empowered to take advantage of built-in supports and reduce reliance on unstructured, unsupervised time that often leads to procrastination or dysregulation.

KEY MESSAGE
Knowing what help is available—and when to access it—is one of the most important skills a student with ADHD can develop.

CLOSING THOUGHT
Support doesn't just appear when you need it most—it's already there. Learning to recognize and use it is a major step toward independence and academic success.

Activity 9.12: Group Work
Executive function skills strengthened: Self-regulation

Group work in school offers a valuable opportunity for students with ADHD to strengthen their social and academic executive functions in a real-world setting. However, it also presents many challenges—especially when it comes to frustration tolerance, flexibility, and managing expectations of others.

This workbook page is designed to proactively structure the group experience for success. It walks the student through the core executive function demands of group work and helps them build a game plan to manage their behavior, understand their role, and engage with peers productively.

This page is to be completed with a teacher, school staff member, or executive function coach before or at the start of a group project. It includes the following sections:

1. **Who is in my group?**
   (List the names of all group members.)
2. **What are my potential concerns about working with this group?**
   (Examples: different work styles, feeling left out, someone talking too much, not agreeing on ideas, distractions, etc.)

3. **What is the plan if those concerns happen?**
   (Examples: ask the teacher for help, take a short break, use kind and respectful words to self-advocate, remind myself of the bigger goal.)
4. **What is our group's goal?**
   (Describe the academic goal of the project or assignment.)
5. **What role will I play in the group?**
   (Examples: note-taker, idea-sharer, presenter, designer, researcher, organizer.)
6. **What does a successful group look like at the end?**
   (Examples: We finish on time, we stay respectful, everyone contributes, we all feel good about our work.)

This worksheet helps students regulate themselves within the demands of group collaboration, while also preparing them to engage in flexible thinking, shared ownership of tasks, and accountability to others. It also explicitly teaches the concept that people can have differences and still work effectively together.

KEY MESSAGE

Working with others requires flexibility, emotional regulation, and shared goals—skills that must be practiced, not assumed.

CLOSING THOUGHT

Group work mirrors real life. We don't always choose who we work with, but we can always choose how we show up, contribute, and grow from the experience.

Activity 9.13: Am I "Ready" to Be in Class?

Executive function skills strengthened: Self-regulation, self-awareness, self-motivation

One of the most essential but underdeveloped executive function skills in students with ADHD is the ability to *self-monitor* their readiness to participate in structured academic environments. Without clear boundaries and accountability, students often rely on impulsive behaviors, struggle to recognize their own dysregulation, and fall into patterns of negative attention-seeking that disrupt their learning and that of their peers.

This workbook page is designed to establish and reinforce classroom readiness by clearly defining teacher expectations and putting the responsibility back on the student to self-assess and self-regulate.

INSTRUCTIONS FOR TEACHER AND STUDENT (COMPLETE TOGETHER)

1. **"When I am *ready* to be in class, I look and act like this:"**
   (The teacher lists specific, observable behaviors that signal the student is calm, regulated, and prepared for classroom learning. Examples: seated in my chair, quiet voice, eyes on the speaker, materials ready, following directions.)

2. **"If I am *not* ready to be in class, I may show these behaviors:"**
   (The teacher and student identify dysregulated or disruptive behaviors. Examples: calling out, refusing work, pacing, making others laugh, ignoring instructions, showing frustration.)

3. **"If the teacher determines I am *not* ready, I will be asked to leave class. I can return when. . ."**
   (This section describes the criteria for returning to class. Examples: I am calm, I agree to follow the expectations, I can name my regulation strategy, I am ready to work.)

Why This Matters

Students with ADHD must learn that participation in a shared learning environment is a privilege tied to their ability to regulate. If they are not "ready," remaining in the classroom often leads to a pattern of repeated behaviors that escalate over time and significantly interfere with academic progress.

By documenting and agreeing upon this plan, the student gains awareness of their role, learns to take ownership of their behavior, and strengthens their internal motivation to meet expectations. It also sends a message that they *can* succeed in the classroom—but only when they are regulated, safe, and respectful of the learning space.

KEY MESSAGE

Readiness is a skill, not a feeling. When we define it, teach it, and hold students accountable to it, they begin to rise to meet it.

CLOSING THOUGHT

Being ready doesn't just help you—it protects your learning, your relationships, and your self-respect. When you're ready, you are powerful.

Activity 9.1: Calling Out in Class

During class, I often feel _____.

This feeling makes me want to interrupt and call out.

I like to do this because _____.

When I interrupt and blurt out, my teacher feels _____.

My classmates feel _____.

Activity 9.2: Self-Advocacy

I don't like feeling _____ at school.

_____ makes me feel _____.

I need help, but I do not know how to ask or get it.

These are three acceptable ways to self-advocate in _____'s
(teacher's name) class:

_____

_____

_____

Activity 9.3: Resources

The following resources are available to me at my school:

_____

_____

_____

_____

_____

_____

_____

On _____ *(date)*, I used _____

(resource) for _____ *(task)*.

It helped me with _____, and made me feel

_____.

Activity 9.4: School Work Becomes Homework

Date	Subject	Assignment name	Reason for incompletion	Due date	Teacher comments (if any)
			Distracted/Needed more time/Absent/Other		
			Distracted/Needed more time/Absent/Other		
			Distracted/Needed more time/Absent/Other		
			Distracted/Needed more time/Absent/Other		
			Distracted/Needed more time/Absent/Other		

Activity 9.5: Study Hall/Work Tracker

Today during _____ *(study hall/free time)*, _____ *(student's*

name) was expected to _____.

Instead, _____ *(student's name)* spent their time _____.

The following is incomplete work that must now be completed at home:

_____.

Teacher/staff initials: _____.

Activity 9.6: School Likes and Dislikes

Three things I enjoy about school:

1. _____

2. _____

3. _____

Three things I do *not* enjoy about school:

1. _____

2. _____

3. _____

Activity 9.7: Natural Consequences

Think about some common behaviors or choices in school that have consequences.

1. When I _____, the natural consequence is

_____.

2. When I _____, the natural consequence is

_____.

3. When I _____, the natural consequence is

_____.

Activity 9.8: Where and Why?

Sometimes in school, I struggle with:

_____

_____

Why do I struggle with this?

_____

_____

To be proactive, we can improve this by:

_____

_____

_____

Activity 9.9: "I Can't Wait!"

At school, I have to work hard through difficult, challenging, and boring things I do not want to do. Here are some of the things I have to work hard at:

_____

_____

I can't wait for school to be over, so I can:

_____

_____

_____

Activity 9.10: School Laptop Monitoring

School Laptop Distraction Log

1. When did the distraction happen? _____

   What websites did I go on? _____

   Why did I go there? _____

   What did I miss while off-task? _____

   How will this affect me? _____

2. When did the distraction happen?_____

   What websites did I go on? _____

   Why did I go there? _____

   What did I miss while off task? _____

   How will this affect me? _____

3. When did the distraction happen? _____

   What websites did I go on? _____

   Why did I go there? _____

   What did I miss while off task? _____

   How will this affect me? _____

Activity 9.11: Resources Available

What is available to me?

Resource name	When and where is this available?	How can it help me?
_____ →	_____ →	_____
_____ →	_____ →	_____
_____ →	_____ →	_____

Activity 9.12: Group Work

1. Who is in my group?

   _____

2. What are my potential concerns about working with this group?

   _____

   _____

3. What is the plan if those concerns happen?

   _____

   _____

4. What is our group's goal?

   _____

   _____

5. What role will I play in the group?

   _____

6. What does a successful group look like at the end?

   _____

   _____

Activity 9.13: Am I "Ready" to Be in Class?

When I am *ready* to be in class, I look and act like this:

\
\
\
\
\

If I am *not* ready to be in class, I may show these behaviors:

\
\
\
\
\

If the teacher determines I am *not* ready, I will be asked to leave class. I can return when:

\
\
\

CHAPTER 10

Social Executive Functioning

Building Real Connection Through Perspective-Taking, Awareness, and Reciprocity

Social success isn't built on scripts or surface skills. It's built on internal thinking—on the ability to read a room, consider someone else's perspective, and adjust behavior in real time.

In *The Executive Function Playbook*, we make a clear distinction between outdated "social skills" training and what actually helps children and teens with ADHD build meaningful relationships. Far too often, traditional social skills groups focus on external behaviors like eye contact, topic maintenance, or turn-taking games. But for many neurodivergent students, those approaches are superficial, disconnected from real-life situations, and ultimately ineffective in producing true growth.

This chapter takes a different approach.

Social executive functioning is about what happens inside the brain, not just what's seen on the outside. The ability to recognize how one's actions impact others, adapt to changing social expectations, and engage in reciprocal back-and-forth interactions is rooted in executive function—not memorized behaviors.

The worksheets in this chapter are designed to be completed with the adult, helping children and teens build:

- ◆ Perspective-taking ("How might they be feeling right now?")
- ◆ Situational awareness ("What's going on around me, and how should I adjust?")
- ◆ Social self-monitoring ("How am I coming across to others?")
- ◆ Reciprocity ("Am I giving as much as I'm getting in this conversation or friendship?")

These activities are not about forcing children to act neurotypical. They are about helping them become more socially competent on their own terms, in ways that improve their real-world relationships and quality of life. This means letting go of checkbox goals like eye contact and instead cultivating deep, lasting skills that empower children to connect meaningfully with others.

In *The Executive Function Playbook*, we introduce the idea that social success is not about masking or compliance—it's about developing the internal executive system that allows for flexible, thoughtful, and respectful engagement. The worksheets in this chapter make that possible by building the skills that matter most.

These pages are ideal for use at home, in therapy, or in school-based coaching. You'll find tools to help your child:

- Reflect on past social situations and what they learned
- Practice noticing and adapting to different social settings
- Think about how their behavior affects others—and themselves
- Plan for social growth and set achievable goals for friendship and inclusion

Above all, this chapter reminds children that they are not "bad at socializing"—they are still learning how to think socially. That learning, when done the right way, can be transformational.

Let's move past scripts and surface skills—and help children develop the social executive functioning that leads to real friendships, real empathy, and real confidence.

Activity 10.1: Video Game Friends or Real-Life Friends?
Executive function skills strengthened: Social perspective taking, social reciprocity

OVERVIEW
Social development is a core pillar of executive functioning, yet it is one of the most misunderstood areas in the lives of students with ADHD. Children and teens often struggle to build and maintain genuine friendships due to difficulties with impulse control, emotional regulation, flexible thinking, and perspective taking. In recent years, this challenge has been compounded by the rapid rise of online gaming and virtual "friendships."

The Executive Function Playbook emphasizes that while technology may appear social on the surface, it often does not translate into meaningful, reciprocal real-world relationships. For many kids and teens, their so-called "friends" are simply people they play games with—yet these interactions rarely foster the skills needed for authentic friendship, such as listening, empathy, problem-solving, or conflict resolution.

This workbook page challenges the myth that gaming is inherently social. It helps students—and more importantly, adults—begin to evaluate the difference between superficial digital interactions and real-life, emotionally connected friendships.

INSTRUCTIONS FOR THE ADULT (PARENT, TEACHER, OR CLINICIAN)

Use this page to open an honest, judgment-free discussion about social connection. This is not about shaming video games, but rather about encouraging social reflection and increasing awareness of what real friendship looks and feels like.

You might begin by saying:

"A lot of kids today spend more time online with their 'friends' than with people in real life. Let's take a closer look at what those friendships are really like, and how we can build stronger connections that help you feel more confident and connected outside of the game."

Then, walk through each of the questions with the child or teen, offering examples, helping with recall, and encouraging thoughtful conversation.

Worksheet Structure

Step 1: Who are my video game friends?

(List three to five usernames or real names of the people your child plays video games with most frequently.)

Step 2: Reflect on each one.

(Use Yes/No and follow-up questions for each listed friend.)

Friend's Name	Do we talk in real life (outside the game)?	Have we ever hung out in person?	Without the game, what would we talk about?	Without the game, what would we do?
	☐ Yes ☐ No	☐ Yes ☐ No		
	☐ Yes ☐ No	☐ Yes ☐ No		
	☐ Yes ☐ No	☐ Yes ☐ No		

Why This Matters

The digital age has blurred the line between real and virtual connection. Tech companies are heavily invested in making screen-based interactions feel rewarding and emotionally engaging—but the truth is, online gaming does not build social skills.

In-person friendships require:

◆ Reading facial expressions and body language
◆ Adjusting behavior based on social cues
◆ Managing turn-taking and compromise
◆ Understanding how your actions impact others

Online play removes most of these elements. There's no eye contact, no physical presence, no shared real-world experience—and therefore, little to no opportunity for social growth.

By asking these reflection questions, students start to realize that many of their "friends" only exist within the context of a game—and that's not enough. This insight is critical for students who feel lonely but can't understand why their hours of gaming aren't filling that social void.

KEY MESSAGE
Video game friends may feel real in the moment, but lasting friendships are built through face-to-face connection, shared experiences, and emotional reciprocity. Social growth requires stepping away from screens and into real life.

CLOSING THOUGHT
True connection happens when we are seen, heard, and supported—not just when we're holding a controller. If we want better friendships, we have to learn how to build them in the real world.

Activity 10.2: Making Friends
Executive function skills strengthened: Social perspective-taking, situational awareness

OVERVIEW
Friendship is not just a natural occurrence—it's a skill that must be learned, practiced, and refined over time. Children and teens with ADHD often struggle to understand the unwritten rules of social interaction: how to initiate a conversation, join a group, keep a conversation going, and manage the give-and-take of real friendships. These are executive function skills that require self-regulation, mental flexibility, self-awareness, and perspective-taking.

This page from *The Executive Function Playbook* emphasizes that social growth is not automatic. In today's screen-saturated world, many students with ADHD are becoming socially passive—waiting for others to initiate and relying on digital connection rather than developing the real-life skills required to form lasting friendships.

This activity supports students in reflecting on their past social behavior, identifying what has worked (or not), and beginning to understand that forming friendships involves active, intentional steps—not just hoping friendships will happen.

INSTRUCTIONS FOR THE ADULT (PARENT, TEACHER, OR CLINICIAN)

Use this page to guide your student or child through an open, supportive conversation. This is not meant to pressure the child into being more social than they're ready for—it's about helping them become more aware of their social patterns, learn what friendship requires, and begin thinking with a growth mindset.

You might begin with:

"Making a new friend is just like learning a new skill—it takes effort, practice, and awareness. Let's take a few minutes to think through what making a friend really looks like, and reflect on how it's gone for you in the past."

Step 1: What Are the Steps to Making a New, Real Friend?

In this section, help the child or teen identify the real-life, observable actions that can lead to friendship. These may include:

- Saying "hi" or giving a compliment
- Asking questions about the other person
- Sharing something about yourself
- Noticing what others are interested in
- Inviting someone to play or hang out
- Offering help or showing kindness
- Following up to keep the connection going

Let the child come up with their own ideas too. These actions help build social insight and initiative.

Step 2: Reflect on Past Efforts

Have the child or teen ask themselves:

- When was the last time I tried to make a new friend?
- Where was I when I tried? (school, sports, camp, etc.)
- How did it go? What worked well?
- What was difficult? What didn't work?
- What would I do differently next time?

Why This Matters

Many children and teens with ADHD develop a fixed mindset about social success. They assume they're "bad at making friends" because of repeated rejections, misunderstandings, or awkward attempts. Over time, this leads to avoidance and withdrawal from real-life social situations.

This page is designed to interrupt that pattern by:

◆ Breaking friendship into small, achievable steps
◆ Encouraging reflective thinking about past experiences
◆ Helping students see social growth as learnable and improvable

This exercise also gives the adult important insight into how the student perceives their social world—and how to better support them without hovering or rescuing.

KEY MESSAGE

Friendship is a skill that can be practiced. The more aware you are of the steps and your own behaviors, the more success you'll have in connecting with others in meaningful ways.

CLOSING THOUGHT

Every real friendship starts with a single act of courage—introducing yourself, asking a question, or offering kindness. Even if it doesn't work the first time, you are learning, growing, and getting better with every step.

Activity 10.3: What Makes a Friend?

Executive function skills strengthened: Social perspective-taking, social reciprocity

OVERVIEW

For children and teens with ADHD, understanding what truly defines a friendship can be a complex and sometimes confusing task. Many equate "friend" with anyone they interact with regularly—classmates, teammates, or even someone they only talk to online. But real, lasting friendships are built on the ability to take another person's perspective, respond with empathy, and share meaningful experiences over time. These are higher-order executive function skills that must be explicitly taught, modeled, and reinforced.

This workbook page helps adults guide students in developing a clearer picture of what makes a real friend, what behaviors foster strong relationships, and what qualities to look for in others. It also highlights that friendship is not just about having fun—it's about connection, trust, and mutual effort.

INSTRUCTIONS FOR THE ADULT (PARENT, TEACHER, OR CLINICIAN)

Use this page to prompt meaningful dialogue with the child or teen. The questions on this sheet aren't just about gathering answers—they are tools for building social insight and emotional literacy.

Introduce the page by saying:

"Friendships are one of the most important parts of our lives, but they're also something we learn how to build and keep. Let's think together about what makes someone a real friend, and how we can become a better friend ourselves."

Take your time with each question. Encourage elaboration, give real-life examples, and offer gentle correction when needed to help the student refine their understanding.

Guided Questions:

1. **How do you know someone is a real friend?**

   Help the child think beyond shared interests. Prompt them to consider trust, loyalty, consistency, and kindness.

   Example responses may include:
   • They care about how I feel.
   • They don't talk about me behind my back.
   • They check on me when I'm upset.
   • They want to spend time with me even when we're not playing a game.

2. **What do friends do together?**

   Emphasize shared experiences that are interactive and meaningful. Not all friend time needs to be activity-based—talking, laughing, and supporting one another count too.

   Example responses:
   • Talk and listen
   • Help each other
   • Invite each other to do things
   • Play games, hang out, or study together

3. **Do friends have to have a lot in common?**

   This is a chance to debunk a common myth. Real friendships are built on mutual respect and shared time—not just having identical interests.

   Reinforce ideas such as:
   • You can learn new things from friends with different interests.
   • Being open-minded helps you make more friends.
   • Some of the best friends don't like all the same things.

4. How do friends make each other feel?

This helps the child develop empathy and reflect on emotional impact—an essential part of social reciprocity.

Guide the student to reflect on:

• Feeling happy, accepted, supported, and safe
• Not feeling judged, ignored, or used
• Wanting to be kind in return

Why This Matters

Children and teens with ADHD often focus on what they get from friendships (e.g., fun, stimulation, distraction) but have difficulty seeing what they give. This mindset can lead to social challenges, rejection, and loneliness. By exploring the qualities of a true friend, they begin to understand the importance of emotional connection, mutual effort, and shared responsibility in a relationship.

This kind of social awareness helps shift the focus from "Who likes me?" to "What kind of friend am I?"—a powerful reframe that promotes growth, self-reflection, and deeper relationships.

KEY MESSAGE

Real friendships are built over time through kindness, effort, and shared connection. They require us to think about others, not just ourselves.

CLOSING THOUGHT

Friendship is more than just fun—it's about being there for someone and letting them be there for you. When we learn to give as much as we get, friendships become something truly special.

Activity 10.4: What Friends Do I Want?

Executive function skills strengthened: Social perspective-taking, social awareness

OVERVIEW

This workbook page helps children and teens begin to clarify what *they truly want* in a friendship—an essential step in developing meaningful and reciprocal relationships. For many students with ADHD and executive function challenges, friendships can be confusing, unstructured, and even overwhelming. They may struggle to articulate what they're looking for in a peer relationship and often gravitate toward the most immediately stimulating or accessible interactions—regardless of whether those interactions are healthy or sustainable.

This activity supports the development of **social awareness**, allowing students to reflect on their personal needs, preferences, and values when it comes to friendships. It also begins to shift the narrative from "Will others like me?" to "What kind of friendships are right for me?"

INSTRUCTIONS FOR THE ADULT (PARENT, TEACHER, OR CLINICIAN)

Use this worksheet to help the child or teen understand that friendship is a two-way street. While it's important to be a good friend to others, it's equally important to know what they themselves want out of a friendship.

Start by explaining:

"Let's think about what kind of friends *you* want. The more you understand what kind of people you enjoy being around, the easier it becomes to find—and build—strong friendships."

Work through each prompt one at a time, encouraging the student to give thoughtful and specific answers. Use follow-up questions to deepen their reflection and explore examples from their own life.

Guided Questions and Prompts

1. **I want friends that I can do _____ with.**
   Encourage the child to list activities that feel natural and enjoyable. This may include sports, creative hobbies, shared interests, or just spending time together.
   • Example: "Play basketball," "draw comics," "ride bikes," "talk about animals."

2. **I want them to talk to me about _____.**
   This helps the child understand the kind of connection they're seeking—emotional, intellectual, light-hearted, or shared interests.
   • Example: "Funny stories," "how I'm feeling," "video games," "what happened at school."

3. **I want them to make me feel _____.**
   Focus on emotional needs like feeling accepted, supported, understood, or safe. This teaches the child to recognize emotional reciprocity.
   • Example: "Happy," "calm," "important," "not alone."

4. **They can make me feel _____ by doing _____.**
   This last prompt bridges emotional awareness with behavior recognition. Help the child connect cause and effect in relationships.
   • Example: "They can make me feel appreciated by inviting me to play."
   • "They can make me feel calm by listening when I'm upset."

Why This Matters

Students with ADHD often have limited insight into how relationships form and evolve. They may seek out others based on proximity, shared interests, or availability—without pausing to consider whether those interactions actually meet their social and emotional needs. This can lead to feelings of rejection, confusion, or even accepting poor treatment from others just to feel included.

This activity provides a foundation for healthy social expectations. By becoming more intentional about who they connect with and *why*, children and teens can begin to move toward friendships that are more rewarding and emotionally sustainable.

Additionally, this page can open important conversations with adults about the difference between real connection vs. just convenience, and how to tell when someone is treating you with respect and care.

KEY MESSAGE

Knowing what you want in a friend helps you make better choices and build stronger, more meaningful relationships.

CLOSING THOUGHT

Friendships should feel good. When you know the kind of connection you're looking for, you can find people who help you grow, smile, and feel like your best self.

Activity 10.5: Perspective-Taking
Executive function skills strengthened: Perspective-taking

OVERVIEW

This workbook page is designed to help children and teens with ADHD begin building one of the most complex and vital social executive function skills: perspective-taking. This skill requires the ability to pause, reflect, and consider how one's own words and actions impact the thoughts and feelings of others. For students with executive function challenges, perspective-taking does not come naturally—it must be explicitly taught, practiced, and scaffolded.

Students with ADHD often operate in a reactive, impulse-driven manner, which means their social behaviors can be unintentionally disruptive, off-putting, or even hurtful—despite their best intentions. Without awareness and reflection, these patterns can become ingrained, leading to peer rejection and persistent difficulty maintaining friendships. This page invites students to slow down and develop insight into how they affect others, and how small changes can lead to stronger, more lasting connections.

INSTRUCTIONS FOR THE ADULT (PARENT, TEACHER, OR CLINICIAN)
Introduce this page by saying:

"Today we're going to talk about something really important—how we make other people feel. This doesn't mean you're doing anything wrong. It means we're learning how to understand others better so we can be a great friend, classmate, and teammate."

Guide the child or teen through the full sentence prompt:

"When I _____, I make others feel _____ because _____. But I want to make others feel _____ around me, so from now on, I will _____."

Break this sentence down step-by-step, using real-life examples. You may need to offer examples or observations to help the child reflect meaningfully. If necessary, frame this discussion with warmth and curiosity—not judgment. Remember, this exercise requires high-level cognitive effort for ADHD brains and should be handled with patience.

Example Prompts to Guide the Discussion:
- **"When I interrupt people a lot. . ."**
  → ". . .I make others feel frustrated because they don't feel heard."
- **"When I talk loudly or blurt out in class. . ."**
  → ". . .I make others feel annoyed or distracted because they are trying to concentrate."
- **"When I make jokes that aren't kind. . ."**
  → ". . .I make others feel embarrassed because they think I don't respect them."
- **"But I want to make others feel..."**
  → ". . .respected," "happy," "safe," "included," "like they can trust me."
- **"So from now on, I will. . ."**
  → ". . .wait my turn to talk."
  → ". . .ask myself, 'Will this help or hurt someone?' before I say something."
  → ". . .use my Brain Coach to tell myself to pause and think."

Let the child come up with at least one full example and then encourage a second or third if they are able. Over time, this repeated reflection will strengthen their ability to self-monitor, adjust, and ultimately build more positive and meaningful social interactions.

Why This Matters

Perspective-taking is one of the core social executive function muscles. It allows students to step outside of themselves and imagine how their behaviors are being received by others. Without this skill, children are at higher risk of social rejection, isolation, and misunderstanding. With this skill, they begin to build empathy, emotional intelligence, and the foundations of lasting friendships.

This worksheet makes a challenging internal process concrete and actionable. It allows adults to walk students through the cognitive and emotional process of understanding cause and effect in social interactions—something that must be modeled repeatedly to become habitual.

KEY MESSAGE

How we act affects how others feel—and when we learn to take their perspective, we can grow stronger relationships.

CLOSING THOUGHT

Being a good friend doesn't mean being perfect. It means trying to understand others, learning from our mistakes, and making choices that help everyone feel seen, safe, and valued.

Activity 10.6: Making Others Laugh

Executive function skills strengthened: Self-awareness, self-regulation, situational awareness, perspective-taking

OVERVIEW

Children and teens with ADHD often love making others laugh. In fact, it may become one of their core identities. Laughter offers immediate feedback, attention, and a quick dopamine hit—making it one of the most reinforcing experiences for the ADHD brain. Unfortunately, the intense pursuit of humor can backfire. The child may begin to rely on impulsive, disruptive, or even inappropriate behaviors to get a laugh. This can result in social confusion, rejection, or strained relationships. While the intention may be playful, the *impact* is what shapes peer perception—and many students with ADHD struggle to recognize this distinction.

This page is designed to help children explore their motivations for humor, reflect on how their jokes are perceived, and build the skills needed to use humor more effectively and appropriately.

INSTRUCTIONS FOR THE ADULT (PARENT, TEACHER, OR CLINICIAN)

Begin by explaining that this page isn't about discouraging the child from being funny—it's about understanding when and how humor is helpful and when it might accidentally push others away. Reassure them that having a great sense of humor is a wonderful trait—but using it in the right way and at the right time is a skill, not just a talent.

Guide the child through the following prompts:

1. "I like the feeling of making others laugh."
2. "I make others laugh by doing: _____."
3. "When I hear others laughing, what do I think their brain is telling them?"

Offer them two possible perspectives:

- **Perspective 1:** "He makes me laugh. I want to be his friend."
- **Perspective 2:** "He makes a lot of jokes and acts pretty wacky. I don't think he would be that much fun to be around. I wish he would joke less."

Ask the child to consider which one is more likely to be true in different situations. Use real-life examples when possible. Encourage honesty without shaming.

Why This Skill Matters

ADHD impacts self-regulation and impulse control—two key traits needed to use humor effectively. Students may act "wacky," call out in class, or dominate conversations in their quest to entertain. Without realizing it, they may become known as the class clown or "the kid who always interrupts," which can lead to missed friendships, lowered teacher trust, and internalized shame.

At the same time, kids with ADHD often have *great* senses of humor—they just need support in learning when and how to use it. This worksheet provides a concrete opportunity to evaluate what type of humor leads to social connection vs. social distance. Over time, this insight can help them regulate their impulses and become more socially effective and emotionally attuned.

Framing Tips for Adults

- **Avoid shame:** Focus on learning and growth, not on punishing humor.
- **Share personal stories:** Talk about times *you* misread a social situation or used humor in the wrong moment.
- **Highlight strengths:** Emphasize that being funny is a *great* quality when used wisely.

Examples to Use During Discussion

- "When I dance around in class to make people laugh, are they laughing because they think I'm cool—or because I look silly?"
- "When I tell jokes over and over again, do people seem more interested—or do they start ignoring me?"
- "If I want to have close friends, how do I know if my humor is helping or hurting?"

Use reflective listening and open-ended questions to help the child process without becoming defensive.

KEY MESSAGE

Humor is powerful—but to build real friendships, we have to understand how our jokes make others feel and what they might be thinking.

CLOSING THOUGHT

Being funny isn't just about getting a laugh—it's about making people feel good, seen, and connected. The most respected people are often the ones who know when to be playful and when to be thoughtful.

Activity 10.7: Social Cause and Effect

Executive function skills strengthened: Self-evaluation, social perspective-taking

OVERVIEW

In *The Executive Function Playbook*, one of the central themes is recognizing how executive functioning varies across three key environments: home, academic, and social. Children with ADHD often behave very differently across these zones—showing more regulation and cooperation in one while struggling in another. This workbook page helps students reflect on their behavior in each zone and develop greater self-awareness by asking: *Who did I affect, how, and why?*

This is an important step toward building a social executive function skillset—understanding how one's actions influence others and how these patterns shift depending on the environment. It also lays the foundation for empathy, accountability, and generalization of positive behaviors across contexts.

INSTRUCTIONS FOR THE ADULT (PARENT, TEACHER, OR CLINICIAN)

Sit with the student and review the three main zones of executive functioning:

1. Home
2. Academic (school)
3. Social (friends and peers)

Ask the student to reflect on a recent event in each zone. For each one, complete the following prompts together:

◆ *Who did I affect?*
◆ *How did I affect them?*
◆ *What specific behavior did I do?*
◆ *How do I think it made them feel?*

This activity is designed to increase social-emotional awareness and self-reflection. It may help to revisit recent examples from the child's life and guide them with open-ended, nonjudgmental prompts.

STEP-BY-STEP GUIDANCE

1. **Introduce the zones.**
   Explain: "There are three big parts of your life where your actions really matter—home, school, and with friends. Today we're going to think about how your actions affect others in each place."

2. **Model the process.**
   Give a clear example:
   "At home, I made my sister cry when I grabbed the remote from her. That probably made her feel disrespected."

3. **Help the student recall events.**
   Use scaffolding questions:
   • "What's something that happened at school this week?"
   • "Did you do something that made someone happy—or upset?"
   • "Was there a time you helped or hurt someone's feelings at home or with a friend?"

4. **Complete the chart together.**
   For each zone, fill in:
   • *Who did I affect?*
   • *What behavior caused it?*
   • *How do I think it made them feel?*

5. Make the connection.

Discuss how success in one area (e.g., being kind at school) means they are capable of doing it in others. Reinforce the idea that skills are transferable.

KEY MESSAGE

If a child can demonstrate executive function success in one setting, they are capable of carrying that same behavior into other areas of life. This worksheet helps children see their influence on others, reflect on their actions, and build internal consistency across environments.

CLOSING THOUGHT

Children with ADHD often struggle to generalize behavior across contexts. But with thoughtful reflection and structured guidance, they can begin to see themselves as active agents in their own lives—shaping not only what they do, but how they make others feel. When they connect behavior to consequence, growth begins.

RESEARCH REFERENCE

Denham, S. A., & Burton, R. (2003). *Social-emotional prevention programs for preschool children's early school success*. Baltimore, MD: Paul H. Brookes Publishing Co.

Activity 10.1: Video Game Friends or Real-Life Friends?

Who are my video game friends?

1. _____

2. _____

3. _____

Reflect on each of them.

1. First video game friend: _____

                                                                Yes   No

Do we talk in real life (outside the game)? ☐ ☐

                                         Yes   No

Have we ever hung out in person? ☐ ☐

Without the game, what would we talk about?

_____

Without the game, what would we do?

_____

2. Second video game friend: _____

                                         Yes   No

Do we talk in real life (outside the game)? ☐ ☐

                                         Yes   No

Have we ever hung out in person? ☐ ☐

Without the game, what would we talk about?

_____

Without the game, what would we do?

_____

3. Third video game friend: _____

Do we talk in real life (outside the game)?   Yes ☐   No ☐

Have we ever hung out in person?   Yes ☐   No ☐

Without the game, what would we talk about?

_____

Without the game, what would we do?

_____

Activity 10.2: Making Friends

What are the steps to making a new, real friend?

_____

_____

_____

_____

_____

Think back on your past efforts to make friends. When was the last time you tried to make a new friend?

_____

Where were you when you tried?

_____

How did it go? What worked well?

_____

_____

What was difficult? What didn't work?

_____

_____

What would you do differently next time?

_____

_____

Activity 10.3: What Makes a Friend?

How do you know someone is a real friend?

_____

_____

What do friends do together?

_____

_____

Do friends have to have a lot in common?

_____

_____

How do friends make each other feel?

_____

_____

Activity 10.4: What Friends Do I Want?

I want friends that I can _____ with.

I want them to talk to me about _____.

I want them to make me feel _____.

They can make me feel _____ by _____.

Activity 10.5: Perspective-Taking

When I _____, I make others feel _____

because _____.

But I want to make others feel _____ around me, so from now

on, I will _____.

Activity 10.6: Making Others Laugh

I like the feeling of making others laugh.

I make others laugh by _____.

When I hear others laughing, what do I think their brain is telling them? Are they thinking: "They make me laugh. I want to be their friend." OR are they thinking: "They make a lot of jokes and act pretty wacky. I don't think they would be that much fun to be around. I wish they would joke less."

_____

_____

Activity 10.7: Social Cause and Effect

Who did I affect?   How? By doing what?   How did it make
                                                       them feel?

Home: _____ → _____ → _____

School: _____ → _____ → _____

Social: _____ → _____ → _____

CHAPTER 11

Screen Time

Ending the Addiction Cycle and Reclaiming Real-World Executive Functioning

If you're holding this workbook, chances are screen time has become a battle in your home. You're not alone—and you're not imagining it. For kids and teens with ADHD, screen time isn't just a distraction. It's a direct threat to the development of the very skills they need to thrive.

This chapter is here to help you take back control.

In *The Executive Function Playbook*, we explain that executive function skills are real-world skills. They develop through face-to-face interaction, frustration tolerance, problem-solving, social negotiation, boredom, delayed gratification, and trial-and-error learning. None of that happens on a screen. When a child spends the majority of their time in the virtual world—whether it's games, apps, videos, or endless scrolling—those opportunities for growth disappear.

That's why this chapter doesn't offer tips on "balance." It offers boundaries.

While many parents dream of their child finding a healthy middle ground—using technology responsibly and still engaging with the real world—the reality for most kids with ADHD is that the concept of balance is a myth. The ADHD brain is wired for stimulation, novelty, and dopamine-seeking. Screens provide all three on demand. Once that pattern is established, it becomes increasingly difficult for the child to choose boredom, effort, or real-world experiences over instant virtual reward.

These worksheets are designed to help you:

◆ Identify the specific screen struggles in your home
◆ Set clear, consistent, and enforceable screen time limits

295

- ◆ Communicate new boundaries without chaos or confusion
- ◆ Replace screens with real, developmentally appropriate activities
- ◆ Stay consistent, even when your child escalates, protests, or manipulates

This chapter is not about shaming parents or villainizing technology. It's about providing the leadership and structure that ADHD kids so desperately need, especially when their developing brains are vulnerable to overexposure. No, removing screens won't "cure" your child—but leaving screens unchecked will make skill-building nearly impossible.

In *The Executive Function Playbook*, we emphasize that building skills like task initiation, self-regulation, and emotional control requires real-world practice. That cannot happen if the child's emotional regulation system is constantly dysregulated by overstimulation. These worksheets help you shift your home environment from reactive to intentional and create a context where executive function growth is actually possible.

You'll find tools to help you:

- ◆ Create family screen time rules that are non-negotiable
- ◆ Replace daily arguments with clear expectations
- ◆ Build a list of screen-free alternatives with your child
- ◆ Establish digital-free zones and tech-free time blocks
- ◆ Follow through with confidence—even when it's hard

Screen time boundaries are not extreme. They are essential. If your child is spending the majority of their time in the virtual world, you are not parenting in the real one. These pages are your roadmap back.

Let's eliminate the noise, end the daily screen battles, and build the real-world executive functioning your child actually needs to succeed.

Introduction

Screens are now an everyday part of life! They provide children with endless access to entertainment.

Unfortunately, screen time often limits a child's opportunity to have more meaningful experiences. Over time, low levels of physical activity and personal engagement can negatively impact their health, brain, and executive functions.

Screen time is the amount of time your child spends using a device that has a screen:

- ◆ iPad or tablet
- ◆ Computer, laptop (including computers issued by their school)

- Cell phone
- Video games

According to Common Sense Media, a nonprofit organization whose mission is to ensure digital well-being for kids, kids are spending nearly five hours or more on their devices every day.

VIDEO GAMES AND SCREENS
Gaming addiction disorder—it's real & it's official!

In 2018, the World Health Organization (WHO) added gaming addiction disorder to its International Classification of Diseases. Video game addiction is an "excessive and compulsive use of computer or video games that results in social and/or emotional problems; despite these problems, the gamer is unable to control this excessive use."

For more than two hours per day, every day, is your child playing video games, computer games, iPad games, or watching excessive YouTube videos of others playing video games? If the answer is a clear and resounding yes, they may have gaming addiction disorder.

GAMING ADDICTION DISORDER
- Thinking about gaming or YouTube videos of gaming throughout the day
- Jeopardizing significant relationships
- Feeling bad when you cannot play
- Emotional withdrawal when gaming privileges are taken away
- Not being able to decrease gaming time without an emotional outburst
- Excessive use despite consistent problems with parents
- Dishonesty and lying regarding gaming
- Using gaming to escape or leave nonpreferred experiences
- Not being able to do various tasks besides gaming

RESEARCH REFERENCE
Lemmens, J. S., Valkenburg, P. M., & Peter, J. (2009). Development and validation of a game addiction scale for adolescents. *Media Psychology, 12*(1), 77–95. doi:10.1080/15213260802669458.

GAMING EFFECTS ON EXECUTIVE FUNCTIONS
Negative Psychological Effects
A number of negative psychological health consequences have been reported in association with video game addiction, such as depression, suicidal ideation, and anxiety.

In addition, one study found that video game–addicted boys had higher levels of sleep disturbance. Youth who were addicted gamers had a greater risk of feeling low, irritable, or in a bad mood; feeling nervous; being tired and exhausted; and feeling afraid, when compared to nonproblem gamers.

Decreased Meaningful Social Interactions

Social media and texting have replaced many face-to-face social activities that older generations grew up with; therefore, teens are spending less time interacting in person leading to higher levels of anxiety, depression, and loneliness.

Today's online games such as *Fortnite* disguise themselves as "social games." Kids log in and play with their friends and many parents rationalize it as a "social experience" by thinking that this is "just how kids socialize today." Incorrect. Many, many kids today still play outside, ride bikes, play sports, exercise, explore, and learn new hands-on hobbies.

These online games are *not* social. They are not a true social experience. Language is crucial to a true social experiment. Take note of the language your child uses while playing online games. The language is quick, concise, mundane, choppy, and solely focused on the game. Boys and girls need emotional connections from their social experiences—there are *no* emotional connections made during online gaming. Social skills are not gained or refined during gaming with peers.

Irritability

When kids play on screens or video games, they get a constant release of the pleasure chemicals in the brain: dopamine, oxytocin, vasopressin, and serotonin. Playing games causes these chemicals to be consistently released at high volumes. By the time they are done gaming, they're spent. Now, nothing can entertain them or hold their attention anymore. Have you ever noticed your child is extra moody and rude after playing games for a few hours? Now you know why.

Lack of Life Skills

Parents complain that they cannot get their kids to do the most basic tasks. They do nothingaround the house, no chores, no responsibilities. If they are able to do some chores, there is no quality to their work. They cannot get their kids to engage in any meaningful physical activity. Hands-on, trial-and-error play is crucial for brain development and maturation. When excessive focus and energy go into gaming, there is nothing left to build more significant skills.

RESEARCH REFERENCE

Choo, H., Gentile, D. A., Sim, T., Dongdong, L., Khoo, A., & Liau, A. K. (2010). Pathological video-gaming among Singaporean youth. *Annals Academy of Medicine*, *39*(11), 822–829.

Mentzoni, R. A., Brunborg, G. S., Molde, H., Myrseth, H., Skouverøe, K. J. M., Hetland, J., & Pallesen, S. (2011). Problematic video game use: estimated prevalence and associations with mental and physical health. *Cyberpsyhology, Behavior and Social Networking*, *14*, 591–596. doi: 10.1089/cyber.2010.0260.

GET PROACTIVE!

Managing Screens

Be proactive by setting clear guidelines and expectations with *all* electronic devices in the home. Consider things like:

- ◆ Who may use it?
- ◆ What may it be used to do?
- ◆ When may it be used?
- ◆ Where may it be used?
- ◆ Why is this rule being set?
- ◆ How will this rule be enforced?

Having a plan and accountability in place will help avoid the mindset of waiting for a problem to surface before you set boundaries with your child and her new device. Stick to your values about violence or other inappropriate content.

- ◆ Watch what you and your kids are doing. Learn the technology they're using.
- ◆ Model good screen time—introduce them to your screen-based interests and look at your own phone/screen use.
- ◆ Ensure they engage in other activities daily. Talk to your children about balance and moderation. Participate in regular, physical activity together—walks, bike rides, trips to the park, etc.
- ◆ Listen/observe what your kids think about screens. Understand their love for technology and have your child teach you to play and play along with them.
- ◆ Enforce screen-free times to make family connection a priority. Times around dinner or before bed are ideal.

Make a Concrete Schedule—Structure Is a Must

One or two hours a day—do *not* exceed two hours per day (recommendation) and only after they complete significant nonpreferred tasks:

- After homework is done
- After chores are done
- After exercise or physical activity is done
- After reading

YOUR CHILD'S REACTIONS

Many parents never enforce screen and video game limits in their home because they are afraid of their child's possible reaction.

- Screaming
- Crying
- Breaking things
- Physical fighting
- Self-harm

All of these are indicators of just how serious video game addiction is. These are the same reactions that drug addicts have during an intervention. Video games are their drug—they negatively impact all aspects of their lives: family, school, health, productivity, and success.

Kids and adolescents are too young and do not yet have the brain development to know when to stop. They do not yet have the ability to choose a nonpreferred task like studying or reading (that will help them in the long run) over gaming.

There are so many things that we do not allow children under the age of 18 to do. Why do we grant them open access to play video games whenever they feel like it?

Especially when we see how much it negatively impacts them and the entire family.

Especially when we know they don't have the self-control to limit themselves.

Especially when we know that those "social" online games they are playing are not real social experiences.

Especially when we see how much it affects their mood, sleep, health, and grades.

Especially when there is a fight every night around games and screens.

Why do we give our children open access to their games?

Ask yourself that question now.

For your own sanity, and your child's future success—this must end *now*.

AUTHORITATIVE PARENTING

Authoritative parenting does not mean there is yelling, screaming, and anger in the home.

This phrase has been widely misunderstood and has gained a poor reputation in today's culture. Authoritative parenting means that you enforce specific guidelines in your home, and you stick to them. Simple as that. You can be an authoritative parent and never yell or scream at your child. You can be as loving as possible and continue to have an incredible relationship with them—even with strict guidelines on screens.

There are decades of research that show the positive effects of family structure and authoritative parenting: studies show that children raised by authoritative parents are more likely to demonstrate independence, self-control, and academic and social success.

As mentioned, many parents never enforce screen and video game limits in their home because they are afraid of their child's possible reaction.

Many parents would rather go through daily battles for years over screens than go through a possible few hours (or days in extreme cases) of behaviors after they introduce them to the new limited screens plan.

What to do when your child has a terrible reaction to the new screen time plan:

1. **Avoid any and all arguments. Decrease and eliminate language.**

   As soon as your child hears the new screens plan, their fight or flight response will instantly kick into gear. Their first thought will be: "I can talk my parents out of this. Either with negotiation, yelling, or behaviors."

   Tell them the plan, and then that's it. No more language. More language will make things much worse. Language can be very anxiety-producing for kids with ADHD or executive function deficits. Stay calm, stay silent, stay strong!

   Remember, when your child is elevated and dysregulated, language does not get through to them at all! You will have to wait it out a significant amount of time before a helpful conversation can take place.

2. **Make sure your child is in a safe room.**

   Some kids will attempt to break things just to show how angry they are. Make sure valuable items are out of their sight and reach. Ensure they are safe and they are unable to hurt others, and most importantly, themselves.

3. **Keep your eyes on the long-term. Remember that these reactionary behaviors are temporary!**

   Focus on long-term and how much this new plan is going to help your child and your entire family. Your child will not be mad forever! This is their initial fight/flight response to losing their drug. Wait it out, stay strong.

Kids can take advantage of the unconditional love of their parents. They know that no matter what they do, their parents will always love them and be there for them. That's why you see the worst of their behaviors and so many people get to see a totally different side of them.

ADHD specialist Ryan Wexelblatt, LCSW, explains the dangers of permissive parenting (allowing kids to have constant and open access to games) in ADDitude Magazine (2020):

Here's how allowing kids with ADHD to make adult decisions may have significant ramifications:

- When parents accommodate a child's inflexibility (i.e., an unwillingness to try new things), this often leads to even greater inflexibility and, ultimately, an unwillingness to accept help.
- Kids with ADHD often say no to anything new or unfamiliar. When they can avoid new experiences, they are denied the opportunity to learn about themselves, develop their strengths, and build confidence through independent experiences.
- When children with ADHD and anxiety are allowed to avoid anxiety-producing situations, they are denied the opportunity to learn that they can move through anxiety, which in turn denies them an important opportunity to develop resiliency and confidence.
- Many kids with ADHD who are unmedicated but should not be, which greatly impacts their ability to learn in school, regulate themselves, and feel successful. Kids do not have the foresight or emotional maturity to know what will help them over the long term. When parents allow their kids to dictate whether they take medication, their learning, social relationships, and overall health and well-being can be greatly impacted. If you allow your child to dictate whether they take medication, you are doing your child a tremendous disservice that may have long-term ramifications.

Find more of Ryan Wexleblatt's (LCSW) work at ADHDDude.com and ADDitudeMag.com.

RESOURCES
Use the following activities and tools to help set boundaries to create healthy screen time habits.

Activities

1. Record your child's screen time. Write it down on the worksheet. Go over it with them.
2. Fill in a record chart for days where screen-free times are enforced.
3. Reward and positive praise for success and compliance.
4. Removing or turning off digital devices in the child's bedroom two hours before bedtime to enforce limits and encourage a consistent sleep routine.

Tools

Create a custom family media plan by using the healthychildren.org planner.

Screen-time tracking and parental control apps on the App Store:

- Zift
- Screen Time
- Space

Apple Screen Time

- Daily Screen Time Downtime
- App Time Limits by Category
- App Use Time Tracking
- Pick Up Tracking
- Content Control
- Share Across Devices Google Family Link
- Daily Screen Time Limits
- App Time Reports
- Remote Lock
- Location Tracking
- App Approvals
- Teacher Recommended Apps

HOW TO SET UP PARENTAL CONTROLS

Using parental controls on devices is an easy and effective way to set usage boundaries.

It is highly recommended you take the time to set up parental controls on *all* the devices in the home—you will thank yourself later! This will eliminate attempts to negotiate and verbal conversations around screens with your child.

The following section provides steps on how to set up the parental controls for each major device.

Xbox

Time limits can be set only through your Microsoft account in your browser. You can make them apply to the console as well as to the PC.

1. Sign in to your Microsoft account.
2. On your family page, scroll to your kid's name and select Screen Time. (If you don't see your kid's name, use "Add a family member" to add their account to your family group or create a new account for them if needed.)
3. To set one limit that applies to both the Xbox and the PC, turn on "Use one screen time schedule."
4. To manage time limits separately, scroll down and turn on screen time for Windows devices or Xbox, whichever you want to set first.
5. Click "Set a time limit." Then choose a start time and an end time for each day of the week.
6. You can program the Xbox to send a notification to your kids when their screen time is ending.
7. To do this, press the Xbox button on the controller.
8. Select System > Settings > Preferences > Notifications > Xbox Notifications > System and turn on "System notifications." Your kid will see the clock count down when time is ending.

How to Turn off Chat on the Xbox One Using the Console   These settings are found in the privacy and online safety section and also turn off other social features.

1. Sign in to your Xbox.
2. Press the Xbox button to open the guide. Then go to System > Settings > Account.
3. Select Family settings > Manage family members.
4. Choose a family member and then select Privacy & online safety > Xbox Live privacy > View details and customize > Communication & multiplayer.
5. Select the setting "You can play with people outside of Xbox Live" and click "block" to turn it off. (This prevents all cross-network play, for example, between your kid on her Xbox and her friends on their PlayStations or Nintendos.)
6. Alternatively, if you're OK with your kid playing cross-network but not OK with them talking and texting with strangers, allow cross-network play but restrict chatting to specific people. Select "You can communicate outside of Xbox Live with voice & text" and designate a player or players with whom your kid can talk within a specific game.

How to Turn off Chat on the Xbox One Using the Browser   These settings are found in the privacy and online safety section and also turn off other social features.

1. Sign in to your Xbox Live account.
2. Choose your kid's gamertag.
3. Select Privacy and Online Settings.
4. Default privacy and safety settings are in place for adults, teens, and children, but you can customize them. Click Custom.
5. Review the settings under Activities, Privacy, and Content.
6. It's safest to block things entirely or limit them to "Friends Only."
7. Save your settings and have your kid log out and log back in for them to take effect.

How to Limit Mature Content on the Xbox One Using the Console   You can limit access to games as well as websites on the Xbox.

1. Sign in to your Xbox.
2. Press the Xbox button to open the guide. Then go to System > Settings > Account > Family.
3. Select "Manage family members" and then find your kid's name and select "Access to content." Select the age limit you feel is appropriate for your child. Microsoft automatically sets default age restrictions for kids, but you can customize them.
4. Go back to the Family page and select "Web filtering." Select the drop-down menu to view the available options.
5. When your kid requests to use a blocked app or game, you can approve it and add it to the "Always allowed" list, which is under Content restrictions. You can also add websites to "Always allowed." You can respond to their requests from your email, from your family profile, or in person, of course.

How to Limit Mature Content on the Xbox One Using the Browser   You may find that using your Microsoft account is the most efficient way of enabling restrictions.

1. Sign in to your Microsoft account.
2. Scroll to your kid's name and select "Content restrictions."
3. Next, go to "Apps, games & media" and turn on "Block inappropriate apps, games & media."
4. Under "Allow apps and games rated for," select the age limit you'd like to apply to your kid.

5. Scroll down to "Web browsing" and turn on "Block inappropriate websites."

6. When your kid requests to use a blocked app or game, you can approve it and add it to the "Always allowed" list, which is under Content restrictions. You can also add websites to "Always allowed." You can respond to their requests from your email, from your family page, or in person, of course.

PlayStation

Add users of your PS4 system or other players to your family. When you set up your family, you can customize parental controls for each child in your family, allowing them to use your PS4 system safely.

◆ Conditions for the use of family features vary by country or region. For details, visit the customer support website for your country or region.

◆ You can configure parental controls from your PC or smartphone; see https://www.playstation.com/acct/family.

◆ You can also set parental controls for users other than family members, if they have never signed in to PlayStation Network. Select (Settings) > [Parental Controls/Family Management], and then from [Users on This PS4], select the user that you want to set parental controls for.

Set up Your Family

The family manager is an adult user who can add and manage family members. Select (Settings) > [Parental Controls/Family Management] > [Family Management] and then follow the on-screen instructions to enter your sign in information. Select [Set Up Now] and then follow the on-screen instructions to add family members.

◆ A user can be in only one family.

◆ You can create new users and add them as family members. If a user is a child, depending on the child's age, a message may appear asking if you want to allow your child to join PlayStation Network. You can set parental controls before allowing your child to join PlayStation Network.

Appointing a Parent/Guardian   As the family manager, you can appoint another adult as a parent or guardian.

Select (Settings) > [Parental Controls/Family Management] > [Family Management] and then follow the on-screen instructions to enter your sign-in information. Select an adult family member that you want to appoint, and then select the checkbox for [Parent/Guardian].

Viewing or Changing Settings   Select (Settings) > [Parental Controls/Family Management] > [Family Management] and then follow the on-screen instructions to enter your sign-in information. Select a family member to view or change the following settings.

Play Time

You can see how long your children play on your PS4™ system or limit when and how long they can play. These settings apply to children who are members of your family. Play time is the amount of time your child is logged in to your PS4™ system, even if games or applications are not running.

To check or restrict play time, you need to set a time zone for each child. Play time is reset at midnight in the time zone you set. Select (Settings) > [Parental Controls/Family Management] > [Family Management] and then follow the on-screen instructions to enter your sign-in information.

Select a user from the screen that appears and then select [Time Zone].

To check your child's total play time for the day and see information for each child, select (Settings) > [Parental Controls/Family Management] > [Family Management]. Children can see how much play time they have on the following screens:

- ◆ Login screen
- ◆ Upper right of the home screen
- ◆ Quick menu (Settings) > [Parental Controls/Family Management] > [Play Time for Today]

To restrict play time, select (Settings) > [Parental Controls/Family Management] and then choose restrictions you want to apply to that user.

To change play time for today, extend or shorten your child's play time on the day they play. Select [Restrict] to set when and how long your child is allowed to play each day. When the set play time ends, a pop-up notification appears repeatedly on the screen to let your child know that they're out of play time. The PS4™ system can also automatically log your child out when play time ends. The default setting is [Notify Only]. You can set the same play times for every day or set specific restrictions for each day of the week.

Nintendo Switch

To set up parental controls for the Nintendo Switch, use the Nintendo Switch Parental Controls mobile app. You can decide which games they can play and you can set limits on how long or how late your child uses the device. You can also limit sharing of in-game text or images and restrict the ability to post screenshots to social media.

Guided Access on iPhone/iPad/iPad

Guided Access limits devices to a single app and lets you control which features are available.

You can turn on Guided Access when you let a child use your device or when accidental gestures might distract you.

Set up Guided Access

1. Go to Settings > Accessibility and then turn on Guided Access.
2. Tap Passcode Settings and then tap Set Guided Access Passcode.
3. Enter a passcode and then re-enter it. From here, you can also turn on Face ID or Touch ID as a way to end a Guided Access session.

Apple–Mac Computer

If your child is going to be using your Mac you may want to set up restrictions to what they have access to. You can manage the following options:

♦ Apps: This menu lets you control access to your Mac's built-in camera, restrict the ability to join multiplayer games in Game Center, restrict use of Mail to known contacts, and limit access to installed apps.
♦ Web: This tab lets you limit access to websites via any browser.
♦ Stores: Here you can manage use of the iTunes Store and limit access to music, movies, TV shows, apps, and books.
♦ Time: Schedule time limits so the account can be used only on weekdays, on weekends, and before bedtime, for example.
♦ Privacy: This menu lets you control which apps and services can access user data.
♦ Other: Options in this menu include disabling use of Siri and Dictation, preventing access to printer and scanner settings, burning discs, hiding profanity in dictionaries and wikis, and preventing the Dock from being modified. You can also opt from here to present a simplified view of the Mac desktop.

How to Manage Restrictions in Parental Controls

1. Click the Apple symbol in the top-left corner of your Mac's screen and select System Preferences.
2. Select the Parental Controls preferences pane.
3. Click the lock in the lower-left corner of the window.
4. Enter your admin password if prompted and click Unlock.
5. Select the user account that you want to set restrictions for from the column on the left.

Windows Computer

Microsoft offers parental controls to help keep children safe when they use the family computer. You can set up restrictions on application types, allowed websites, and how much time they can spend on the computer and other Windows-based devices. Detailed reporting is also provided after parental controls are set.

The parental controls are applied only when your child logs in to a Windows device using their own Microsoft Account. These settings do not prevent what they do on their friends' computers, school computers, or their Apple or Android devices, or when they access a computer under someone else's account, including your own.

Follow these steps to set up the controls:

1. Select Start and choose Settings to launch the Windows Settings app.
2. Select Accounts.
3. In the left pane, select Family & Other Users.
4. Select Add a Family Member if your child does not have a separate account on your device. This step launches a Microsoft Account wizard.
5. Select Add a Child then enter your child's email address or select The Person I Want To Add Doesn't Have an Email Address.
6. Read the information offered (what you see here depends on what you selected in Step 5), and choose Close.

How to Prevent Arguing During Nongaming Times

It is highly recommended that you completely remove access to the controllers, cords, etc., so that the child cannot sneak in gaming during off-hours. As we know, our kids can be very creative, sneaky, and sometimes manipulative! They love to negotiate increasing gaming time, so here is a way to eliminate that.

For additional management, consider purchasing and using a lockable storage trunk. This will ensure that controllers remain in parent's possession during nongaming times. One good option is Sterilite 16 Gallon Storage Trunk (Footlocker).

SUMMARY

1. Create a family/household screen time structure plan today! Do not wait!
2. Figure out exactly how you want to limit screen time in the home:
   Two hours per day (recommended)
   A specific amount of hours per day
   Only on certain days
   Only on weekends
3. Use the appropriate schedule worksheet to display the times for screens that you decide upon for your family. You may want to print, laminate, and post.

4. Screen time must always be earned and given after nonpreferred tasks are completed. Use the Earn Your Screen Time Worksheet to track completion of tasks.

5. Parents should be in full possession of controllers/cords during nongaming times. It is crucial that you control the environment. If the console is available and gaming is possible in the environment, it will be too difficult for the child to resist and it will create opportunities for manipulation and sneaking. Look into purchasing the locking trunk.

6. To help them with their time management skills, use the Clock Worksheet to help them visualize their time.

7. For negative and unexpected behaviors, use the Unexpected Behaviors Worksheet to create a system of accountability. Children with Executive Function challenges require increased structure and accountability.

8. Use the Schedule and Agenda Worksheets to help your child plan their days and keep track of school assignments.

9. Do not allow *any* gaming on a school-issued computer. Contact the school's IT department immediately to ensure all gaming websites are blocked. Children are very creative in sneaking in gaming during school time and also then deleting their web browsing history.

10. Take the time to set up Parental Controls on all gaming systems, iPhone, iPad, and computers.

11. Stay strong. The behaviors will be temporary. Focus on long-term growth!

Activity 11.1: Visual Schedule
Executive function skills strengthened: Self-regulation

OVERVIEW
In *The Executive Function Playbook*, a central theme is helping parents externalize boundaries so the child can begin to internalize them over time. This workbook page provides parents with a clear, visual system for managing screen time—an area that frequently becomes a source of conflict, power struggles, and emotional dysregulation in homes with children who have ADHD.

Children with ADHD often struggle with internal timing, delay of gratification, and transitions—especially when it comes to ending preferred activities like video games or YouTube. These transitions become even more difficult when expectations are unclear or inconsistently enforced. This screen time visual schedule addresses those challenges by externalizing the rules in a clear and non-negotiable format that removes the need for ongoing verbal prompts or arguments.

By creating, displaying, and consistently following this schedule, families establish a predictable structure that reduces emotional reactivity and supports healthier screen habits.

INSTRUCTIONS FOR THE ADULT (PARENT, TEACHER, OR CLINICIAN)

- ◆ Fill in the specific days and start/end times during which screen time is permitted. Be as concrete and specific as possible.
- ◆ Laminate the sheet and display it clearly in the room or space where screen time happens.
- ◆ Remind the child that this is now "family law"—meaning it is not up for discussion or negotiation.
- ◆ If your child argues or complains, simply point silently to the visual schedule rather than engaging verbally. Let the structure speak for itself.

STEP-BY-STEP GUIDANCE

1. **Determine screen-time windows.**

   Decide with your partner or co-caregiver exactly when screen time will be permitted. Stick to consistent timeframes based on your family values (e.g., no screen time before school, only after chores/homework, never during meals, etc.).

2. **Fill out the visual schedule.**
   - Write the allowed screen time blocks clearly on the sheet (e.g., "Monday–Friday: 4–5:30 p.m." or "Saturday: 10 a.m.–12 p.m.").
   - If possible, include a visual clock or time icons to support nonverbal working memory.

3. **Discuss once—then enforce visually.**

   Hold a family meeting to review the schedule together. Explain that this is not a punishment—it's a plan to support healthy habits and reduce arguments.

4. **Laminated = final.**

   Once the schedule is laminated and posted, it should be treated like a contract. Make changes only when necessary, and not in response to child complaints.

5. **Reinforce with consistency.**

   When the screen time window ends, say, "Check the chart—we're done for today." Do not elaborate, explain, or negotiate. Walk away if needed.

Why This Matters

For kids with ADHD, impulsivity and emotional dysregulation make screen time a highly sensitive topic. Visual schedules provide a *nonverbal boundary* that reduces conflict and increases independence. They are a critical tool for reducing the chaos and inconsistency that can come from verbal-only parenting.

This structure also supports the development of time-awareness, self-regulation, and internal restraint—skills that will help the child in school, at home, and in future relationships.

KEY MESSAGE
Visuals replace battles. When screen time rules are clearly posted and enforced with consistency—not emotion—children learn to self-regulate within structured limits.

CLOSING THOUGHT
You don't need to argue about screen time anymore. When the rules are clear, written, and visible, the conversation ends—and growth begins.

Activity 11.2: Earn Your Screen Time
Executive function skills strengthened: *Self-motivation*

OVERVIEW
The Executive Function Playbook emphasizes that children with ADHD thrive when they are working toward something rather than simply receiving it by default. This is especially important in the case of screens—an incredibly powerful source of instant gratification that often undermines motivation, attention span, and reciprocity. When screens are handed out "for free," with no effort required, children quickly become prompt-dependent, reward-driven, and increasingly disinterested in any task that doesn't deliver immediate stimulation.

This worksheet provides parents with a simple, clear framework to help children earn their screen time through meaningful, age-appropriate effort. When implemented consistently, it teaches the child that access to screen time is a reward—not a right—and that completing real-world, nonpreferred tasks is a part of life.

INSTRUCTIONS FOR THE ADULT (PARENT, TEACHER, OR CLINICIAN)
- With your child, identify **three to five tasks** that must be completed each day to earn screen time. These may include household chores, homework, personal hygiene routines, or social behaviors like being respectful or following directions.
- Write these expectations on the worksheet in clear, age-appropriate language.
- Choose the amount of screen time to be earned (e.g., 30 minutes, 1 hour) and write that clearly at the bottom.
- Screen time is not given unless all listed tasks are completed.
- Praise effort—not just completion—when your child earns their screen time.

STEP-BY-STEP GUIDANCE

1. **Set clear daily expectations.**
   - Examples:
     - "Put away all clean laundry."
     - "Complete math homework and check for errors."
     - "Take out the trash without reminders."
     - "Get ready for school without arguing."
   - Be specific. Vague tasks like "be good" don't help with executive function growth.

2. **Be consistent and unemotional.**
   When a task is not done, do not bargain or negotiate. Simply say:
   "Screens are earned after your tasks are complete. Let me know when it's done."

3. **Track completion.**
   Use checkboxes to mark off tasks each day. You may also laminate this page and use a dry-erase marker to reset it daily.

4. **Celebrate earning, not receiving.**
   When screen time is earned, acknowledge the effort:
   "You followed through today—nice job earning it. That's how we do things in this house."

Why This Matters

Many children with ADHD become intensely focused on screens because screens require no effort and deliver constant dopamine. But life does not work that way—and parenting cannot follow that model. To raise capable, independent, and motivated individuals, we must teach them that effort leads to reward—not entitlement.

This simple, daily routine promotes:

- A work-before-play mindset
- Internal satisfaction from completing real-world tasks
- Reduced screen dependence and fewer power struggles

KEY MESSAGE

When screen time is earned—not given—children begin to understand effort, responsibility, and true cause and effect. This is how we raise capable, not comfortable, kids.

CLOSING THOUGHT

It's not about punishing your child by taking screens away—it's about teaching them the value of earning, striving, and contributing before enjoying a reward. That's the path to lasting motivation.

RESEARCH REFERENCE

Barkley, R. A. (2015). *Taking Charge of ADHD: The Complete Authoritative Guide for Parents* (3rd ed.). Guilford Press.

Activity 11.3: Analog Clock

Executive function skills strengthened: Self-regulation, time management

OVERVIEW

Children with ADHD often struggle with time blindness—the inability to *feel* or *sense* the passage of time. This contributes to major challenges with task initiation, transitions, planning, and persistence. The analog clock is one of the most powerful tools we can use to make time visual and concrete.

In *The Executive Function Playbook*, we emphasize the critical need for children to *externalize time* through visual means. Time, by nature, is invisible and abstract—but children with executive function deficits need time to be *seen* in order to *manage* it.

This worksheet provides a blank analog clock that adults can use to help children visualize the duration of any task, whether it's a 20-minute chore, a 30-minute screen session, or a homework block. When children *see* how much time is passing, their brains can begin to better regulate their behavior and expectations.

INSTRUCTIONS FOR THE ADULT (PARENT, TEACHER, OR CLINICIAN)

1. Print the worksheet and use a highlighter or colored marker to **shade in the "time wedge"** that represents how long the child will engage in the task.
2. Label the start and end times clearly.
3. Use consistent color coding—for example, green for screen time, blue for homework, red for chores.
4. Post the clock in a visible location during the task (e.g., desk, kitchen, screen area).
5. Refer to the shaded portion frequently:
   "This is how much time you have left."
   or
   "This wedge shows how long you'll need to stick with this task."

STEP-BY-STEP GUIDANCE

1. **Choose the task.**
   Pick a single task or activity (e.g., screen time, reading, cleaning room).
2. **Set the duration.**
   Agree on how long the task will last (e.g., 25 minutes). Be realistic and consistent.

3. **Draw the time block.**

Shade in the start-to-end portion of the analog clock. Example: If screen time is from 3 to 3:30 p.m., you will shade in that specific portion of the clock.

4. **Reinforce the visual.**

Prompt your child to look at the wedge throughout the task. For children who struggle with transitions, give a five-minute warning by pointing to the portion that's left.

5. **Reset for the next task.**

After the task ends, use a new clock sheet or erase the markings and start again.

Why This Matters

Children with ADHD often operate based on emotion, not time. If something feels long or boring, they may give up quickly. If something feels short and fun, they may want it to last forever. By creating a visual representation of time, we help them regulate expectations and behaviors—and gradually develop independence with time management.

This strategy is especially useful for:

◆ Reducing resistance to nonpreferred tasks
◆ Creating predictability and structure
◆ Minimizing verbal prompts and power struggles

KEY MESSAGE

Time isn't felt by default—it's learned. When we make time visible, we give children with ADHD the tools they need to regulate themselves, plan ahead, and transition more successfully.

CLOSING THOUGHT

Your child's future independence hinges on their ability to manage time. You don't need more timers or apps—you need to make time something they can see, understand, and work with.

RESEARCH REFERENCE

Ward, S., & Jacobsen, G. (2022). *Seeing My Time: A Time-Management Curriculum for Teens and Adults with Executive Function Weaknesses* (2nd ed.). Cognitive Connections, LLP.

Activity 11.4: Unexpected Choices

Executive function skills strengthened: Self-regulation, self-awareness

OVERVIEW

Children with ADHD often struggle to connect choices to consequences, especially when emotions are high. Their impulsivity, time blindness, and underdeveloped internal language make it difficult to anticipate outcomes or remember previous consequences. As a result, they may repeat the same behaviors—like arguing, refusing, or breaking a rule—without internalizing the pattern or learning from it.

In *The Executive Function Playbook*, we emphasize the value of predictability, visual supports, and consistent follow-through. This worksheet helps children and parents predetermine the consequence of specific "unexpected choices" before they happen. This removes negotiation from the equation, reduces emotional escalation, and promotes a sense of structure and safety.

Rather than waiting for a behavior to occur and then scrambling to come up with a consequence, this tool makes the consequences visual, predictable, and automatic. It allows the child to take ownership over their behavior—and prepares the adult to respond with calm consistency.

INSTRUCTIONS FOR THE ADULT (PARENT, TEACHER, OR CLINICIAN)

1. Review the sheet together with the child during a calm, neutral time—not in the middle of a meltdown or conflict.
2. Identify three to five common "unexpected choices" that frequently occur at home or school (e.g., refusing to end screen time, yelling, lying, physical aggression).
3. Collaboratively determine a fair, firm, and clear consequence for each behavior. These must be consistent, reasonable, and enforced 100% of the time.
4. Write each behavior and consequence pair clearly. Post the sheet in a visible spot (e.g., refrigerator, bedroom door, homework area).
5. Refer to the sheet during the moment of dysregulation by pointing, not lecturing. Let the consequence speak for itself.

STEP-BY-STEP GUIDANCE

1. **Name the unexpected behaviors.**

   Example behaviors might include:
   - Ignoring a parent when asked to put device away
   - Screaming or using aggressive language

- Refusing to get out of bed or get ready for school
- Lying about homework

2. **Determine the natural or logical consequence.**
   - No screen access for 24 hours
   - Early bedtime that evening
   - Parent not helping with any missed assignments
   - Privileges withheld (e.g., no playdate, outing canceled)

3. **Keep it short and clear.**

   Use language like:
   - "If I do ____, then ____ will happen."
   - "If I break this rule, I will lose ____ until ____."

4. **Write it down and post it visibly.**

   Make sure both the child and all caregivers agree on and understand the terms. Consistency is key.

Why This Matters

Children with ADHD thrive in environments that are structured, predictable, and low in unnecessary language. When consequences are visual and agreed upon ahead of time, there's no need for long lectures, bargaining, or escalating power struggles. This promotes self-regulation in the child and calm authority in the parent.

KEY MESSAGE

Clear expectations create calm homes. When consequences are predetermined and visual, children learn to self-monitor and make better choices—not because they're scared of punishment but because they understand the cause-and-effect relationship between behavior and outcome.

CLOSING THOUGHT

Children with ADHD will push boundaries—that's developmentally normal. What matters most is that the boundaries don't move. Consistent, calm consequences build trust, structure, and long-term behavior change.

RESEARCH REFERENCE

Barkley, R. A. (2013). *Taking charge of ADHD: The complete, authoritative guide for parents* (3rd ed.). Guilford Press.

Activity 11.5: Complete Schedule
Executive function skills strengthened: Self-evaluation

OVERVIEW
Children and teens with ADHD often struggle with *time blindness*—a neurological trait that makes it difficult to sense how time is passing, estimate how long tasks will take, or reflect on how they've used their time. Without strong internal time management skills, they may procrastinate, become absorbed in screen-based activities, or avoid nonpreferred tasks altogether.

This worksheet provides a full-day schedule template in 30-minute increments, allowing for flexible use depending on the needs of the student and adult. Whether it is used for real-time tracking, retrospective analysis, or pre-planning, the goal is to help the child *visualize, evaluate, and eventually take ownership* of how they spend their time.

This exercise builds awareness around time usage and promotes metacognitive reflection—helping the child answer essential executive function questions like:

- ◆ "Where did my time go today?"
- ◆ "How much time am I spending on the things that matter?"
- ◆ "What would I do differently tomorrow?"

INSTRUCTIONS FOR THE ADULT (PARENT, TEACHER, OR CLINICIAN)
1. Determine how you want to use the worksheet—pre-planning, real-time tracking, or self-reporting after the fact.
2. Print the full-day schedule and explain how the sheet works. Each row represents 30 minutes from wake-up to bedtime.
3. Clarify expectations. For example, "We'll fill this out every hour today," or "You'll use this tonight to tell me how you spent your day."
4. Review the completed sheet together at the end of the day (or week), using it as a tool for reflection, discussion, and problem-solving—not punishment.

STEP-BY-STEP GUIDANCE
Option 1: Self-Reporting
Let the child record what they do every 30 minutes throughout the day. Set a reminder or visual timer to help them check in regularly.

- ◆ Morning example: "8–8:30: Got dressed and ate breakfast."
- ◆ Afternoon: "2:30–3: Played Roblox."
- ◆ Evening: "7:30–8: Watched TV."

Option 2: Adult Observation

Parents or teachers can use the sheet to log what they see the child doing, especially if the child resists completing it themselves. This can be reviewed together to highlight patterns and discuss changes.

Option 3: Pre-planning

The adult maps out the child's day ahead of time, showing clear blocks for play, chores, meals, downtime, homework, etc. This promotes structure and sets expectations early.

Reflection Activity

Once the sheet is complete, guide the child through a reflection:

*   "How many blocks today were spent on screens?"
*   "What time of day were you the most productive?"
*   "What's one time block you want to use differently tomorrow?"
    This is a powerful self-evaluation habit that builds metacognition and internal accountability.

Why This Matters

ADHD brains struggle with seeing the full picture of a day. Without visual scheduling tools, kids live moment-to-moment and have little awareness of how they're spending their time. This worksheet bridges that gap, making the invisible visible. When children see their schedule laid out and compare intention to action, they begin to take more responsibility for how their day unfolds.

KEY MESSAGE

You can't change how you use your time if you don't know how you're using it. By tracking and reflecting on daily time blocks, kids with ADHD build the critical skill of self-evaluation and move closer to independent time management.

CLOSING THOUGHT

Time is one of the most valuable resources we have—and yet for children with ADHD, it often slips away unnoticed. This page teaches them to notice, reflect, and begin to take control.

RESEARCH REFERENCE

Barkley, R. A. (2012). *Executive functions: What they are, how they work, and why they evolved.* Guilford Press.

Activity 11.1: Visual Schedule

WORKSHEETS - PRINT & USE!

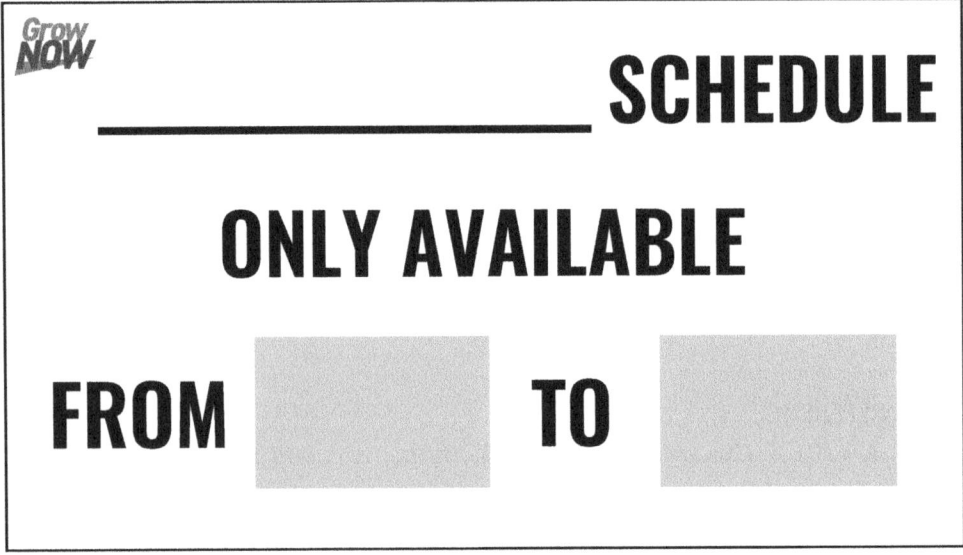

Grow NOW

_____ SCHEDULE

	SUNDAY	MONDAY	TUESDAY	WEDNESDAY	THURSDAY	FRIDAY	SATURDAY
Week 1							
Week 2							
Week 3							
Week 4							

Grow NOW

_____ SCHEDULE

ONLY AVAILABLE

FROM ▢ TO ▢

Activity 11.2: Earn Your Screen Time

EARN YOUR SCREEN TIME

HAVE YOU? CHECK IT OFF WHEN IT'S DONE	M	T	W	T	F

YOU CAN EARN SCREEN TIME!

Activity 11.3: Analog Clock

Activity 11.4: Unexpected Choices

UNEXPECTED CHOICES

Parents Own & Determine the Screen Time

UNEXPECTED CHOICE	RESULT

Grow NOW

Activity 11.5: Complete Schedule

DAILY AGENDA					
SUBJECT	**ASSIGNMENT**	**DONE?** ☑		**TURNED IN?** ☑	
		YES	NO	YES	NO

CHAPTER 12

ADHD Hope

Finding Hope, Healing, and Executive Function Progress—One Day at a Time

You've made it to the final pages of *The Executive Function Playbook in Action*. And if no one has told you this yet: you are doing an extraordinary job.

We know how heavy this journey can feel—how easy it is to fall into doubt, exhaustion, and fear when every day brings power struggles, emotional outbursts, incomplete homework, and deep concern for your child's future. But right now, by simply committing to learn, reflect, and show up again and again, you are planting seeds of change. And those seeds matter more than you know.

This workbook wasn't written to make your life harder. It was written to make your path clearer. To put language around the things you've seen but didn't know how to explain. To give structure to the chaos, and to replace endless reminders, lectures, and meltdowns with tools that actually build the skills your child needs to grow.

Let's be honest, this work is not glamorous. You won't always see immediate results. There may be days when you finish a worksheet and your child still slams the door. There may be weeks when the growth feels slow, invisible, or undone. But here's the truth we want you to hold onto: progress in the ADHD brain happens in layers. Quietly. Gradually. And then, suddenly, something clicks.

That "click" doesn't come from a single conversation or reward chart. It comes from repetition, safety, structure, and your steady presence. It comes when your child begins to internalize the routines, the language, and the expectations you've modeled again and again—even when it felt like they weren't listening.

In *The Executive Function Playbook*, we talk about the difference between behavior management and skill development. These worksheets have helped you step into the deeper work of building real skills—internal systems like self-awareness, working memory, motivation, and regulation. These are not things your child will "grow out of." These are things they will grow into, because you chose to coach instead of react, lead instead of lecture, and hold the boundary instead of backing down.

You've now seen:

♦ How self-regulation doesn't come from punishment—it comes from modeling and coaching
♦ How motivation grows from small, consistent routines—not big rewards
♦ How screens don't just entertain—they compete with executive function development
♦ How parenting on the same page is not just helpful—it's essential
♦ How structure at home can be just as strong (and often more healing) than structure at school
♦ And how your child is not broken—they are simply building, brick by brick

This workbook has given you the blueprint. But the real power has always been in your hands.

You Are the Most Powerful Tool

We want to remind you of this: there is no one better equipped to lead your child than you.

Not because you're perfect, but because you're committed.

Because you're learning to stay calm when your child loses it.

Because you're choosing connection over control.

Because you're willing to hold a boundary—even when it's hard.

Because you know that structure is not harsh—it's loving.

Because you're showing your child what it looks like to stay, to care, and to try again.

You may not always feel confident, but this workbook is a reflection of your courage. Every time you sat down to complete a page, reflect on a parenting pattern, or guide your child through an activity, you were doing what so many parents never do: you were choosing intention over reactivity. And that's what changes lives.

If your child could put their growth into words, they might say:

"Thank you for not giving up on me."

"Thank you for not rescuing me every time it got hard."

"Thank you for showing me what calm looks like—even when I couldn't feel it myself."

"Thank you for believing I can do hard things—even when I didn't believe it yet."

A Vision of What's to Come

There will still be hard days. That's the truth of raising a child with ADHD and executive function challenges. But the difference now is that you have the tools to respond—not react. You have the clarity to see the behavior for what it is: communication of a lagging skill. And you have the confidence to know that your consistency will outlast your child's testing.

So when your child starts initiating tasks without reminders, celebrate.

When they catch themselves before yelling, acknowledge it.

When they use one of your phrases, one of your boundaries, one of your strategies, smile quietly. That means it's working.

But even on the days when nothing seems to work, remember this: you are changing the story. And that kind of change takes time, courage, and heart.

So revisit these pages when things unravel. Use them to reset when you feel lost. And most importantly, come back to the *why*:

You're not doing this to have a perfect child.

You're doing this to raise a capable, compassionate, and confident human being—someone who knows how to reflect, regulate, and own their path.

That's executive functioning. That's the long game. That's the power of parenting with a playbook.

Hope

You are not alone.

You are doing sacred, foundational work that will echo in your child's future relationships, success, and sense of self.

You don't have to do everything all at once. Choose a few worksheets to return to. Focus on one routine. One pattern. One goal. Small steps, repeated daily, will create the transformation you're hoping for.

And if you need to hear this again:

You're not just surviving—you are showing your child how to build a life.

Not a life free of struggle, but a life full of tools to meet it.

Thank you for showing up. Thank you for doing the work.

This workbook may be coming to a close, but your leadership—and your child's growth—are just getting started.

With love,

Mike

Index